Lecture Notes in Computer Science 13474

More information about this series at https://link.springer.com/bookseries/558

Alicia Villanueva (Ed.)

Logic-Based Program Synthesis and Transformation

32nd International Symposium, LOPSTR 2022
Tbilisi, Georgia, September 21–23, 2022
Proceedings

 Springer

Editor
Alicia Villanueva 🆔
Universitat Politècnica de València
Valencia, Spain

ISSN 0302-9743   ISSN 1611-3349 (electronic)
Lecture Notes in Computer Science
ISBN 978-3-031-16766-9   ISBN 978-3-031-16767-6 (eBook)
https://doi.org/10.1007/978-3-031-16767-6

This Springer imprint is published by the registered company Springer Nature Switzerland AG
The registered company address is: Gewerbestrasse 11, 6330 Cham, Switzerland

Preface

The International Symposium on Logic-based Program Synthesis and Transformation (LOPSTR) gathers researchers interested in logic-based program development. The LOPSTR series stimulates and promotes international research and collaboration in all aspects of this area, including all stages of the software life cycle and dealing with issues related to both programming-in-the-small and programming-in-the-large.

The 32nd edition of LOPSTR was held in the city of Tbilisi in Georgia as a hybrid (blended) meeting during September 21–23, 2022. It was organized in the context of the Computational Logic Autumn Summit (CLAS 2022), and co-located with the 24th International ACM SIGPLAN Symposium on Principles and Practice of Declarative Programming (PPDP 2022). Previous LOPSTR symposia were held in Tallin (2021, as a hybrid event), Bologna (2020, as a virtual meeting), Porto (2019), Frankfurt am Main (2018), Namur (2017), Edinburgh (2016), Siena (2015), Canterbury (2014), Madrid (2013 and 2002), Leuven (2012 and 1997), Odense (2011), Hagenberg (2010), Coimbra (2009), Valencia (2008), Lyngby (2007), Venice (2006 and 1999), London (2005 and 2000), Verona (2004), Uppsala (2003), Paphos (2001), Manchester (1998, 1992 and 1991), Stockholm (1996), Arnhem (1995), Pisa (1994), and Louvain-la-Neuve (1993). More information about the symposium can be found at https://lopstr2022.webs.upv.es/.

LOPSTR traditionally solicits contributions, in any programming language paradigm, in the areas of synthesis, specification, transformation, analysis and verification, specialization, testing and certification, composition, program and model manipulation, optimization, transformational techniques in software engineering, inversion, artificial intelligence methods for program development, verification and testing of AI-based systems, applications, and tools. LOPSTR has a reputation for being a lively, friendly forum that allows for the presentation and discussion of both finished work and work in progress.

In response to the call for papers, 18 contributions were submitted from authors in 17 different countries. One of the submissions was withdrawn by the authors, and each of the remaining submissions was reviewed by at least three Program Committee members or external referees. After two rounds of reviewing, eight papers were selected for inclusion in the formal proceedings and presented at the conference. Four additional papers were accepted for presentation at the symposium, leading to an attractive scientific program. In addition, the symposium program included invited talks by three outstanding speakers: Robert Hierons (University of Sheffield, UK) and two joint PPDP-LOPSTR speakers, Florian Zuleger (Technische Universität Wien, Austria), and Niki Vazou (IMDEA Software Institute, Spain). In addition to the eight accepted papers, this volume includes the abstracts of the invited talks.

I want to thank the Program Committee members, who worked diligently to produce high-quality reviews for the submitted papers, as well as all the external reviewers involved in the paper selection. LOPSTR 2022 was hosted and sponsored by the Ivane Javakhishvili Tbilisi State University and the Kurt Gödel Society. I am very grateful to the local organizer, Besik Dundua, and his team for the great job they did in managing the CLAS 2022 event. Many thanks also to Manuel Hermenegildo and Beniamino Accattoli, the Program Committee chairs of PPDP, with whom I interacted for coordinating the events, and to the Steering Committee, chaired by Maurizio Proietti, for their support. I would also like to thank Andrei Voronkov for his excellent EasyChair conference management system that automates many of the tasks involved in chairing a conference. Special thanks go to the invited speakers and to all the authors who submitted and presented their papers at LOPSTR 2022. I also thank our sponsor, Springer, for the LOPSTR 2022 award and the cooperation and support in the organization of the symposium.

August 2022   Alicia Villanueva

Organization

Steering Committee

Emanuele De Angelis	National Research Council, Italy
Maribel Fernández	King's College London, UK
Fabio Fioravanti	Università degli Studi G. d'Annunzio, Italy
Maurizio Gabbrielli	University of Bologna, Italy
John Gallagher	Roskilde University, Denmark
Manuel Hermenegildo	IMDEA, Spain
Pedro López	IMDEA, Spain
Fred Mesnard	Université de la Réunion, France
Maurizio Proietti (Chair)	National Research Council, Italy
Peter Stuckey	Monash University, Australia
Wim Vanhoof	University of Namur, Belgium
Germán Vidal	Universitat Politècnica de València, Spain

Organizing Committee

Sedat Akleylek	Ondokuz Mayis University, Turkey
Sandra Alves	University of Porto, Portugal
Matthias Baaz	TU Wien, Austria
Besik Dundua (Chair)	Tbilisi State University/Kutaisi International University, Georgia
Santiago Escobar	Universitat Politècnica de València, Spain
Temur Kutsia	Johannes Kepler University Linz, Austria
Mircea Marin	West University of Timisoara, Romania
Konstantine Pkhakadze	Georgian Technical University, Georgia
Mikheil Rukhaia	Tbilisi State University, Georgia

Program Committee

Elvira Albert	Complutense University of Madrid, Spain
Roberto Amadini	University of Bologna, Italy
Emanuele De Angelis	National Research Council, Italy
Włodzimierz Drabent	IPI PAN, Poland/Linköping University, Sweden
Catherine Dubois	ENSIIE-Samovar, France
Fabio Fioravanti	Università degli Studi G. d'Annunzio, Italy
Gopal Gupta	University of Texas at Dallas, USA

Geoff Hamilton	Dublin City University, Ireland
Michael Hanus	Kiel University, Germany
Maja Kirkeby	Roskilde University, Denmark
Ekaterina Komendantskaya	Heriot-Watt University, UK
Temur Kutsia	Johannes Kepler University of Linz, Austria
Maria Chiara Meo	Università degli Studi G. d'Annunzio, Italy
Fred Mesnard	Université de la Réunion, France
Alberto Momigliano	University of Milan, Italy
Naoki Nishida	Nagoya University, Japan
Laura Panizo	University of Málaga, Spain
Laura Titolo	National Institute of Aerospace, USA
Wim Vanhoof	University of Namur, Belgium
Alicia Villanueva (Chair)	Universitat Politècnica de València, Spain

Additional Reviewers

Serdar Erbatur
Marco Antonio Feliú Gabaldón
Samir Genaim
Kenji Hashimoto
Abdel-Rahman Hedar
Alejandro Hernández-Cerezo
Michał Knapik
Clara Rodríguez-Núñez

Keynotes

Systematic Testing for Robotic Systems

Robert Hierons

The University of Sheffield, UK
r.hierons@sheffield.ac.uk

Robotic systems form the basis for advances in areas such as manufacturing, health-care, and transport. A number of areas in which robotic systems are being used are safety-critical and so there is a need for software development processes that lead to robotic systems that are safe, reliable and trusted. Testing will inevitably be an important component.

We describe recent work on automated testing of robotic systems. The work is model-based: it takes as input a state-based model that describes the required behaviour of the system under test. Models are written in either RoboChart, a state-based language for robotics, or RoboSim, a simulation language for robotics. These languages have been given a formal semantics, making it possible to reason about models in a sound manner. We describe how the development of robotic software can be formalised based on such languages and how this can lead to the potential to automate the generation of sound test cases. Such test cases can be used for testing within a simulation and possibly also for testing the deployed system. Testing is systematic since test cases target potential faults.

Automated Termination and Complexity Analysis

Florian Zuleger

Technische Universität Wien, Austria
florian.zuleger@tuwien.ac.at

We overview two techniques that are suitable for automated termination and computational complexity analysis. 1) We are interested in abstract program models for which we are able to obtain decidability and expressivity results. Such program models can be used as backends in automated analyzers. Results will be presented on the size-change abstraction (SCA), which maintains only inequalities between sizes on the program state, and on vector addition systems with states (VASS), which are an equivalent representation of Petri nets with finite state. 2) Building on a line of previous work, we present an approach based on potential function templates with unknown coefficients. The analysis is stated as a type-and-effect system where the typing rules generate constraints over the unknown coefficients. Our work targets the performance analysis of self-adjusting data structures such as (randomized) splay trees, which requires sophisticated potential functions that include logarithmic expressions.

Contents

Analysis of Rewrite Systems

Analysing Parallel Complexity of Term Rewriting

Thaïs Baudon[1], Carsten Fuhs[2], and Laure Gonnord[1,3(✉)]

[1] LIP (UMR CNRS/ENS Lyon/UCB Lyon1/INRIA), Lyon, France
Laure.Gonnord@grenoble-inp.fr
[2] Birkbeck, University of London, London, UK
[3] LCIS (UGA/Grenoble INP/Ésisar), Valence, France

Abstract. We revisit parallel-innermost term rewriting as a model of parallel computation on inductive data structures and provide a corresponding notion of runtime complexity parametric in the size of the start term. We propose automatic techniques to derive both upper and lower bounds on parallel complexity of rewriting that enable a direct reuse of existing techniques for sequential complexity. The applicability and the precision of the method are demonstrated by the relatively light effort in extending the program analysis tool APROVE and by experiments on numerous benchmarks from the literature.

1 Introduction

Automated inference of complexity bounds for parallel computation has seen a surge of attention in recent years [5,11,12,17,30,31]. While techniques and tools for a variety of computational models have been introduced, so far there does not seem to be any paper in this area for complexity of *term rewriting* with parallel evaluation strategies. This paper addresses this gap in the literature. We consider term rewrite systems (TRSs) as *intermediate representation* for programs with *pattern-matching* operating on *algebraic data types* like the one depicted in Fig. 1.

```
fn size(&self) -> int {
  match self {
    &Tree::Node { v, ref left, ref right }
      => left.size() + right.size() + 1,
    &Tree::Empty => 0 , }     }
```

Fig. 1. Tree size computation in Rust

In this particular example, the recursive calls to `left.size()` and `right.size()` can be done in parallel. Building on previous work on parallel-innermost rewriting [19,40], and first ideas about parallel complexity [6], we propose a

This work was partially funded by the French National Agency of Research in the CODAS Project (ANR-17-CE23-0004-01). For Open Access purposes, our extended authors' accepted manuscript [14] of this paper is available under Creative Commons CC BY licence.

A. Villanueva (Ed.): LOPSTR 2022, LNCS 13474, pp. 3–23, 2022.
https://doi.org/10.1007/978-3-031-16767-6_1

new notion of Parallel Dependency Tuples that captures such a behaviour, and methods to compute both upper and lower *parallel complexity bounds*.

Bounds on parallel complexity can provide insights about the potentiality of parallelisation: if sequential and parallel complexity of a function (asymptotically) coincide, this information can be useful for a parallelising compiler to refrain from parallelising the evaluation of this function. Moreover, evaluation of TRSs (as a simple functional programming language) in massively parallel settings such as GPUs is currently a topic of active research [18]. In this context, a static analysis of parallel complexity can be helpful to determine whether to rewrite on a (fast, but not very parallel) CPU or on a (slower, but massively parallel) GPU.

A preliminary version of this work with an initial notion of parallel complexity was presented in an informal extended abstract [13]. We now propose a more formal version accompanied by extensions, proofs, implementation, experiments, and related work. Section 2 recalls term rewriting and Dependency Tuples [37] as the basis of our approach. In Sect. 3, we introduce a notion of runtime complexity for parallel-innermost rewriting, and we harness the existing Dependency Tuple framework to compute asymptotic upper bounds on this complexity. In Sect. 4, we provide a transformation to innermost term rewriting that lets any tool for (sequential) innermost runtime complexity be reused to find upper bounds for parallel-innermost runtime complexity and, for confluent parallel-innermost rewriting, also lower bounds. Section 5 gives experimental evidence of the practicality of our method on a large standard benchmark set. We discuss related work in Sect. 6. Our extended authors' accepted manuscript [14] additionally has full proofs of our theorems.

2   Term Rewriting and Innermost Runtime Complexity

We assume basic familiarity with term rewriting (see, e.g., [10]) and recall standard definitions to fix notation. As customary for analysis of runtime complexity of rewriting, we consider terms as *tree-shaped* objects, without sharing of subtrees.

We first define *Term Rewrite Systems* and *Innermost Rewriting*. $\mathcal{T}(\Sigma, \mathcal{V})$ denotes the set of *terms* over a finite signature Σ and the set of variables $\mathcal{V}$. For a term t, its *size* $|t|$ is defined by: (a) if $t \in \mathcal{V}$, $|t| = 1$; (b) if $t = f(t_1, \ldots, t_n)$, then $|t| = 1 + \sum_{i=1}^{n} |t_i|$. The set $\mathcal{P}os(t)$ of the *positions* of t is defined by: (a) if $t \in \mathcal{V}$, then $\mathcal{P}os(t) = \{\varepsilon\}$, and (b) if $t = f(t_1, \ldots, t_n)$, then $\mathcal{P}os(t) = \{\varepsilon\} \cup \bigcup_{1 \leq i \leq n} \{i\pi \mid \pi \in \mathcal{P}os(t_i)\}$. The position ε is the *root position* of term t. If $t = f(t_1, \ldots, t_n)$, $\text{root}(t) = f$ is the *root symbol* of t. The *(strict) prefix order* $>$ on positions is the strict partial order given by: $\tau > \pi$ iff there exists $\pi' \neq \varepsilon$ such that $\pi\pi' = \tau$. Two positions π and τ are *parallel* iff neither $\pi > \tau$ nor $\pi = \tau$ nor $\tau > \pi$ hold. For $\pi \in \mathcal{P}os(t)$, $t|_\pi$ is the subterm of t at position π, and we write $t[s]_\pi$ for the term that results from t by replacing the subterm $t|_\pi$ at position π by the term s.

A substitution σ is a mapping from $\mathcal{V}$ to $\mathcal{T}(\Sigma, \mathcal{V})$ with finite domain $Dom(\sigma) = \{x \in \mathcal{V} \mid \sigma(x) \neq x\}$. We write $\{x_1 \mapsto t_1; \ldots; x_n \mapsto t_n\}$ for a substitution σ with $\sigma(x_i) = t_i$ for $1 \leq i \leq n$ and $\sigma(x) = x$ for all other $x \in \mathcal{V}$. We extend substitutions to terms by $\sigma(f(t_1, \ldots, f_n)) = f(\sigma(t_1), \ldots, \sigma(t_n))$. We may write $t\sigma$ for $\sigma(t)$.

For a term t, $\mathcal{V}(t)$ is the set of variables in t. A *term rewrite system (TRS)* $\mathcal{R}$ is a set of rules $\{\ell_1 \to r_1, \ldots, \ell_n \to r_n\}$ with $\ell_i, r_i \in \mathcal{T}(\Sigma, \mathcal{V})$, $\ell_i \notin \mathcal{V}$, and $\mathcal{V}(r_i) \subseteq \mathcal{V}(\ell_i)$ for all $1 \le i \le n$. The *rewrite relation* of $\mathcal{R}$ is $s \to_{\mathcal{R}} t$ iff there are a rule $\ell \to r \in \mathcal{R}$, a position $\pi \in \mathcal{P}os(s)$, and a substitution σ such that $s = s[\ell\sigma]_\pi$ and $t = s[r\sigma]_\pi$. Here, σ is called the *matcher* and the term $\ell\sigma$ the *redex* of the rewrite step. If no proper subterm of $\ell\sigma$ is a possible redex, $\ell\sigma$ is an *innermost redex*, and the rewrite step is an *innermost rewrite step*, denoted by $s \xrightarrow{i}_{\mathcal{R}} t$.

$\Sigma_d^{\mathcal{R}} = \{f \mid f(\ell_1, \ldots, \ell_n) \to r \in \mathcal{R}\}$ and $\Sigma_c^{\mathcal{R}} = \Sigma \setminus \Sigma_d^{\mathcal{R}}$ are the *defined* and *constructor* symbols of $\mathcal{R}$. We may also just write Σ_d and Σ_c. The set of positions with defined symbols of t is $\mathcal{P}os_d(t) = \{\pi \mid \pi \in \mathcal{P}os(t), \mathrm{root}(t|_\pi) \in \Sigma_d\}$.

For a relation $\to$, $\to^+$ is its transitive closure and $\to^*$ its reflexive-transitive closure. An object o is a *normal form* wrt a relation $\to$ iff there is no o' with $o \to o'$. A relation $\to$ is *confluent* iff $s \to^* t$ and $s \to^* u$ implies that there exists an object v with $t \to^* v$ and $u \to^* v$. A relation $\to$ is *terminating* iff there is no infinite sequence $t_0 \to t_1 \to t_2 \to \cdots$.

Example 1 (size). Consider the TRS $\mathcal{R}$ with the following rules modelling the code of Fig. 1.

$$\mathsf{plus}(\mathsf{Zero}, y) \to y \qquad\qquad \mathsf{size}(\mathsf{Nil}) \to \mathsf{Zero}$$
$$\mathsf{plus}(\mathsf{S}(x), y) \to \mathsf{S}(\mathsf{plus}(x, y)) \qquad \mathsf{size}(\mathsf{Tree}(v, l, r)) \to \mathsf{S}(\mathsf{plus}(\mathsf{size}(l), \mathsf{size}(r)))$$

Here $\Sigma_d^{\mathcal{R}} = \{\mathsf{plus}, \mathsf{size}\}$ and $\Sigma_c^{\mathcal{R}} = \{\mathsf{Zero}, \mathsf{S}, \mathsf{Nil}, \mathsf{Tree}\}$. We have the following innermost rewrite sequence, where the used innermost redexes are underlined:

$$\mathsf{size}(\mathsf{Tree}(\mathsf{Zero}, \mathsf{Nil}, \mathsf{Tree}(\mathsf{Zero}, \mathsf{Nil}, \mathsf{Nil})))$$
$$\xrightarrow{i}_{\mathcal{R}} \mathsf{S}(\mathsf{plus}(\underline{\mathsf{size}(\mathsf{Nil})}, \mathsf{size}(\mathsf{Tree}(\mathsf{Zero}, \mathsf{Nil}, \mathsf{Nil})))))$$
$$\xrightarrow{i}_{\mathcal{R}} \mathsf{S}(\mathsf{plus}(\mathsf{Zero}, \underline{\mathsf{size}(\mathsf{Tree}(\mathsf{Zero}, \mathsf{Nil}, \mathsf{Nil})))))$$
$$\xrightarrow{i}_{\mathcal{R}} \mathsf{S}(\mathsf{plus}(\mathsf{Zero}, \mathsf{S}(\mathsf{plus}(\underline{\mathsf{size}(\mathsf{Nil})}, \mathsf{size}(\mathsf{Nil})))))$$
$$\xrightarrow{i}_{\mathcal{R}} \mathsf{S}(\mathsf{plus}(\mathsf{Zero}, \mathsf{S}(\mathsf{plus}(\mathsf{Zero}, \underline{\mathsf{size}(\mathsf{Nil})})))))$$
$$\xrightarrow{i}_{\mathcal{R}} \mathsf{S}(\mathsf{plus}(\mathsf{Zero}, \mathsf{S}(\underline{\mathsf{plus}(\mathsf{Zero}, \mathsf{Zero})})))$$
$$\xrightarrow{i}_{\mathcal{R}} \mathsf{S}(\underline{\mathsf{plus}(\mathsf{Zero}, \mathsf{S}(\mathsf{Zero}))})$$
$$\xrightarrow{i}_{\mathcal{R}} \mathsf{S}(\mathsf{S}(\mathsf{Zero}))$$

This rewrite sequence uses 7 steps to reach a normal form.

We wish to provide static bounds on the length of the longest rewrite sequence from terms of a specific size. Here we use innermost evaluation strategies, which closely correspond to call-by-value strategies used in many programming languages. We focus on rewrite sequences that start with *basic terms*, corresponding to function calls where a function is applied to data objects. The resulting notion of complexity for term rewriting is known as *innermost runtime complexity*.

Definition 1 (Innermost Runtime Complexity irc [26,37]**).** *The deriva-tion height of a term t wrt a relation $\rightarrow$ is the length of the longest sequence of $\rightarrow$-steps from t:* $\mathrm{dh}(t, \rightarrow) = \sup\{e \mid \exists t' \in \mathcal{T}(\Sigma, \mathcal{V}).\ t \rightarrow^e t'\}$ *where $\rightarrow^e$ is the eth iterate of $\rightarrow$. If t starts an infinite $\rightarrow$-sequence, we write $\mathrm{dh}(t, \rightarrow) = \omega$. Here, ω is the smallest infinite ordinal, i.e., $\omega > n$ holds for all $n \in \mathbb{N}$.*

A term $f(t_1, \ldots, t_k)$ is basic *(for a TRS $\mathcal{R}$) iff $f \in \Sigma_d^{\mathcal{R}}$ and $t_1, \ldots, t_k \in \mathcal{T}(\Sigma_c^{\mathcal{R}}, \mathcal{V})$. $\mathcal{T}_{\mathrm{basic}}^{\mathcal{R}}$ is the set of basic terms for a TRS $\mathcal{R}$. For $n \in \mathbb{N}$, the* innermost runtime complexity *function is $\mathrm{irc}_{\mathcal{R}}(n) = \sup\{\mathrm{dh}(t, \xrightarrow{i}_{\mathcal{R}}) \mid t \in \mathcal{T}_{\mathrm{basic}}^{\mathcal{R}}, |t| \leq n\}$. For all $P \subseteq \mathbb{N} \cup \{\omega\}$, $\sup P$ is the least upper bound of P, where $\sup \emptyset = 0$.*

Many automated techniques are available [8,26,27,35–37] to analyse $\mathrm{irc}_{\mathcal{R}}$. We build on Dependency Tuples [37], originally designed to find upper bounds for (sequential) innermost runtime complexity. A central idea is to group all function calls by a rewrite rule *together* rather than to separate them (as with DPs for proving termination [7]). We use *sharp terms* to represent these function calls.

Definition 2 (Sharp Terms $\mathcal{T}^\sharp$). *For every $f \in \Sigma_d$, we introduce a fresh symbol $f^\sharp$ of the same arity, called a* sharp symbol. *For a term $t = f(t_1, \ldots, t_n)$ with $f \in \Sigma_d$, we define $t^\sharp = f^\sharp(t_1, \ldots, t_n)$. For all other terms t, we define $t^\sharp = t$. $\mathcal{T}^\sharp = \{t^\sharp \mid t \in \mathcal{T}(\Sigma, \mathcal{V}), \mathrm{root}(t) \in \Sigma_d\}$ denotes the set of* sharp terms.

To get an upper bound for sequential complexity, we "count" how often each rewrite rule is used. The idea is that when a rule $\ell \rightarrow r$ is used, the cost (i.e., number of rewrite steps for the evaluation) of the function call to the instance of ℓ is 1 + the sum of the costs of all the function calls in the resulting instance of r, counted separately in some fixed order. To group k function calls together, we use "compound symbols" Com_k of arity k, which intuitively represent the sum of the runtimes of their arguments.

Definition 3 (Dependency Tuple, DT [37]**).** *A dependency tuple (DT) is a rule of the form $s^\sharp \rightarrow \mathsf{Com}_n(t_1^\sharp, \ldots, t_n^\sharp)$ where $s^\sharp, t_1^\sharp, \ldots, t_n^\sharp \in \mathcal{T}^\sharp$. Let $\ell \rightarrow r$ be a rule with $\mathcal{P}os_d(r) = \{\pi_1, \ldots, \pi_n\}$ and $\pi_1 > \ldots > \pi_n$ for a total order $>$ (e.g., lex-icographic order) on positions. Then $DT(\ell \rightarrow r) = \ell^\sharp \rightarrow \mathsf{Com}_n(r|_{\pi_1}^\sharp, \ldots, r|_{\pi_n}^\sharp)$.[1] For a TRS $\mathcal{R}$, let $DT(\mathcal{R}) = \{DT(\ell \rightarrow r) \mid \ell \rightarrow r \in \mathcal{R}\}$.*

Example 2. For $\mathcal{R}$ from Example 1, $DT(\mathcal{R})$ consists of the following DTs:

$$\mathsf{plus}^\sharp(\mathsf{Zero}, y) \rightarrow \mathsf{Com}_0$$
$$\mathsf{plus}^\sharp(\mathsf{S}(x), y) \rightarrow \mathsf{Com}_1(\mathsf{plus}^\sharp(x, y))$$
$$\mathsf{size}^\sharp(\mathsf{Nil}) \rightarrow \mathsf{Com}_0$$
$$\mathsf{size}^\sharp(\mathsf{Tree}(v, l, r)) \rightarrow \mathsf{Com}_3(\mathsf{size}^\sharp(l), \mathsf{size}^\sharp(r), \mathsf{plus}^\sharp(\mathsf{size}(l), \mathsf{size}(r)))$$

To represent the complexity of a sharp term for a set of DTs and a TRS $\mathcal{R}$, *chain trees* are used [37]. Intuitively, a chain tree for some sharp term is

---

[1] The order $>$ must be total to ensure that the function DT is well defined wrt the order of the arguments of Com_n. The (partial!) prefix order $>$ is not sufficient here.

a dependency tree of the computations involved in evaluating this term. Each node represents a computation (the DT) on some arguments (defined by the substitution).

Definition 4 (Chain Tree, *Cplx* [37]). *Let $\mathcal{D}$ be a set of DTs and $\mathcal{R}$ be a TRS. Let T be a (possibly infinite) tree where each node is labelled with a DT $q^\sharp \to \mathsf{Com}_n(w_1^\sharp, \ldots, w_n^\sharp)$ from $\mathcal{D}$ and a substitution ν, written $(q^\sharp \to \mathsf{Com}_n(w_1^\sharp, \ldots, w_n^\sharp) \mid \nu)$. Let the root node be labelled with $(s^\sharp \to \mathsf{Com}_e(r_1^\sharp, \ldots, r_e^\sharp) \mid \sigma)$. Then T is a $(\mathcal{D}, \mathcal{R})$-chain tree for $s^\sharp \sigma$ iff the following conditions hold for any node of T, where $(u^\sharp \to \mathsf{Com}_m(v_1^\sharp, \ldots, v_m^\sharp) \mid \mu)$ is the label of the node:*

- *$u^\sharp \mu$ is in normal form wrt $\mathcal{R}$;*
- *if this node has the children $(p_1^\sharp \to \mathsf{Com}_{m_1}(\ldots) \mid \delta_1), \ldots, (p_k^\sharp \to \mathsf{Com}_{m_k}(\ldots) \mid \delta_k)$, then there are pairwise different $i_1, \ldots, i_k \in \{1, \ldots, m\}$ with $v_{i_j}^\sharp \mu \xrightarrow{i}{}_{\mathcal{R}}^* p_j^\sharp \delta_j$ for all $j \in \{1, \ldots, k\}$.*

Let $\mathcal{S} \subseteq \mathcal{D}$ and $s^\sharp \in T^\sharp$. For a chain tree T, $|T|_{\mathcal{S}} \in \mathbb{N} \cup \{\omega\}$ is the number of nodes in T labelled with a DT from $\mathcal{S}$. We define $Cplx_{\langle \mathcal{D}, \mathcal{S}, \mathcal{R} \rangle}(s^\sharp) = \sup\{|T|_{\mathcal{S}} \mid T$ is a $(\mathcal{D}, \mathcal{R})$-chain tree for $s^\sharp\}$. For terms $s^\sharp$ without a $(\mathcal{D}, \mathcal{R})$-chain tree, we define $Cplx_{\langle \mathcal{D}, \mathcal{S}, \mathcal{R} \rangle}(s^\sharp) = 0$.

Example 3. For $\mathcal{R}$ from Example 1 and $\mathcal{D} = DT(\mathcal{R})$ from Example 2, the following is a chain tree for the term $\mathsf{size}^\sharp(\mathsf{Tree}(\mathsf{Zero}, \mathsf{Nil}, \mathsf{Nil}))$:

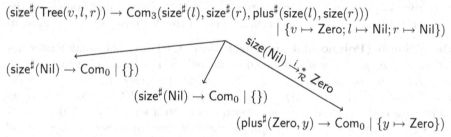

$(\mathsf{size}^\sharp(\mathsf{Tree}(v, l, r)) \to \mathsf{Com}_3(\mathsf{size}^\sharp(l), \mathsf{size}^\sharp(r), \mathsf{plus}^\sharp(\mathsf{size}(l), \mathsf{size}(r)))$
$\mid \{v \mapsto \mathsf{Zero}; l \mapsto \mathsf{Nil}; r \mapsto \mathsf{Nil}\})$

$(\mathsf{size}^\sharp(\mathsf{Nil}) \to \mathsf{Com}_0 \mid \{\})$

$(\mathsf{size}^\sharp(\mathsf{Nil}) \to \mathsf{Com}_0 \mid \{\})$

$(\mathsf{plus}^\sharp(\mathsf{Zero}, y) \to \mathsf{Com}_0 \mid \{y \mapsto \mathsf{Zero}\})$

The main correctness statement in the sequential case is the following:

Theorem 1 (*Cplx* bounds Derivation Height for $\xrightarrow{i}{}_{\mathcal{R}}$ [37]). *Let $\mathcal{R}$ be a TRS, let $t = f(t_1, \ldots, t_n) \in \mathcal{T}(\Sigma, \mathcal{V})$ such that all t_i are in normal form (this includes all $t \in \mathcal{T}_{\text{basic}}^{\mathcal{R}}$). Then we have $\mathrm{dh}(t, \xrightarrow{i}{}_{\mathcal{R}}) \leq Cplx_{\langle DT(\mathcal{R}), DT(\mathcal{R}), \mathcal{R} \rangle}(t^\sharp)$. If $\xrightarrow{i}{}_{\mathcal{R}}$ is confluent, then $\mathrm{dh}(t, \xrightarrow{i}{}_{\mathcal{R}}) = Cplx_{\langle DT(\mathcal{R}), DT(\mathcal{R}), \mathcal{R} \rangle}(t^\sharp)$.*

For automated complexity analysis with DTs, the following notion of *DT problems* is used as a characterisation of DTs that we reduce in incremental proof steps to a trivially solved problem.

Definition 5 (DT Problem, Complexity of DT Problem [37]). *Let $\mathcal{R}$ be a TRS, $\mathcal{D}$ be a set of DTs, $\mathcal{S} \subseteq \mathcal{D}$. Then $\langle \mathcal{D}, \mathcal{S}, \mathcal{R} \rangle$ is a DT problem. Its complexity function is $\mathrm{irc}_{\langle \mathcal{D}, \mathcal{S}, \mathcal{R} \rangle}(n) = \sup\{Cplx_{\langle \mathcal{D}, \mathcal{S}, \mathcal{R} \rangle}(t^\sharp) \mid t \in \mathcal{T}_{\text{basic}}^{\mathcal{R}}, |t| \leq n\}$. The DT problem $\langle DT(\mathcal{R}), DT(\mathcal{R}), \mathcal{R} \rangle$ is called the* canonical DT problem for $\mathcal{R}$.

For a DT problem $\langle \mathcal{D}, \mathcal{S}, \mathcal{R} \rangle$, the set $\mathcal{D}$ contains all DTs that can be used in chain trees. $\mathcal{S}$ contains the DTs whose complexity remains to be analysed. $\mathcal{R}$ contains the rewrite rules for evaluating the arguments of DTs. Here we focus on simplifying $\mathcal{S}$ (thus $\mathcal{D}$ and $\mathcal{R}$ are fixed during the process) but techniques to simplify $\mathcal{D}$ and $\mathcal{R}$ are available as well [8, 37].

Theorem 1 implies the following link between $\mathrm{irc}_{\mathcal{R}}$ and $\mathrm{irc}_{\langle DT(\mathcal{R}), DT(\mathcal{R}), \mathcal{R} \rangle}$:

Theorem 2 (Complexity Bounds for TRSs via Canonical DT Problems [37]). *Let $\mathcal{R}$ be a TRS with canonical DT problem $\langle DT(\mathcal{R}), DT(\mathcal{R}), \mathcal{R} \rangle$. Then we have $\mathrm{irc}_{\mathcal{R}}(n) \leq \mathrm{irc}_{\langle DT(\mathcal{R}), DT(\mathcal{R}), \mathcal{R} \rangle}(n)$. If $\xrightarrow{i}_{\mathcal{R}}$ is confluent, we have $\mathrm{irc}_{\mathcal{R}}(n) = \mathrm{irc}_{\langle DT(\mathcal{R}), DT(\mathcal{R}), \mathcal{R} \rangle}(n)$.*

In practice, the focus is on finding asymptotic bounds for $\mathrm{irc}_{\mathcal{R}}$. For example, Example 4 will show that for our TRS $\mathcal{R}$ from Example 1 we have $\mathrm{irc}_{\mathcal{R}}(n) \in \mathcal{O}(n^2)$.

A DT problem $\langle \mathcal{D}, \mathcal{S}, \mathcal{R} \rangle$ is said to be *solved* iff $\mathcal{S} = \emptyset$: we always have $\mathrm{irc}_{\langle \mathcal{D}, \emptyset, \mathcal{R} \rangle}(n) = 0$. To simplify and finally solve DT problems in an incremental fashion, complexity analysis techniques called *DT processors* are used. A DT processor takes a DT problem as input and returns a (hopefully simpler) DT problem as well as an asymptotic complexity bound as an output. The largest asymptotic complexity bound returned over this incremental process is then also an upper bound for $\mathrm{irc}_{\mathcal{R}}(n)$ [37, Corollary 21].

The reduction pair processor using polynomial interpretations [37] applies a restriction of polynomial interpretations to $\mathbb{N}$ [34] to infer upper bounds on the number of times that DTs can occur in a chain tree for terms of size at most n.

Definition 6 (Polynomial Interpretation, CPI). *A polynomial interpretation $\mathcal{P}ol$ maps every n-ary function symbol to a polynomial with variables $x_1, \ldots, x_n$ and coefficients from $\mathbb{N}$. $\mathcal{P}ol$ extends to terms via $\mathcal{P}ol(x) = x$ for $x \in \mathcal{V}$ and $\mathcal{P}ol(f(t_1, \ldots, t_n)) = \mathcal{P}ol(f)(\mathcal{P}ol(t_1), \ldots, \mathcal{P}ol(t_n))$. $\mathcal{P}ol$ induces an order $\succ_{\mathcal{P}ol}$ and a quasi-order $\succsim_{\mathcal{P}ol}$ over terms where $s \succ_{\mathcal{P}ol} t$ iff $\mathcal{P}ol(s) > \mathcal{P}ol(t)$ and $s \succsim_{\mathcal{P}ol} t$ iff $\mathcal{P}ol(s) \geq \mathcal{P}ol(t)$ for all instantiations of variables with natural numbers.*

A complexity polynomial interpretation (CPI) $\mathcal{P}ol$ is a polynomial interpretation where: $\mathcal{P}ol(\mathsf{Com}_n(x_1, \ldots, x_n)) = x_1 + \cdots + x_n$, and for all $f \in \Sigma_c$, $\mathcal{P}ol(f(x_1, \ldots, x_n)) = a_1 \cdot x_1 + \cdots + a_n \cdot x_n + b$ for some $a_i \in \{0, 1\}$ and $b \in \mathbb{N}$.

The restriction for CPIs regarding constructor symbols enforces that the interpretation of a constructor term t (as an argument of a term for which a chain tree is constructed) can exceed its size $|t|$ only by at most a constant factor. This is crucial for soundness. Using a CPI, we can now define and state correctness of the corresponding reduction pair processor [37, Theorem 27].

Theorem 3 (Reduction Pair Processor with CPIs [37]). *Let $\langle \mathcal{D}, \mathcal{S}, \mathcal{R} \rangle$ be a DT problem, let $\succsim$ and $\succ$ be induced by a CPI $\mathcal{P}ol$. Let $k \in \mathbb{N}$ be the maximal degree of all polynomials $\mathcal{P}ol(f^\sharp)$ for all $f \in \Sigma_d$. Let $\mathcal{D} \cup \mathcal{R} \subseteq \succsim$. If $\mathcal{S} \cap \succ \neq \emptyset$, the reduction pair processor returns the DT problem $\langle \mathcal{D}, \mathcal{S} \backslash \succ, \mathcal{R} \rangle$ and the complexity $\mathcal{O}(n^k)$. Then the reduction pair processor is sound.*

Example 4 (Example 2 continued). For our running example, consider the CPI $\mathcal{P}ol$ with: $\mathcal{P}ol(\text{plus}^{\sharp}(x_1, x_2)) = \mathcal{P}ol(\text{size}(x_1)) = x_1$, $\mathcal{P}ol(\text{size}^{\sharp}(x_1)) = 2x_1 + x_1^2$, $\mathcal{P}ol(\text{plus}(x_1, x_2)) = x_1 + x_2$, $\mathcal{P}ol(\text{Tree}(x_1, x_2, x_3)) = 1 + x_2 + x_3$, $\mathcal{P}ol(\text{S}(x_1)) = 1 + x_1$, $\mathcal{P}ol(\text{Zero}) = \mathcal{P}ol(\text{Nil}) = 1$. $\mathcal{P}ol$ orients all DTs in $\mathcal{S} = DT(\mathcal{R})$ with $\succ$ and all rules in $\mathcal{R}$ with $\succsim$. This proves $\text{irc}_{\mathcal{R}}(n) \in \mathcal{O}(n^2)$: since the maximal degree of the CPI for a symbol $f^{\sharp}$ is 2, the upper bound of $\mathcal{O}(n^2)$ follows by Theorem 3.

3   Finding Upper Bounds for Parallel Complexity

In this section we present our main contribution: an application of the DT framework from innermost runtime complexity to *parallel-innermost rewriting*.

The notion of parallel-innermost rewriting dates back at least to [40]. Informally, in a parallel-innermost rewrite step, all innermost redexes are rewritten simultaneously. This corresponds to executing all function calls in parallel using a call-by-value strategy on a machine with unbounded parallelism [15]. In the literature [39], this strategy is also known as "max-parallel-innermost rewriting".

Definition 7 (Parallel-Innermost Rewriting [19]). *A term s rewrites innermost in parallel to t with a TRS $\mathcal{R}$, written $s \xrightarrow{\,i\,}\!\!\!+\!\!\!\!\rightarrow_{\mathcal{R}} t$, iff $s \xrightarrow{\,i\,}^{+}_{\mathcal{R}} t$, and either (a) $s \xrightarrow{\,i\,}_{\mathcal{R}} t$ with s an innermost redex, or (b) $s = f(s_1, \ldots, s_n)$, $t = f(t_1, \ldots, t_n)$, and for all $1 \le k \le n$ either $s_k \xrightarrow{\,i\,}\!\!\!+\!\!\!\!\rightarrow_{\mathcal{R}} t_k$ or $s_k = t_k$ is a normal form.*

Example 5 (Example 1 continued). The TRS $\mathcal{R}$ from Example 1 allows the following parallel-innermost rewrite sequence, where innermost redexes are underlined:

$$\underline{\text{size}(\text{Tree}(\text{Zero}, \text{Nil}, \text{Tree}(\text{Zero}, \text{Nil}, \text{Nil}))))}$$
$$\xrightarrow{\,i\,}\!\!\!+\!\!\!\!\rightarrow_{\mathcal{R}} \text{S}(\text{plus}(\underline{\text{size}(\text{Nil})}, \underline{\text{size}(\text{Tree}(\text{Zero}, \text{Nil}, \text{Nil}))}))$$
$$\xrightarrow{\,i\,}\!\!\!+\!\!\!\!\rightarrow_{\mathcal{R}} \text{S}(\text{plus}(\text{Zero}, \text{S}(\text{plus}(\underline{\text{size}(\text{Nil})}, \underline{\text{size}(\text{Nil})}))))$$
$$\xrightarrow{\,i\,}\!\!\!+\!\!\!\!\rightarrow_{\mathcal{R}} \text{S}(\text{plus}(\text{Zero}, \text{S}(\underline{\text{plus}(\text{Zero}, \text{Zero})})))$$
$$\xrightarrow{\,i\,}\!\!\!+\!\!\!\!\rightarrow_{\mathcal{R}} \text{S}(\underline{\text{plus}(\text{Zero}, \text{S}(\text{Zero}))})$$
$$\xrightarrow{\,i\,}\!\!\!+\!\!\!\!\rightarrow_{\mathcal{R}} \text{S}(\text{S}(\text{Zero}))$$

In the second and in the third step, two innermost steps each happen in parallel (which is not possible with standard innermost rewriting: $\xrightarrow{\,i\,}\!\!\!+\!\!\!\!\rightarrow_{\mathcal{R}} \not\subseteq \xrightarrow{\,i\,}_{\mathcal{R}}$). An innermost rewrite sequence without parallel evaluation necessarily needs two more steps to a normal form from this start term, as in Example 1.

Note that for all TRSs $\mathcal{R}$, $\xrightarrow{\,i\,}\!\!\!+\!\!\!\!\rightarrow_{\mathcal{R}}$ is terminating iff $\xrightarrow{\,i\,}_{\mathcal{R}}$ is terminating [19]. Example 5 shows that such an equivalence does *not* hold for the derivation height of a term. The question now is: given a TRS $\mathcal{R}$, how much of a speed-up might we get by a switch from innermost to parallel-innermost rewriting? To investigate, we extend the notion of innermost runtime complexity to parallel-innermost rewriting.

Definition 8 (Parallel-Innermost Runtime Complexity pirc). *For $n \in \mathbb{N}$, we define the* parallel-innermost runtime complexity *function as* $\text{pirc}_{\mathcal{R}}(n) = \sup\{\text{dh}(t, \xrightarrow{\,i\,}\!\!\!+\!\!\!\!\rightarrow_{\mathcal{R}}) \mid t \in \mathcal{T}^{\mathcal{R}}_{\text{basic}}, |t| \le n\}$.

In the literature on parallel computing [11,15,30], the terms *depth* or *span* are commonly used for the concept of the runtime of a function on a machine with unbounded parallelism ("wall time"), corresponding to the complexity measure of $\mathrm{pirc}_{\mathcal{R}}$. In contrast, $\mathrm{irc}_{\mathcal{R}}$ would describe the *work* of a function ("CPU time").

In the following, given a TRS $\mathcal{R}$, our goal shall be to infer (asymptotic) upper bounds for $\mathrm{pirc}_{\mathcal{R}}$ fully automatically. Of course, an upper bound for (sequential) $\mathrm{irc}_{\mathcal{R}}$ is also an upper bound for $\mathrm{pirc}_{\mathcal{R}}$. We will now introduce techniques to find upper bounds for $\mathrm{pirc}_{\mathcal{R}}$ that are strictly tighter than these trivial bounds.

To find upper bounds for runtime complexity of parallel-innermost rewriting, we can *reuse* the notion of DTs from Definition 3 for sequential innermost rewriting along with existing techniques [37] as illustrated in the following example.

Example 6. In the recursive size-rule, the two calls to size(l) and size(r) happen *in parallel* (they are *structurally independent*) and take place at *parallel positions* in the term. Thus, the cost (number of rewrite steps with $\xrightarrow{\mathrm{i}}_{\mathcal{R}}$ until a normal form is reached) for these two calls is not the *sum*, but the *maximum* of their individual costs. Regardless of which of these two calls has the higher cost, we still need to add the cost for the call to plus on the results of the two calls: plus starts evaluating only after both calls to size have finished. With σ as the used matcher for the rule and with $t \downarrow$ as the (here unique) normal form resulting from repeatedly rewriting a term t with $\xrightarrow{\mathrm{i}}_{\mathcal{R}}$ (the "result" of evaluating t), we have:

$$\mathrm{dh}(\mathrm{size}(\mathrm{Tree}(v,l,r))\sigma, \xrightarrow{\mathrm{i}}_{\mathcal{R}})$$
$$= 1 + \max(\mathrm{dh}(\mathrm{size}(l)\sigma, \xrightarrow{\mathrm{i}}_{\mathcal{R}}), \mathrm{dh}(\mathrm{size}(r)\sigma, \xrightarrow{\mathrm{i}}_{\mathcal{R}}))$$
$$+ \mathrm{dh}(\mathrm{plus}(\mathrm{size}(l)\sigma\downarrow, \mathrm{size}(r)\sigma\downarrow), \xrightarrow{\mathrm{i}}_{\mathcal{R}})$$

In the DT setting, we could introduce a new symbol ComPar_k that explicitly expresses that its arguments are evaluated in parallel. This symbol would then be interpreted as the maximum of its arguments in an extension of Theorem 3:

$$\mathrm{size}^\sharp(\mathrm{Tree}(v,l,r)) \to \mathrm{Com}_2(\mathrm{ComPar}_2(\mathrm{size}^\sharp(l), \mathrm{size}^\sharp(r)), \mathrm{plus}^\sharp(\mathrm{size}(l), \mathrm{size}(r)))$$

Although automation of the search for polynomial interpretations extended by the maximum function is readily available [23], we would still have to extend the notion of Dependency Tuples and also adapt all existing techniques in the Dependency Tuple framework to work with ComPar_k.

This is why we have chosen the following alternative approach, which is equally powerful on theoretical level and enables immediate reuse of existing techniques in the DT framework. Equivalently to the above, we can "factor in" the cost of calling plus into the maximum function:

$$\mathrm{dh}(\mathrm{size}(\mathrm{Tree}(v,l,r))\sigma, \xrightarrow{\mathrm{i}}_{\mathcal{R}})$$
$$= \max(1 + \mathrm{dh}(\mathrm{size}(l)\sigma, \xrightarrow{\mathrm{i}}_{\mathcal{R}}) + \mathrm{dh}(\mathrm{plus}(\mathrm{size}(l)\sigma\downarrow, \mathrm{size}(r)\sigma\downarrow), \xrightarrow{\mathrm{i}}_{\mathcal{R}}),$$
$$1 + \mathrm{dh}(\mathrm{size}(r)\sigma, \xrightarrow{\mathrm{i}}_{\mathcal{R}}) + \mathrm{dh}(\mathrm{plus}(\mathrm{size}(l)\sigma\downarrow, \mathrm{size}(r)\sigma\downarrow), \xrightarrow{\mathrm{i}}_{\mathcal{R}}))$$

Intuitively, this would correspond to evaluating plus($\ldots$, $\ldots$) twice, in two parallel threads of execution, which costs the same amount of (wall) time as evaluating plus($\ldots$, $\ldots$) once. We can represent this maximum of the execution times of two threads by introducing *two* DTs for our recursive size-rule:

$$\text{size}^\sharp(\text{Tree}(v, l, r)) \rightarrow \text{Com}_2(\text{size}^\sharp(l), \text{plus}^\sharp(\text{size}(l), \text{size}(r)))$$
$$\text{size}^\sharp(\text{Tree}(v, l, r)) \rightarrow \text{Com}_2(\text{size}^\sharp(r), \text{plus}^\sharp(\text{size}(l), \text{size}(r)))$$

To express the cost of a concrete rewrite sequence, we would non-deterministically choose the DT that corresponds to the "slower thread".

In other words, when a rule $\ell \rightarrow r$ is used, the cost of the function call to the instance of ℓ is 1 + the sum of the costs of the function calls in the resulting instance of r *that are in structural dependency with each other*. The actual cost of the function call to the instance of ℓ in a concrete rewrite sequence is the *maximum* of all the possible costs caused by such *chains* of structural dependency (based on the prefix order $>$ on positions of defined function symbols in r). Thus, *structurally independent* function calls are considered in separate DTs, whose non-determinism models the parallelism of these function calls.

The notion of *structural dependency* of function calls is captured by Definition 9. Basically, it comes from the fact that a term cannot be evaluated before all its subterms have been reduced to normal forms (innermost rewriting/*call by value*). This induces a "happens-before" relation for the computation [33].

Definition 9 (Structural Dependency, *MSDC*). *For positions $\pi_1, \ldots, \pi_k$, we call $\langle \pi_1, \ldots, \pi_k \rangle$ a structural dependency chain for a term t iff $\pi_1, \ldots, \pi_k \in \mathcal{P}os_d(t)$ and $\pi_1 > \ldots > \pi_k$. Here π_i structurally depends on π_j in t iff $j < i$. A structural dependency chain $\langle \pi_1, \ldots, \pi_k \rangle$ for a term t is* maximal *iff $k = 0$ and $\mathcal{P}os_d(t) = \emptyset$, or $k > 0$ and $\forall \pi \in \mathcal{P}os_d(t) . \pi \not> \pi_1 \wedge (\pi_1 > \pi \Rightarrow \pi \in \{\pi_2, \ldots, \pi_k\})$. We write $MSDC(t)$ for the set of all maximal structural dependency chains for t.*

Note that $MSDC(t) \neq \emptyset$ always holds: if $\mathcal{P}os_d(t) = \emptyset$, then $MSDC(t) = \{\langle \rangle\}$.

Example 7. Let $t = \text{S}(\text{plus}(\text{size}(\text{Nil}), \text{plus}(\text{size}(x), \text{Zero})))$. In our running example, t has the following structural dependencies: $MSDC(t) = \{\langle 11, 1 \rangle, \langle 121, 12, 1 \rangle\}$. The chain $\langle 11, 1 \rangle$ corresponds to the nesting of $t|_{11} = \text{size}(\text{Nil})$ below $t|_1 = \text{plus}(\text{size}(\text{Nil}), \text{plus}(\text{size}(x), \text{Zero}))$, so the evaluation of $t|_1$ will have to wait at least until $t|_{11}$ has been fully evaluated.

If π structurally depends on τ in a term t, neither $t|_\tau$ nor $t|_\pi$ need to be a redex. Rather, $t|_\tau$ could be *instantiated* to a redex and an instance of $t|_\pi$ could become a redex after its subterms, including the instance of $t|_\tau$, have been evaluated.

We thus revisit the notion of DTs, which now embed structural dependencies in addition to the algorithmic dependencies already captured in DTs.

Definition 10 (Parallel Dependency Tuples *PDT*, Canonical Parallel DT Problem). *For a rewrite rule $\ell \rightarrow r$, we define the set of its* Parallel Dependency Tuples (PDTs) $PDT(\ell \rightarrow r)$: $PDT(\ell \rightarrow r) = \{\ell^\sharp \rightarrow \text{Com}_k(r|^\sharp_{\pi_1}, \ldots, r|^\sharp_{\pi_k})\mid$

$\langle \pi_1, \ldots, \pi_k \rangle \in MSDC(r)\}$. For a TRS $\mathcal{R}$, let $PDT(\mathcal{R}) = \bigcup_{\ell \to r \in \mathcal{R}} PDT(\ell \to r)$. The canonical parallel DT problem *for* $\mathcal{R}$ *is* $\langle PDT(\mathcal{R}), PDT(\mathcal{R}), \mathcal{R} \rangle$.

Example 8. For our recursive size-rule $\ell \to r$, we have $\mathcal{P}os_d(r) = \{1, 11, 12\}$ and $MSDC(r) = \{\langle 11, 1 \rangle, \langle 12, 1 \rangle\}$. With $r|_1 = \mathsf{plus}(\mathsf{size}(l), \mathsf{size}(r))$, $r|_{11} = \mathsf{size}(l)$, and $r|_{12} = \mathsf{size}(r)$, we get the PDTs from Example 6. For the rule $\mathsf{size}(\mathsf{Nil}) \to \mathsf{Zero}$, we have $MSDC(\mathsf{Zero}) = \{\langle\rangle\}$, so we get $PDT(\mathsf{size}(\mathsf{Nil}) \to \mathsf{Zero}) = \{\mathsf{size}^\sharp(\mathsf{Nil}) \to \mathsf{Com}_0\}$.

We can now make our main correctness statement:

Theorem 4 (*Cplx* bounds Derivation Height for $\Vdash^i_{\mathcal{R}}$). *Let $\mathcal{R}$ be a TRS, let $t = f(t_1, \ldots, t_n) \in \mathcal{T}(\Sigma, \mathcal{V})$ such that all t_i are in normal form (e.g., when $t \in \mathcal{T}^{\mathcal{R}}_{\mathrm{basic}}$). Then we have* $\mathrm{dh}(t, \Vdash^i_{\mathcal{R}}) \leq Cplx_{\langle PDT(\mathcal{R}), PDT(\mathcal{R}), \mathcal{R} \rangle}(t^\sharp)$. *If $\Vdash^i_{\mathcal{R}}$ is confluent, then* $\mathrm{dh}(t, \Vdash^i_{\mathcal{R}}) = Cplx_{\langle PDT(\mathcal{R}), PDT(\mathcal{R}), \mathcal{R} \rangle}(t^\sharp)$.[2]

From Theorem 4, the soundness of our approach to parallel complexity analysis via the DT framework follows analogously to [37]:

Theorem 5 (Parallel Complexity Bounds for TRSs via Canonical Parallel DT Problems). *Let $\mathcal{R}$ be a TRS with canonical parallel DT problem $\langle PDT(\mathcal{R}), PDT(\mathcal{R}), \mathcal{R} \rangle$. Then we have* $\mathrm{pirc}_{\mathcal{R}}(n) \leq \mathrm{irc}_{\langle PDT(\mathcal{R}), PDT(\mathcal{R}), \mathcal{R} \rangle}(n)$. *If $\Vdash^i_{\mathcal{R}}$ is confluent, we have* $\mathrm{pirc}_{\mathcal{R}}(n) = \mathrm{irc}_{\langle PDT(\mathcal{R}), PDT(\mathcal{R}), \mathcal{R} \rangle}(n)$.

This theorem implies that we can reuse arbitrary techniques to find upper bounds for *sequential* complexity in the DT framework also to find upper bounds for *parallel* complexity, without requiring any modification to the framework.

Thus, via Theorem 3, in particular we can use polynomial interpretations in the DT framework for our PDTs to get upper bounds for $\mathrm{pirc}_{\mathcal{R}}$.

Example 9 (Example 6 continued). For our TRS $\mathcal{R}$ computing the size function on trees, we get the set $PDT(\mathcal{R})$ with the following PDTs:

$$
\begin{aligned}
\mathsf{plus}^\sharp(\mathsf{Zero}, y) &\to \mathsf{Com}_0 \\
\mathsf{plus}^\sharp(\mathsf{S}(x), y) &\to \mathsf{Com}_1(\mathsf{plus}^\sharp(x, y)) \\
\mathsf{size}^\sharp(\mathsf{Nil}) &\to \mathsf{Com}_0 \\
\mathsf{size}^\sharp(\mathsf{Tree}(v, l, r)) &\to \mathsf{Com}_2(\mathsf{size}^\sharp(l), \mathsf{plus}^\sharp(\mathsf{size}(l), \mathsf{size}(r))) \\
\mathsf{size}^\sharp(\mathsf{Tree}(v, l, r)) &\to \mathsf{Com}_2(\mathsf{size}^\sharp(r), \mathsf{plus}^\sharp(\mathsf{size}(l), \mathsf{size}(r)))
\end{aligned}
$$

The interpretation $\mathcal{P}ol$ from Example 4 implies $\mathrm{pirc}_{\mathcal{R}}(n) \in \mathcal{O}(n^2)$. This bound is tight: consider $\mathsf{size}(t)$ for a comb-shaped tree t where the first argument of Tree is always Zero and the third is always Nil. The function plus, which needs time linear in its first argument, is called linearly often on data linear in the size of the start term. Due to the structural dependencies, these calls do not happen in parallel (so call $k + 1$ to plus must wait for call k).

---

[2] The proof uses the confluence of $\mathcal{R}$ as a sufficient criterion for *unique normal forms*.

Example 10. Note that $\mathrm{pirc}_{\mathcal{R}}(n)$ can be asymptotically lower than $\mathrm{irc}_{\mathcal{R}}(n)$, for instance for the TRS $\mathcal{R}$ with the following rules:

doubles(Zero) $\to$ Nil	d(Zero) $\to$ Zero
doubles(S(x)) $\to$ Cons(d(S(x)), doubles(x))	d(S(x)) $\to$ S(S(d(x)))

The upper bound $\mathrm{irc}_{\mathcal{R}}(n) \in \mathcal{O}(n^2)$ is tight: from doubles(S(S(...S(Zero)...))), we get linearly many calls to the linear-time function d on arguments of size linear in the start term. However, the Parallel Dependency Tuples in this example are:

doubles$^\sharp$(Zero) $\to$ Com$_0$	d$^\sharp$(Zero) $\to$ Com$_0$
doubles$^\sharp$(S(x)) $\to$ Com$_1$(d$^\sharp$(S(x)))	d$^\sharp$(S(x)) $\to$ Com$_1$(d$^\sharp$(x))
doubles$^\sharp$(S(x)) $\to$ Com$_1$(doubles$^\sharp$(x))	

Then the following polynomial interpretation, which orients all DTs with $\succ$ and all rules from $\mathcal{R}$ with $\succsim$, proves $\mathrm{pirc}_{\mathcal{R}}(n) \in \mathcal{O}(n)$: $\mathcal{P}ol(\text{doubles}^\sharp(x_1)) = \mathcal{P}ol(\text{d}(x_1)) = 2x_1, \mathcal{P}ol(\text{d}^\sharp(x_1)) = x_1, \mathcal{P}ol(\text{doubles}(x_1)) = \mathcal{P}ol(\text{Cons}(x_1, x_2)) = \mathcal{P}ol(\text{Zero}) = \mathcal{P}ol(\text{Nil}) = 1, \mathcal{P}ol(\text{S}(x_1)) = 1 + x_1$.

Interestingly enough, Parallel Dependency Tuples also allow us to identify TRSs that have *no* potential for parallelisation by parallel-innermost rewriting.

Theorem 6 (Absence of Parallelism by PDTs). *Let $\mathcal{R}$ be a TRS such that for all rules $\ell \to r \in \mathcal{R}$, $|MSDC(r)| = 1$. Then: (a) $PDT(\mathcal{R}) = DT(\mathcal{R})$; (b) for all basic terms t_0 and rewrite sequences $t_0 \xLeftrightarrow{\text{i}}_{\mathcal{R}} t_1 \xLeftrightarrow{\text{i}}_{\mathcal{R}} t_2 \xLeftrightarrow{\text{i}}_{\mathcal{R}} \ldots$, also $t_0 \xrightarrow{\text{i}}_{\mathcal{R}} t_1 \xrightarrow{\text{i}}_{\mathcal{R}} t_2 \xrightarrow{\text{i}}_{\mathcal{R}} \ldots$ holds (i.e., from basic terms, $\xLeftrightarrow{\text{i}}_{\mathcal{R}}$ and $\xrightarrow{\text{i}}_{\mathcal{R}}$ coincide); (c) $\mathrm{pirc}_{\mathcal{R}}(n) = \mathrm{irc}_{\mathcal{R}}(n)$.*

Thus, for TRSs $\mathcal{R}$ where Theorem 6 applies, no rewrite rule can introduce parallel redexes, and specific analysis techniques for $\mathrm{pirc}_{\mathcal{R}}$ are not needed.

4 From Parallel DTs to Innermost Rewriting

As we have seen in the previous section, we can transform a TRS $\mathcal{R}$ with parallel-innermost rewrite relation to a DT problem whose complexity provides an upper bound of $\mathrm{pirc}_{\mathcal{R}}$ (or, for confluent $\xLeftrightarrow{\text{i}}_{\mathcal{R}}$, corresponds exactly to $\mathrm{pirc}_{\mathcal{R}}$). However, DTs are only one of many available techniques to find bounds for $\mathrm{irc}_{\mathcal{R}}$. Other techniques include, e.g., Weak Dependency Pairs [26], usable replacement maps [27], the Combination Framework [8], a transformation to complexity problems for integer transition systems [36], amortised complexity analysis [35], or techniques for finding *lower* bounds [22]. Thus, can we benefit also from other techniques for (sequential) innermost complexity to analyse parallel complexity?

In this section, we answer the question in the affirmative, via a generic transformation from Dependency Tuple problems back to rewrite systems whose innermost complexity can then be analysed using arbitrary existing techniques.

We use *relative rewriting*, which allows for labelling some of the rewrite rules such that their use does not contribute to the derivation height of a term. In other words, rewrite steps with these rewrite rules are "for free" from the perspective of complexity. Existing state-of-the-art tools like APROVE [24] and TCT [9] are able to find bounds on (innermost) runtime complexity of such rewrite systems.

Definition 11 (Relative Rewriting). *For two TRSs $\mathcal{R}_1$ and $\mathcal{R}_2$, $\mathcal{R}_1/\mathcal{R}_2$ is a relative TRS. Its rewrite relation $\to_{\mathcal{R}_1/\mathcal{R}_2}$ is $\to^*_{\mathcal{R}_2} \circ \to_{\mathcal{R}_1} \circ \to^*_{\mathcal{R}_2}$, i.e., rewriting with $\mathcal{R}_2$ is allowed before and after each $\mathcal{R}_1$-step. We define the innermost rewrite relation by $s \xrightarrow{i}_{\mathcal{R}_1/\mathcal{R}_2} t$ iff $s \to^*_{\mathcal{R}_2} s' \to_{\mathcal{R}_1} s'' \to^*_{\mathcal{R}_2} t$ for some terms s', s'' such that the proper subterms of the redexes of each step with $\to_{\mathcal{R}_2}$ or $\to_{\mathcal{R}_1}$ are in normal form wrt $\mathcal{R}_1 \cup \mathcal{R}_2$.*

The set $\mathcal{T}_{\text{basic}}^{\mathcal{R}_1/\mathcal{R}_2}$ of basic terms for a relative TRS $\mathcal{R}_1/\mathcal{R}_2$ is $\mathcal{T}_{\text{basic}}^{\mathcal{R}_1/\mathcal{R}_2} = \mathcal{T}_{\text{basic}}^{\mathcal{R}_1 \cup \mathcal{R}_2}$. The notion of innermost runtime complexity extends to relative TRSs in the natural way: $\text{irc}_{\mathcal{R}_1/\mathcal{R}_2}(n) = \sup\{\text{dh}(t, \xrightarrow{i}_{\mathcal{R}_1/\mathcal{R}_2}) \mid t \in \mathcal{T}_{\text{basic}}^{\mathcal{R}_1/\mathcal{R}_2}, |t| \le n\}$

The rewrite relation $\xrightarrow{i}_{\mathcal{R}_1/\mathcal{R}_2}$ is essentially the same as $\xrightarrow{i}_{\mathcal{R}_1 \cup \mathcal{R}_2}$, but only steps using rules from $\mathcal{R}_1$ count towards the complexity; steps using rules from $\mathcal{R}_2$ have no cost. This can be useful, e.g., for representing that built-in functions from programming languages modelled as recursive functions have constant cost.

Example 11. Consider a variant of Example 1 where $\text{plus}(S(x), y) \to S(\text{plus}(x, y))$ is moved to $\mathcal{R}_2$, but all other rules are elements of $\mathcal{R}_1$. Then $\mathcal{R}_1/\mathcal{R}_2$ would provide a modelling of the size function that is closer to the Rust function from Sect. 1. Let $S^n(\text{Zero})$ denote the term obtained by n-fold application of S to Zero (e.g., $S^2(\text{Zero}) = S(S(\text{Zero}))$). Although $\text{dh}(\text{plus}(S^n(\text{Zero}), S^m(\text{Zero})), \xrightarrow{i}_{\mathcal{R}_1 \cup \mathcal{R}_2}) = n + 1$, we would then get $\text{dh}(\text{plus}(S^n(\text{Zero}), S^m(\text{Zero})), \xrightarrow{i}_{\mathcal{R}_1/\mathcal{R}_2}) = 1$, corresponding to a machine model where the time of evaluating addition for integers is constant.

Note the similarity of a relative TRS and a Dependency Tuple problem: only certain rewrite steps count towards the analysed complexity. We make use of this observation for the following transformation.

Definition 12 (Relative TRS for a Dependency Tuple Problem, δ). *Let $\langle \mathcal{D}, \mathcal{S}, \mathcal{R} \rangle$ be a Dependency Tuple problem. We define the corresponding relative TRS $\delta(\langle \mathcal{D}, \mathcal{S}, \mathcal{R} \rangle) = \mathcal{S}/((\mathcal{D} \setminus \mathcal{S}) \cup \mathcal{R})$.*

In other words, we omit the information that steps with our dependency tuples can happen only on top level (possibly below constructors Com_n, but above $\to_{\mathcal{R}}$ steps). (As we shall see in Theorem 8, this information can be recovered.)

The following example is taken from the *Termination Problem Data Base (TPDB)* [42], a collection of examples used at the annual *Termination and Complexity Competition (termCOMP)* [25,41] (see also Sect. 5):

Example 12 (TPDB, `HirokawaMiddeldorp_04/t002`). Consider the following TRS $\mathcal{R}$ from category `Innermost_Runtime_Complexity` of the TPDB:

$$
\begin{array}{ll}
\mathsf{leq}(0, y) \rightarrow \mathsf{true} & \mathsf{if}(\mathsf{true}, x, y) \rightarrow x \\
\mathsf{leq}(\mathsf{s}(x), 0) \rightarrow \mathsf{false} & \mathsf{if}(\mathsf{false}, x, y) \rightarrow y \\
\mathsf{leq}(\mathsf{s}(x), \mathsf{s}(y)) \rightarrow \mathsf{leq}(x, y) & -(x, 0) \rightarrow x \\
\mathsf{mod}(0, y) \rightarrow 0 & -(\mathsf{s}(x), \mathsf{s}(y)) \rightarrow -(x, y) \\
\mathsf{mod}(\mathsf{s}(x), 0) \rightarrow 0 & \\
\multicolumn{2}{l}{\mathsf{mod}(\mathsf{s}(x), \mathsf{s}(y)) \rightarrow \mathsf{if}(\mathsf{leq}(y, x), \mathsf{mod}(-(\mathsf{s}(x), \mathsf{s}(y)), \mathsf{s}(y)), \mathsf{s}(x))}
\end{array}
$$

This TRS has the following PDTs $PDT(\mathcal{R})$:

$$
\begin{array}{ll}
\mathsf{leq}^{\sharp}(0, y) \rightarrow \mathsf{Com}_0 & \mathsf{if}^{\sharp}(\mathsf{true}, x, y) \rightarrow \mathsf{Com}_0 \\
\mathsf{leq}^{\sharp}(\mathsf{s}(x), 0) \rightarrow \mathsf{Com}_0 & \mathsf{if}^{\sharp}(\mathsf{false}, x, y) \rightarrow \mathsf{Com}_0 \\
\mathsf{leq}^{\sharp}(\mathsf{s}(x), \mathsf{s}(y)) \rightarrow \mathsf{Com}_1(\mathsf{leq}^{\sharp}(x, y)) & -^{\sharp}(x, 0) \rightarrow \mathsf{Com}_0 \\
\mathsf{mod}^{\sharp}(0, y) \rightarrow \mathsf{Com}_0 & -^{\sharp}(\mathsf{s}(x), \mathsf{s}(y)) \rightarrow \mathsf{Com}_1(-^{\sharp}(x, y)) \\
\mathsf{mod}^{\sharp}(\mathsf{s}(x), 0) \rightarrow \mathsf{Com}_0 &
\end{array}
$$

$$
\mathsf{mod}^{\sharp}(\mathsf{s}(x), \mathsf{s}(y)) \rightarrow \mathsf{Com}_2(\mathsf{leq}^{\sharp}(y, x), \mathsf{if}^{\sharp}(\mathsf{leq}(y, x), \mathsf{mod}(-(\mathsf{s}(x), \mathsf{s}(y)), \mathsf{s}(y)), \mathsf{s}(x)))
$$

$$
\mathsf{mod}^{\sharp}(\mathsf{s}(x), \mathsf{s}(y)) \rightarrow \mathsf{Com}_3(-^{\sharp}(\mathsf{s}(x), \mathsf{s}(y)), \mathsf{mod}^{\sharp}(-(\mathsf{s}(x), \mathsf{s}(y)), \mathsf{s}(y)),
$$
$$
\mathsf{if}^{\sharp}(\mathsf{leq}(y, x), \mathsf{mod}(-(\mathsf{s}(x), \mathsf{s}(y)), \mathsf{s}(y)), \mathsf{s}(x)))
$$

The canonical parallel DT problem is $\langle PDT(\mathcal{R}), PDT(\mathcal{R}), \mathcal{R} \rangle$. We get the relative TRS $\delta(\langle PDT(\mathcal{R}), PDT(\mathcal{R}), \mathcal{R} \rangle) = PDT(\mathcal{R})/\mathcal{R}$.

Theorem 7 (Upper Complexity Bounds for $\delta(\langle \mathcal{D}, \mathcal{S}, \mathcal{R} \rangle)$ from $\langle \mathcal{D}, \mathcal{S}, \mathcal{R} \rangle$). *Let $\langle \mathcal{D}, \mathcal{S}, \mathcal{R} \rangle$ be a DT problem. Then (a) for all $t^{\sharp} \in \mathcal{T}^{\sharp}$ with $t \in \mathcal{T}_{\mathrm{basic}}^{\mathcal{R}}$, we have $Cplx_{\langle \mathcal{D}, \mathcal{S}, \mathcal{R} \rangle}(t^{\sharp}) \leq dh(t^{\sharp}, \xrightarrow{\mathrm{i}}_{\mathcal{S}/((\mathcal{D} \backslash \mathcal{S}) \cup \mathcal{R})})$, and (b) $irc_{\langle \mathcal{D}, \mathcal{S}, \mathcal{R} \rangle}(n) \leq irc_{\mathcal{S}/((\mathcal{D} \backslash \mathcal{S}) \cup \mathcal{R})}(n)$.*

Example 13 (Example 12 continued). For the relative TRS $PDT(\mathcal{R})/\mathcal{R}$ from Example 12, the tool APROVE uses a transformation to integer transition systems [36] followed by an application of the complexity analysis tool COFLOCO [20, 21] to find a bound $irc_{PDT(\mathcal{R})/\mathcal{R}}(n) \in \mathcal{O}(n)$ and to deduce the bound $pirc_{\mathcal{R}}(n) \in \mathcal{O}(n)$ for the original TRS $\mathcal{R}$ from the TPDB. In contrast, using the techniques of Sect. 3 without the transformation to a relative TRS from Definition 12, APROVE finds only a bound $pirc_{\mathcal{R}}(n) \in \mathcal{O}(n^2)$.

Intriguingly, we can use our transformation from Definition 12 not only for finding upper bounds, but also for *lower* bounds on $pirc_{\mathcal{R}}$.

Theorem 8 (Lower Complexity Bounds for $\delta(\langle \mathcal{D}, \mathcal{S}, \mathcal{R} \rangle)$ from $\langle \mathcal{D}, \mathcal{S}, \mathcal{R} \rangle$). *Let $\langle \mathcal{D}, \mathcal{S}, \mathcal{R} \rangle$ be a DT problem. Then (a) there is a type assignment s.t. for all $\ell \rightarrow r \in \mathcal{D} \cup \mathcal{R}$, ℓ and r get the same type, and for all well-typed $t \in \mathcal{T}_{\mathrm{basic}}^{\mathcal{D} \cup \mathcal{R}}$, $Cplx_{\langle \mathcal{D}, \mathcal{S}, \mathcal{R} \rangle}(t^{\sharp}) \geq dh(t, \xrightarrow{\mathrm{i}}_{\mathcal{S}/((\mathcal{D} \backslash \mathcal{S}) \cup \mathcal{R})})$, and (b) $irc_{\langle \mathcal{D}, \mathcal{S}, \mathcal{R} \rangle}(n) \geq irc_{\mathcal{S}/((\mathcal{D} \backslash \mathcal{S}) \cup \mathcal{R})}(n)$.*

Theorem 7 and Theorem 8 hold regardless of whether the original DT problem was obtained from a TRS with sequential or with parallel evaluation. So while this kind of connection between DT (or DP) problems and relative rewriting may be folklore in the community, its application to convert a TRS whose *parallel* complexity is sought to a TRS with the same *sequential* complexity is new.

Note that Theorem 5 requires confluence of $\xmapsto{i}_{\mathcal{R}}$ to derive lower bounds for $\mathrm{pirc}_{\mathcal{R}}$ from lower complexity bounds of the canonical parallel DT problem. So to use Theorem 8 to search for *lower* complexity bounds with existing techniques [22], we need a criterion for confluence of parallel-innermost rewriting.

Example 14 (Confluence of $\xrightarrow{i}_{\mathcal{R}}$ does not Imply Confluence of $\xmapsto{i}_{\mathcal{R}}$). To see that we cannot prove confluence of $\xmapsto{i}_{\mathcal{R}}$ just by using a standard off-the-shelf tool for confluence analysis of innermost or full rewriting [16], consider the TRS $\mathcal{R} = \{a \to f(b,b), a \to f(b,c), b \to c, c \to b\}$. For this TRS, both $\xrightarrow{i}_{\mathcal{R}}$ and $\to_{\mathcal{R}}$ are confluent. However, $\xmapsto{i}_{\mathcal{R}}$ is not confluent: we can rewrite both $a \xmapsto{i}_{\mathcal{R}} f(b,b)$ and $a \xmapsto{i}_{\mathcal{R}} f(b,c)$, yet there is no term v such that $f(b,b) \xmapsto{i}{}^{*}_{\mathcal{R}} v$ and $f(b,c) \xmapsto{i}{}^{*}_{\mathcal{R}} v$. The reason is that the only possible rewrite sequences with $\xmapsto{i}_{\mathcal{R}}$ from these terms are $f(b,b) \xmapsto{i}_{\mathcal{R}} f(c,c) \xmapsto{i}_{\mathcal{R}} f(b,b) \xmapsto{i}_{\mathcal{R}} \ldots$ and $f(b,c) \xmapsto{i}_{\mathcal{R}} f(c,b) \xmapsto{i}_{\mathcal{R}} f(b,c) \xmapsto{i}_{\mathcal{R}} \ldots$, with no terms in common.

Conjecture 1. If $\xmapsto{i}_{\mathcal{R}}$ is confluent, then $\xrightarrow{i}_{\mathcal{R}}$ is confluent.

Confluence means: if a term s can be rewritten to two different terms t_1 and t_2 in 0 or more steps, it is always possible to rewrite t_1 and t_2 in 0 or more steps to a term u. For $\xmapsto{i}_{\mathcal{R}}$, the redexes that get rewritten are fixed: all innermost redexes simultaneously. Thus, s can rewrite to two *different* terms t_1 and t_2 only if at least one of these redexes can be rewritten in two different ways using $\xrightarrow{i}_{\mathcal{R}}$.

Towards a sufficient criterion for confluence of parallel-innermost rewriting, we introduce the following standard definition:

Definition 13 (Non-Overlapping). *A TRS $\mathcal{R}$ is* non-overlapping *iff for any two rules $\ell \to r, u \to v \in \mathcal{R}$ where variables have been renamed apart between the rules, there is no position π in ℓ such that $\ell|_\pi \notin \mathcal{V}$ and the terms $\ell|_\pi$ and u unify.*

A sufficient criterion that a given redex has a unique result from a rewrite step is given in the following.

Lemma 1 ([10], Lemma 6.3.9). *If a TRS $\mathcal{R}$ is non-overlapping, $s \to_{\mathcal{R}} t_1$ and $s \to_{\mathcal{R}} t_2$ with the redex of both rewrite steps at the same position, then $t_1 = t_2$.*

With the above reasoning, this lemma directly gives us a sufficient criterion for confluence of *parallel-innermost* rewriting.

Corollary 1 (Confluence of Parallel-Innermost Rewriting). *If a TRS $\mathcal{R}$ is non-overlapping, then $\xmapsto{i}_{\mathcal{R}}$ is confluent.*

So, in those cases we can actually use this sequence of transformations from a parallel-innermost TRS via a DT problem to an innermost (relative) TRS to analyse both upper and lower bounds for the original. Conveniently, these cases correspond to deterministic programs, our motivation for this work!

Example 15 (Example 13 *continued).* Corollary 1 and Theorem 8 imply that a lower bound for $\mathrm{irc}_{PDT(\mathcal{R})/\mathcal{R}}(n)$ of the relative TRS $PDT(\mathcal{R})/\mathcal{R}$ from Example 12 carries over to $\mathrm{pirc}_{\mathcal{R}}(n)$ of the original TRS $\mathcal{R}$ from the TPDB. APROVE uses rewrite lemmas [22] to find the lower bound $\mathrm{irc}_{PDT(\mathcal{R})/\mathcal{R}}(n) \in \Omega(n)$. Together with Example 13, we have automatically inferred that this complexity bound is *tight*: $\mathrm{pirc}_{\mathcal{R}}(n) \in \Theta(n)$.

5   Implementation and Experiments

We have implemented the contributions of this paper in the automated termination and complexity analysis tool APROVE [24]. We added or modified 620 lines of Java code, including 1. the framework of parallel-innermost rewriting; 2. the generation of parallel DTs (Theorem 5); 3. a processor to convert them to TRSs with the same complexity (Theorem 7, Theorem 8); 4. the confluence test of Corollary 1. As far as we are aware, this is the first implementation of a fully automated inference of complexity bounds for parallel-innermost rewriting. To demonstrate the effectiveness of our implementation, we have considered the 663 TRSs from category Runtime_Complexity_Innermost_Rewriting of the TPDB, version 11.2 [42]. This category of the TPDB is the benchmark collection used at termCOMP to compare tools that infer complexity bounds for runtime complexity of innermost rewriting, $\mathrm{irc}_{\mathcal{R}}$. To get meaningful results, we first applied Theorem 6 to exclude TRSs $\mathcal{R}$ where $\mathrm{pirc}_{\mathcal{R}}(n) = \mathrm{irc}_{\mathcal{R}}(n)$ trivially holds. We obtained 294 TRSs with potential for parallelism as our benchmark set. We conducted our experiments on the STAREXEC compute cluster [38] in the all.q queue. The timeout per example and tool configuration was set to 300 s. Our experimental data with analysis times and all examples are available online [1].

As remarked earlier, we always have $\mathrm{pirc}_{\mathcal{R}}(n) \leq \mathrm{irc}_{\mathcal{R}}(n)$, so an upper bound for $\mathrm{irc}_{\mathcal{R}}(n)$ is always a legitimate upper bound for $\mathrm{pirc}_{\mathcal{R}}(n)$. Thus, we include upper bounds for $\mathrm{irc}_{\mathcal{R}}$ found by the state-of-the-art tools APROVE and TCT [2,9]. from termCOMP 2021 as a "baseline" in our evaluation. We compare with several configurations of APROVE and TCT that use the techniques of this paper for $\mathrm{pirc}_{\mathcal{R}}$: "APROVE $\mathrm{pirc}_{\mathcal{R}}$ Sect. 3" also uses Theorem 5 to produce canonical parallel DT problems as input for the DT framework. "APROVE $\mathrm{pirc}_{\mathcal{R}}$ Sects. 3 & 4" additionally uses the transformation from Definition 12 to convert a TRS $\mathcal{R}$ to a relative TRS $PDT(\mathcal{R})/\mathcal{R}$ and then to analyse $\mathrm{irc}_{PDT(\mathcal{R})/\mathcal{R}}(n)$ (for lower bounds only together with a confluence proof via Corollary 1). We also extracted each of the TRSs $PDT(\mathcal{R})/\mathcal{R}$ and used the files as inputs for APROVE and TCT from termCOMP 2021. "APROVE $\mathrm{pirc}_{\mathcal{R}}$ Sect. 4" and "TCT $\mathrm{pirc}_{\mathcal{R}}$ Sect. 4" provide the results for $\mathrm{irc}_{PDT(\mathcal{R})/\mathcal{R}}$ (for lower bounds, only where $\stackrel{i}{\Vdash}\!\!\rightarrow_{\mathcal{R}}$ had been proved confluent).

Table 1 gives an overview over our experimental results for upper bounds. For each configuration, we state the number of examples for which the corresponding asymptotic complexity bound was inferred. A column "$\leq \mathcal{O}(n^k)$" means that the corresponding tools proved a bound $\leq \mathcal{O}(n^k)$ (e.g., the configuration "APROVE $\mathrm{irc}_{\mathcal{R}}$" proved constant or linear upper bounds in 50 cases). Maximum values in

Table 1. Upper bounds for runtime complexity of (parallel-)innermost rewriting

Tool	$\mathcal{O}(1)$	$\leq \mathcal{O}(n)$	$\leq \mathcal{O}(n^2)$	$\leq \mathcal{O}(n^3)$	$\leq \mathcal{O}(n^{\geq 4})$
TcT irc$_\mathcal{R}$	4	28	39	44	44
APROVE irc$_\mathcal{R}$	5	50	110	123	127
APROVE pirc$_\mathcal{R}$ Sect. 3	5	65	**125**	**140**	**142**
APROVE pirc$_\mathcal{R}$ Sects. 3 & 4	5	**69**	125	139	141
TcT pirc$_\mathcal{R}$ Sect. 4	3	39	52	56	57
APROVE pirc$_\mathcal{R}$ Sect. 4	5	62	96	105	105

Table 2. Lower bounds for runtime complexity of parallel-innermost rewriting

Tool	confluent	$\geq \Omega(n)$	$\geq \Omega(n^2)$	$\geq \Omega(n^3)$	$\geq \Omega(n^{\geq 4})$
APROVE pirc$_\mathcal{R}$ Sects. 3 & 4	**186**	133	**23**	5	**1**
TcT pirc$_\mathcal{R}$ Sect. 4	**186**	59	0	0	0
APROVE pirc$_\mathcal{R}$ Sect. 4	**186**	**155**	22	5	**1**

Table 3. Tight bounds for runtime complexity of parallel-innermost rewriting

Tool	$\Theta(1)$	$\Theta(n)$	$\Theta(n^2)$	$\Theta(n^3)$	Total
APROVE pirc$_\mathcal{R}$ Sects. 3 & 4	5	32	1	3	41
TcT pirc$_\mathcal{R}$ Sect. 4	3	21	0	0	24
APROVE pirc$_\mathcal{R}$ Sect. 4	5	37	1	3	46

a column are highlighted in bold. We observe that upper complexity bounds improve in a noticeable number of cases, e.g., linear bounds on pirc$_\mathcal{R}$ can now be inferred for 69 TRSs rather than for 50 TRSs (using upper bounds on irc$_\mathcal{R}$ as an over-approximation), an improvement by 38%. Note that this does *not* indicate deficiencies in the existing tools for irc$_\mathcal{R}$, which had not been designed with analysis of pirc$_\mathcal{R}$ in mind – rather, it shows that specialised techniques for analysing pirc$_\mathcal{R}$ are a worthwhile subject of investigation. Note also that Example 4 and Example 9 show that even for TRSs with potential for parallelism, the actual parallel and sequential complexity may still be asymptotically identical, which further highlights the need for dedicated analysis techniques for pirc$_\mathcal{R}$.

The improvement from irc$_\mathcal{R}$ to pirc$_\mathcal{R}$ can be drastic: for example, for the TRS TCT_12/recursion_10, the bounds found by APROVE change from an upper bound of sequential complexity of $\mathcal{O}(n^{10})$ to a (tight) upper bound for parallel complexity of $\mathcal{O}(n)$. (This TRS models a specific recursion structure, with rules $\{f_0(x) \to a\} \cup \{f_i(x) \to g_i(x,x), g_i(s(x),y) \to b(f_{i-1}(y), g_i(x,y)) \mid 1 \leq i \leq 10\}$, and is highly amenable to parallelisation.) We observe that adding the techniques from Sect. 4 to the techniques from Sect. 3 leads to only few examples for which better upper bounds can be found (one of them is Example 13).

Table 2 shows our results for lower bounds on $\text{pirc}_{\mathcal{R}}$. Here we evaluated only configurations including Definition 12 to make inference techniques for lower bounds of $\text{irc}_{\mathcal{R}}$ applicable to $\text{pirc}_{\mathcal{R}}$. The reason is that a lower bound on $\text{irc}_{\mathcal{R}}$ is not necessarily also a lower bound for $\text{pirc}_{\mathcal{R}}$ (the whole *point* of performing innermost rewriting in parallel is to reduce the asymptotic complexity!), so using results by tools that compute lower bounds on $\text{irc}_{\mathcal{R}}$ for comparison would not make sense. We observe that non-trivial lower bounds can be inferred for 155 out of the 186 examples proved confluent via Corollary 1. This shows that our transformation from Sect. 4 has practical value since it produces relative TRSs that are generally amenable to analysis by existing program analysis tools. Finally, Table 3 shows that for overall 46 TRSs, the bounds that were found are asymptotically *precise*.

6   Related Work, Conclusion, and Future Work

Related Work. We provide pointers to work on automated analysis of (sequential) innermost runtime complexity of TRSs at the start of Sect. 4. We now focus on automated techniques for complexity analysis of parallel/concurrent computation.

Our notion of parallel complexity follows a large tradition of static *cost analysis*, notably for concurrent programming. The two notable works [4,5] address async/finish programs where tasks are explicitly launched. The authors propose several metrics such as the total number of spawned tasks (in any execution of the program) and a notion of parallel complexity that is roughly the same as ours. They provide static analyses that build on techniques for estimating costs of imperative languages with functions calls [3], and/or recurrence equations. Recent approaches for the Pi Calculus [11,12] compute the *span* (our parallel complexity) through a new typing system. Another type-based calculus for the same purpose has been proposed with session types [17].

For logic programs, which – like TRSs – express an implicit parallelism, parallel complexity can be inferred using recurrence solving [31].

The tool RAML [29] derives bounds on the worst-case evaluation cost of first-order functional programs with list and pair constructors as well as pattern matching and both sequential and parallel composition [30]. They use two typing derivations with specially annotated types, one for the *work* and one for the *depth* (parallel complexity). Our setting is more flexible wrt the shape of user-defined data structures (we allow for tree constructors of arbitrary arity), and our analysis deals with both data structure and control in an integrated manner.

Conclusion and Future Work. We have defined parallel-innermost runtime complexity for TRSs and proposed an approach to its automated analysis. Our approach allows for finding both upper and lower bounds and builds on existing techniques and tools. Our experiments on the TPDB indicate that our approach is practically usable, and we are confident that it captures the potential parallelism of programs with pattern matching.

Parallel rewriting is a topic of active research, e.g., for GPU-based massively parallel rewrite engines [18]. Here our work could be useful to determine which functions to evaluate on the GPU. More generally, parallelising compilers which need to determine which function calls should be compiled into parallel code may benefit from an analysis of parallel-innermost runtime complexity such as ours.

DTs have been used [43] in runtime complexity analysis of *Logically Constrained TRSs (LCTRSs)* [32], an extension of TRSs by built-in data types from SMT theories (integers, arrays, ...). This work could be extended to parallel rewriting. Moreover, analysis of *derivational complexity* [28] of parallel-innermost term rewriting can be a promising direction. Derivational complexity considers the length of rewrite sequences from arbitrary start terms, e.g., $d(d(\ldots(d(S(\mathsf{Zero})))\ldots))$ in Example 10, which can have longer derivations than basic terms of the same size. Finally, towards automated parallelisation we aim to infer complexity bounds wrt term *height* (terms = trees!), as suggested in [6].

Acknowledgements. We thank the anonymous reviewers for helpful comments.

References

1. https://www.dcs.bbk.ac.uk/carsten/eval/parallel_complexity/
2. https://www.starexec.org/starexec/secure/details/solver.jsp?id=29575
3. Albert, E., Arenas, P., Genaim, S., Puebla, G., Zanardini, D.: Cost analysis of object-oriented bytecode programs. Theor. Comput. Sci. **413**(1), 142–159 (2012). https://doi.org/10.1016/j.tcs.2011.07.009
4. Albert, E., Arenas, P., Genaim, S., Zanardini, D.: Task-level analysis for a language with async/finish parallelism. In: Vitek, J., Sutter, B.D. (eds.) Proceedings of the ACM SIGPLAN/SIGBED 2011 Conference on Languages, Compilers, and Tools for Embedded Systems, LCTES 2011, Chicago, IL, USA, 11–14 April 2011, pp. 21–30. ACM (2011). https://doi.org/10.1145/1967677.1967681
5. Albert, E., Correas, J., Johnsen, E.B., Pun, V.K.I., Román-Díez, G.: Parallel cost analysis. ACM Trans. Comput. Log. **19**(4), 31:1–31:37 (2018). https://doi.org/10.1145/3274278
6. Alias, C., Fuhs, C., Gonnord, L.: Estimation of parallel complexity with rewriting techniques. In: Proceedings of the 15th Workshop on Termination (WST 2016), pp. 2:1–2:5 (2016). https://hal.archives-ouvertes.fr/hal-01345914
7. Arts, T., Giesl, J.: Termination of term rewriting using dependency pairs. Theoret. Comput. Sci. **236**, 133–178 (2000)
8. Avanzini, M., Moser, G.: A combination framework for complexity. Inf. Comput. **248**, 22–55 (2016). https://doi.org/10.1016/j.ic.2015.12.007
9. Avanzini, M., Moser, G., Schaper, M.: TcT: Tyrolean complexity tool. In: Chechik, M., Raskin, J.-F. (eds.) TACAS 2016. LNCS, vol. 9636, pp. 407–423. Springer, Heidelberg (2016). https://doi.org/10.1007/978-3-662-49674-9_24
10. Baader, F., Nipkow, T.: Term Rewriting and All That. Cambridge University Press, Cambridge (1998)
11. Baillot, P., Ghyselen, A.: Types for complexity of parallel computation in Pi-Calculus. In: ESOP 2021. LNCS, vol. 12648, pp. 59–86. Springer, Cham (2021). https://doi.org/10.1007/978-3-030-72019-3_3

12. Baillot, P., Ghyselen, A., Kobayashi, N.: Sized types with usages for parallel complexity of Pi-Calculus processes. In: Haddad, S., Varacca, D. (eds.) 32nd International Conference on Concurrency Theory, CONCUR 2021, 24–27 August 2021, Virtual Conference. LIPIcs, vol. 203, pp. 34:1–34:22. Schloss Dagstuhl - Leibniz-Zentrum für Informatik (2021). https://doi.org/10.4230/LIPIcs.CONCUR.2021.34

13. Baudon, T., Fuhs, C., Gonnord, L.: Parallel complexity of term rewriting systems. In: 17th International Workshop on Termination (WST 2021), pp. 45–50 (2021). https://hal.archives-ouvertes.fr/hal-03418400/document

14. Baudon, T., Fuhs, C., Gonnord, L.: Analysing parallel complexity of term rewriting (2022). https://doi.org/10.48550/ARXIV.2208.01005. https://arxiv.org/abs/2208.01005

15. Blelloch, G.E., Greiner, J.: Parallelism in sequential functional languages. In: Williams, J. (ed.) Proceedings of the Seventh International Conference on Functional Programming Languages and Computer Architecture, FPCA 1995, La Jolla, California, USA, 25–28 June 1995, pp. 226–237. ACM (1995). https://doi.org/10.1145/224164.224210

16. Community: The international Confluence Competition (CoCo). http://project-coco.uibk.ac.at/

17. Das, A., Hoffmann, J., Pfenning, F.: Parallel complexity analysis with temporal session types. Proc. ACM Program. Lang. 2(ICFP), 91:1–91:30 (2018). https://doi.org/10.1145/3236786

18. van Eerd, J., Groote, J.F., Hijma, P., Martens, J., Wijs, A.: Term rewriting on GPUs. In: Hojjat, H., Massink, M. (eds.) FSEN 2021. LNCS, vol. 12818, pp. 175–189. Springer, Cham (2021). https://doi.org/10.1007/978-3-030-89247-0_12

19. Fernández, M.-L., Godoy, G., Rubio, A.: Orderings for innermost termination. In: Giesl, J. (ed.) RTA 2005. LNCS, vol. 3467, pp. 17–31. Springer, Heidelberg (2005). https://doi.org/10.1007/978-3-540-32033-3_3

20. Flores-Montoya, A.: Upper and lower amortized cost bounds of programs expressed as cost relations. In: Fitzgerald, J., Heitmeyer, C., Gnesi, S., Philippou, A. (eds.) FM 2016. LNCS, vol. 9995, pp. 254–273. Springer, Cham (2016). https://doi.org/10.1007/978-3-319-48989-6_16

21. Flores-Montoya, A., Hähnle, R.: Resource analysis of complex programs with cost equations. In: Garrigue, J. (ed.) APLAS 2014. LNCS, vol. 8858, pp. 275–295. Springer, Cham (2014). https://doi.org/10.1007/978-3-319-12736-1_15

22. Frohn, F., Giesl, J., Hensel, J., Aschermann, C., Ströder, T.: Lower bounds for runtime complexity of term rewriting. J. Autom. Reason. 59(1), 121–163 (2016). https://doi.org/10.1007/s10817-016-9397-x

23. Fuhs, C., Giesl, J., Middeldorp, A., Schneider-Kamp, P., Thiemann, R., Zankl, H.: Maximal termination. In: Voronkov, A. (ed.) RTA 2008. LNCS, vol. 5117, pp. 110–125. Springer, Heidelberg (2008). https://doi.org/10.1007/978-3-540-70590-1_8

24. Giesl, J., et al.: Analyzing program termination and complexity automatically with AProVE. J. Autom. Reason. 58(1), 3–31 (2016). https://doi.org/10.1007/s10817-016-9388-y

25. Giesl, J., Rubio, A., Sternagel, C., Waldmann, J., Yamada, A.: The termination and complexity competition. In: Beyer, D., Huisman, M., Kordon, F., Steffen, B. (eds.) TACAS 2019. LNCS, vol. 11429, pp. 156–166. Springer, Cham (2019). https://doi.org/10.1007/978-3-030-17502-3_10

26. Hirokawa, N., Moser, G.: Automated complexity analysis based on the dependency pair method. In: Armando, A., Baumgartner, P., Dowek, G. (eds.) IJCAR 2008. LNCS (LNAI), vol. 5195, pp. 364–379. Springer, Heidelberg (2008). https://doi.org/10.1007/978-3-540-71070-7_32

27. Hirokawa, N., Moser, G.: Automated complexity analysis based on context-sensitive rewriting. In: Dowek, G. (ed.) RTA 2014. LNCS, vol. 8560, pp. 257–271. Springer, Cham (2014). https://doi.org/10.1007/978-3-319-08918-8_18

28. Hofbauer, D., Lautemann, C.: Termination proofs and the length of derivations. In: Dershowitz, N. (ed.) RTA 1989. LNCS, vol. 355, pp. 167–177. Springer, Heidelberg (1989). https://doi.org/10.1007/3-540-51081-8_107

29. Hoffmann, J., Aehlig, K., Hofmann, M.: Resource aware ML. In: Madhusudan, P., Seshia, S.A. (eds.) CAV 2012. LNCS, vol. 7358, pp. 781–786. Springer, Heidelberg (2012). https://doi.org/10.1007/978-3-642-31424-7_64

30. Hoffmann, J., Shao, Z.: Automatic static cost analysis for parallel programs. In: Vitek, J. (ed.) ESOP 2015. LNCS, vol. 9032, pp. 132–157. Springer, Heidelberg (2015). https://doi.org/10.1007/978-3-662-46669-8_6

31. Klemen, M., López-García, P., Gallagher, J.P., Morales, J.F., Hermenegildo, M.V.: A general framework for static cost analysis of parallel logic programs. In: Gabbrielli, M. (ed.) LOPSTR 2019. LNCS, vol. 12042, pp. 19–35. Springer, Cham (2020). https://doi.org/10.1007/978-3-030-45260-5_2

32. Kop, C., Nishida, N.: Term rewriting with logical constraints. In: Fontaine, P., Ringeissen, C., Schmidt, R.A. (eds.) FroCoS 2013. LNCS (LNAI), vol. 8152, pp. 343–358. Springer, Heidelberg (2013). https://doi.org/10.1007/978-3-642-40885-4_24

33. Lamport, L.: Time, clocks, and the ordering of events in a distributed system. Commun. ACM 21(7), 558–565 (1978). https://doi.org/10.1145/359545.359563

34. Lankford, D.S.: Canonical algebraic simplification in computational logic. Technical report, ATP-25, University of Texas (1975)

35. Moser, G., Schneckenreither, M.: Automated amortised resource analysis for term rewrite systems. Sci. Comput. Program. 185 (2020). https://doi.org/10.1016/j.scico.2019.102306

36. Naaf, M., Frohn, F., Brockschmidt, M., Fuhs, C., Giesl, J.: Complexity analysis for term rewriting by integer transition systems. In: Dixon, C., Finger, M. (eds.) FroCoS 2017. LNCS (LNAI), vol. 10483, pp. 132–150. Springer, Cham (2017). https://doi.org/10.1007/978-3-319-66167-4_8

37. Noschinski, L., Emmes, F., Giesl, J.: Analyzing innermost runtime complexity of term rewriting by dependency pairs. J. Autom. Reason. 51(1), 27–56 (2013). https://doi.org/10.1007/s10817-013-9277-6

38. Stump, A., Sutcliffe, G., Tinelli, C.: StarExec: a cross-community infrastructure for logic solving. In: Demri, S., Kapur, D., Weidenbach, C. (eds.) IJCAR 2014. LNCS (LNAI), vol. 8562, pp. 367–373. Springer, Cham (2014). https://doi.org/10.1007/978-3-319-08587-6_28. https://www.starexec.org/

39. Thiemann, R., Sternagel, C., Giesl, J., Schneider-Kamp, P.: Loops under strategies ... continued. In: Kirchner, H., Muñoz, C.A. (eds.) Proceedings International Workshop on Strategies in Rewriting, Proving, and Programming, IWS 2010, Edinburgh, UK, 9th July 2010. EPTCS, vol. 44, pp. 51–65 (2010). https://doi.org/10.4204/EPTCS.44.4

40. Vuillemin, J.: Correct and optimal implementations of recursion in a simple programming language. J. Comput. Syst. Sci. 9(3), 332–354 (1974). https://doi.org/10.1016/S0022-0000(74)80048-6

41. Wiki: The International Termination Competition (TermComp). http://termination-portal.org/wiki/Termination_Competition
42. Wiki: Termination Problems DataBase (TPDB). http://termination-portal.org/wiki/TPDB
43. Winkler, S., Moser, G.: Runtime complexity analysis of logically constrained rewriting. In: LOPSTR 2020. LNCS, vol. 12561, pp. 37–55. Springer, Cham (2021). https://doi.org/10.1007/978-3-030-68446-4_2

Confluence Framework: Proving Confluence with CONFident

Raúl Gutiérrez[2] , Miguel Vítores[1], and Salvador Lucas[1]([⊠])

[1] DSIC & VRAIN, Universitat Politècnica de València, Valencia, Spain
slucas@dsic.upv.es
[2] DLSIIS, Universidad Politécnica de Madrid, Madrid, Spain
r.gutierrez@upm.es

Abstract. This paper describes CONFident, a tool which is able to automatically prove and disprove confluence of variants of rewrite systems: *term rewriting systems*, *conditional term rewriting systems* (using *join*, *oriented*, or *semi-equational* semantics), and *context-sensitive term rewriting systems*. We introduce a new proof framework to generate proof trees by combining different techniques for proving confluence (including modular decompositions, checking joinability of (conditional) critical pairs, transformations, etc.). We also use external tools for proving termination and operational termination (MU-TERM), or feasibility (infChecker) and deducibility (Prover9).

Keywords: Confluence · Program analysis · Rewriting

1 Introduction

Reduction relations $\rightarrow$ are pervasive in computer science and semantics of programming languages as suitable means to describe computations $s \rightarrow^* t$, where $\rightarrow^*$ denotes zero or more steps issued with $\rightarrow$. In general, s and t are abstract values (i.e., elements of an arbitrary set A), but often denote program expressions: terms, lambda expressions, configurations in imperative programming, etc. If $s \rightarrow^* t$ holds, we say that s *reduces* to t or that t is a *reduct* of s. Confluence is the property of reduction relations guaranteeing that whenever s has two different reducts t and t' (i.e., $s \rightarrow^* t$ and $s \rightarrow^* t'$), both t and t' are *joinable*, i.e., they have a common reduct u (hence $t \rightarrow^* u$ and $t' \rightarrow^* u$ holds for some u). Confluence is one of the most important properties of reduction relations: for instance, (i) it ensures that for all expressions s, *at most* one irreducible reduct t of s can be obtained; and (ii) it ensures that two divergent computations can always join in the future. Thus, the semantics and implementation of rewriting-based languages is less dependent on specific strategies to implement reductions.

Confluence has been investigated for several reduction-based formalisms and systems. Confluence is *undecidable* already for Term Rewriting Systems (TRSs [2]), see,

Partially supported by grants PID2021-122830OB-C42 and PID2021-122830OB-C44 funded by MCIN/AEI/10.13039/501100011033 and by "ERDF A way of making Europe" and PROMETEO/2019/098.

A. Villanueva (Ed.): LOPSTR 2022, LNCS 13474, pp. 24–43, 2022.
https://doi.org/10.1007/978-3-031-16767-6_2

e.g., [27, Section 4.1]. Since TRSs are subclasses of Conditional Term Rewriting Systems (CTRSs, see [27, Chapter 7]), and also of Context-Sensitive TRSs (CS-TRSs [16]), this means that, in general, no algorithm is able to prove or disprove confluence of the reduction relation associated to all such systems. Thus, existing techniques for proving and disproving confluence are *partial*, i.e., they succeed on some kinds of systems and fail on others. However, the combination of techniques in a certain order or the use of auxiliary properties can help to prove or disprove confluence.

CONFident is able to prove confluence of TRSs, CS-TRSs, and CTRSs. For this purpose, in this paper, we introduce and briefly describe a *Confluence Framework*, inspired by the *Dependency Pair Framework*, originally developed for proving (innermost) termination of TRSs [5,6]. In the Confluence Framework, we define two kinds of problems: *confluence problems* and *joinability problems*. *Confluence problems* encapsulate the system $\mathscr{R}$ whose confluence is tested. Such confluence problems are transformed, decomposed, simplified, etc., into other (possibly different) problems by using the so-called *processors*. Besides, *joinability problems* are produced by some processors acting on confluence problems. They are used to prove or disprove the joinability of, e.g., (possibly conditional) critical pairs. They are also treated by appropriate processors. Processors apply on the obtained problems until (i) a trivial problem is obtained (which is then labeled with YES) and the proof either continues by considering pending problems, or else *finishes* and YES is returned if no problem remains to be solved; (ii) a counterexample is obtained and the problem is then labeled with NO and the proof *finishes* as well but NO is returned; (iii) the processor fails and then some other processor is attempted if possible or, otherwise, the proof is finished and MAYBE is returned; or (iv) the ongoing proof is eventually interrupted due to a *timeout*, which is usually prescribed in this kind of proof processes whose termination is not guaranteed or could last too much time, and the whole proof fails. The use of processors often require calls to external tools to solve proof obligations like *termination*, etc.

The confluence framework allows us to use existing techniques to prove confluence of a rewriting system as a black box (processor) that can be plugged in and out in a proof strategy, allowing us to find the best place to apply a proving technique in practice. The obtained proof is depicted as a *proof tree* from which the (non-)confluence of the targetted rewrite system can be proved. As explained above, the construction of such a proof tree successfully finishes whenever *some* problem is given a label NO, or *all* problems have been labeled with YES. Figure 1 below illustrates the proof trees obtained for the running Examples 1 and 2 introduced below. The applied processors are shown in Examples 3 and 4 respectively. This paper provides a description of how CONFident implements the Confluence Framework.

After some preliminaries in Sect. 2, Sect. 3 describes the variants of rewrite systems supported by CONFident. Section 4 defines the problems and processors used in the Confluence Framework. Section 5 gives a list of processors implemented in the tool. Section 6 explains how to prove and disprove confluence in the Confluence Framework. Section 7 presents the proof strategy of CONFident. Section 8 provides some details about the implementation. Section 9 provides an experimental evaluation of the tool. Section 10 discusses related work. Section 11 concludes.

2 Preliminaries

In the following, *w.r.t.* means *with respect to* and *iff* means *if and only if*. Given a binary relation $R \subseteq A \times A$ on a set A, we often write $a \, R \, b$ instead of $(a, b) \in R$. The *transitive closure* of R is denoted by R^+, and its *reflexive and transitive* closure by R^*. An element $a \in A$ is *irreducible* if there is no b such that $a \, R \, b$; we say that b is an R-normal form of a (written $a \, R^! \, b$), if $a \, R^* b$ and b is irreducible. Given $a \in A$, if there is no infinite sequence $a = a_1 \, R \, a_2 \, R \cdots R \, a_n \, R \cdots$, then a is R-*terminating* (or *well-founded*); R is *terminating* if a is R-terminating for all $a \in A$. We say that R is (locally) *confluent* if, for every $a, b, c \in A$, whenever $a \, R^* b$ and $a \, R^* c$ (resp. $a \, R \, b$ and $a \, R \, c$), there exists $d \in A$ such that $b \, R^* d$ and $c \, R^* d$.

In this paper, $\mathscr{X}$ denotes a countable set of *variables* and $\mathscr{F}$ denotes a *signature*, i.e., a set of *function symbols* $\{f, g, \ldots\}$, each with a fixed *arity* given by a mapping $ar : \mathscr{F} \to \mathbb{N}$. The set of terms built from $\mathscr{F}$ and $\mathscr{X}$ is $\mathscr{T}(\mathscr{F}, \mathscr{X})$. The set of variables occurring in t is $\mathscr{V}ar(t)$. Terms are viewed as labeled trees in the usual way. *Positions* p are represented by chains of positive natural numbers used to address subterms $t|_p$ of t. The *set of positions* of a term t is $\mathscr{P}os(t)$. The set of positions of a subterm s in t is denoted $\mathscr{P}os_s(t)$. The set of positions of non-variable symbols in t are denoted as $\mathscr{P}os_{\mathscr{F}}(t)$, and $\mathscr{P}os_{\mathscr{X}}(t)$ is the set of variable positions of t.

Given a signature $\mathscr{F}$, a *replacement map* is a mapping μ satisfying that, for all symbols f in $\mathscr{F}$, $\mu(f) \subseteq \{1, \ldots, ar(f)\}$ [16]. The set of replacement maps for the signature $\mathscr{F}$ is $M_{\mathscr{F}}$. The set $\mathscr{P}os^{\mu}(t)$ of μ-*replacing (or* active*) positions* of t is $\mathscr{P}os^{\mu}(t) = \{\Lambda\}$, if $t \in \mathscr{X}$, and $\mathscr{P}os^{\mu}(t) = \{\Lambda\} \cup \{i.p \mid i \in \mu(f), p \in \mathscr{P}os^{\mu}(t_i)\}$, if $t = f(t_1, \ldots, t_k)$. The set of *non-μ-replacing* (or *frozen*) positions of t is $\overline{\mathscr{P}os^{\mu}}(t) = \mathscr{P}os(t) - \mathscr{P}os^{\mu}(t)$.

A *renaming* ρ is a bijection from $\mathscr{X}$ to $\mathscr{X}$. A *substitution* σ is a mapping $\sigma : \mathscr{X} \to \mathscr{T}(\mathscr{F}, \mathscr{X})$ from variables into terms which is homomorphically extended to a mapping (also denoted σ) $\sigma : \mathscr{T}(\mathscr{F}, \mathscr{X}) \to \mathscr{T}(\mathscr{F}, \mathscr{X})$. It is standard to assume that substitutions σ satisfy $\sigma(x) = x$ except for a *finite* set of variables, usually called the *domain* of the substitution, and denoted $\mathscr{D}om(\sigma)$. Thus, we often write $\sigma = \{x_1 \mapsto t_1, \ldots, x_n \mapsto t_n\}$ to denote a substitution. Two terms s and t *unify* if there is a substitution σ (i.e., a *unifier*) such that $\sigma(s) = \sigma(t)$. If s and t unify, then there is a *most general unifier* (*mgu*) θ of s and t satisfying that, for any other unifier σ of s and t, there is a substitution τ such that, for all $x \in \mathscr{X}$, $\sigma(x) = \tau(\theta(x))$. Moreover, *mgu*'s are unique up to variable renaming.

An *atom* is an expression $P(t_1, \ldots, t_n)$ where P is a predicate symbol and $t_1, \ldots, t_n$ are terms. A *literal* is an expression $\neg A$ where A is an atom. A first-order formula can be seen as a (possibly quantified, using $\forall$ and $\exists$) combination of literals using logical connectives $\wedge$, $\vee$, etc. A first-order formula whose variables are all quantified is called a *sentence*. A *theory* Th is a set of sentences. A sequence $A_1, \ldots, A_n$ of *atoms* is *feasible* w.r.t. a theory Th if there is a substitution σ such that for all $1 \leq i \leq n$, $\sigma(A_i)$ can be proved in Th. Otherwise, it is called *infeasible*.

3 Supported Variants of Rewrite Systems

CONFident can be used to prove and disprove confluence of:

Term Rewriting Systems (TRSs), which can be thought of as sets of rules $\ell \rightarrow r$, where ℓ and r are terms such that all variables in r already occur in ℓ.[1] The definition of a rewriting step $s \rightarrow_{\mathscr{R}} t$ is the usual one, see, e.g., [27, Section 3.2].

Context-Sensitive Term Rewriting Systems (CS-TRSs), which are TRSs $\mathscr{R}$ built on a signature $\mathscr{F}$ equipped with a *replacement map* μ. We often write $(\mathscr{R}, \mu)$ to denote a CS-TRS. *Context-sensitive rewriting (CSR)* is the restriction of rewriting obtained when a replacement map μ is used to restrict reductions: s μ-rewrites to t, written $s \xrightarrow{p}_{\mathscr{R},\mu} t$ (or $s \hookrightarrow_{\mathscr{R},\mu} t$, $s \hookrightarrow_{\mu} t$, or even $s \hookrightarrow t$), if $s \xrightarrow{p}_{\mathscr{R}} t$ and p is active in s (i.e., $p \in \mathscr{P}os^{\mu}(s)$).

Conditional Term Rewriting Systems (CTRSs), consisting of rules $\ell \rightarrow r \Leftarrow c$ where c is the *conditional part* of the rule, i.e., a (possibly empty) sequence $s_1 \approx t_1, \ldots, s_n \approx t_n$ of $n \geq 0$ conditions $s_i \approx t_i$, where s_i and t_i are terms for all $1 \leq i \leq n$. If $n = 0$ the rule is unconditional and we write $\ell \rightarrow r$ rather than $\ell \rightarrow r \Leftarrow$. Different interpretations of $\approx$ can be considered, leading to different subclasses of CTRSs [27, Definition 7.1.3]:

- *Join* CTRSs (J-CTRSs) if $\approx$ is interpreted as *joinability* of terms (two terms s and t are joinable if there is u such that both $s \rightarrow^* u$ and $t \rightarrow^* u$ hold).
- *Oriented* CTRSs (O-CTRSs) if $\approx$ is interpreted as *reachability* (a term t is reachable from s if $s \rightarrow^* t$ holds).
- *Semi-equational* CTRSs (SE-CTRSs) if $\approx$ is interpreted as *conversion* $\leftrightarrow^*$ (where $\leftrightarrow$ is the union $\rightarrow \cup \leftarrow$ of direct ($\rightarrow$) and inverse ($\leftarrow$) rewriting steps).

These classes of rewriting-based systems have been used and investigated in the last decades, see [2, 16, 27] and the references therein.

3.1 Logic-Based Description of Rewriting Computations

In [13, Section 3.1], we have provided a homogeneous, logic-based treatment to the three aforementioned kinds of CTRSs $\mathscr{R}$ leading to appropriate theories $\overline{\mathscr{R}}_J$, $\overline{\mathscr{R}}_O$, and $\overline{\mathscr{R}}_{SE}$ (which we often just denote as $\overline{\mathscr{R}}$ if no confusion arises) depending on the interpretation of $\approx$. This is used to define the one-step and many-step rewrite relations $\rightarrow_{\mathscr{R}}$ and $\rightarrow^*_{\mathscr{R}}$ of a CTRS $\mathscr{R}$ as follows: $s \rightarrow_{\mathscr{R}} t$ (resp. $s \rightarrow^*_{\mathscr{R}} t$) if and only if $s \rightarrow t$ (resp. $s \rightarrow^* t$) can be proved in $\overline{\mathscr{R}}$.

Since TRSs are particular cases of CTRSs where all rules are unconditional, we have a corresponding theory $\overline{\mathscr{R}}$ associated to a TRS $\mathscr{R}$. Similarly happens for a CS-TRS $(\mathscr{R}, \mu)$ with associated theory $\overline{\mathscr{R}}^{\mu}$, see [16, Section 4.1]. In the following, though, for simplicity the first-order theory associated to a system $\mathscr{R}$ (whether it is a TRS, a CS-TRS, or a J-,O-,or SE-CTRS) will be denoted $\overline{\mathscr{R}}$ if no confusion arises; furthermore,

---

[1] *String rewriting systems* (SRSs), which are rewrite systems where only monadic or constant function symbols are used, are also supported in CONFident.

we assume it as (not explicitly) *given* when necessary to give full meaning to some of the deployed techniques (e.g., infeasibility of rules and pairs, see Definition 2, and joinability as feasibility, see Example 3).

Definition 1 (Confluence and termination). *For TRSs and CTRSs $\mathscr{R}$, we say that $\mathscr{R}$ is (locally) confluent iff $\rightarrow_{\mathscr{R}}$ is (locally) confluent; $\mathscr{R}$ is terminating iff $\rightarrow_{\mathscr{R}}$ is terminating.*

For CS-TRSs $\mathscr{R}$ with replacement map μ, we say that $\mathscr{R}$ is (locally) μ-confluent iff $\hookrightarrow_{\mathscr{R},\mu}$ is (locally) confluent; $\mathscr{R}$ is μ-terminating iff $\hookrightarrow_{\mathscr{R},\mu}$ is terminating.

Note that we pay no attention to the considered *type* of CTRSs according to the distribution of variables in rules (1-, 2-, 3- or 4-CTRSs, see [23, Definition 6.1]).

3.2 Conditional Critical Pairs and Extended μ-Critical Pairs

Two terms s and t are (μ-)joinable if there is a term u such that $s \rightarrow_{\mathscr{R}}^* u$ and $t \rightarrow_{\mathscr{R}}^* u$ (resp. $s \hookrightarrow_{\mathscr{R},\mu}^* u$ and $t \hookrightarrow_{\mathscr{R},\mu}^* u$). In the following, we consider *conditional pairs* $\pi = \langle s,t \rangle \Leftarrow c$, where s and t are terms and c is a (possibly empty) condition consisting of a sequence of atomic conditions of the form $u \rightarrow^* v$, $u \downarrow v$, $u \leftrightarrow^* v$, and also one-step μ-rewriting conditions $u \hookrightarrow v$. If c is empty, we just write $\langle s,t \rangle$ (and we often call it an *unconditional* pair). We say that π is *joinable* if for all substitutions σ such that $\sigma(c)$ holds (i.e., each instantiated condition in c can be proved in $\overline{\mathscr{R}}$), terms $\sigma(s)$ and $\sigma(t)$ are joinable (or μ-joinable, for CS-TRSs). In order to simplify we just use *joinable* if no confusion arises.

Definition 2 (((In)easible rules and pairs). *For a TRS $\mathscr{R}$, CS-TRS $(\mathscr{R},\mu)$, or CTRS $\mathscr{R}$,*

- *A conditional rule $\ell \rightarrow r \Leftarrow c$ is (in)feasible if c is (in)feasible w.r.t. $\overline{\mathscr{R}}$.*
- *A conditional pair $\langle s,t \rangle \Leftarrow c$ is (in)feasible if c is (in)feasible w.r.t. $\overline{\mathscr{R}}$ (or $\overline{\mathscr{R}}^{\mu}$).*

Infeasible conditional pairs are trivially (μ-)joinable. This notion of conditional pair covers several specific notions which are important in proofs of confluence.

1. For CTRSs, a *conditional critical pair* $\langle s,t \rangle \Leftarrow c$ with label π is obtained from two conditional rules $\ell \rightarrow r \Leftarrow d, \ell' \rightarrow r' \Leftarrow d'$ with labels α and α', sharing no variable (rename if necessary) iff there is a non-variable position $p \in \mathscr{P}os_{\mathscr{F}}(\ell)$ (usually called *critical position*) such that $\ell|_p$ and ℓ' unify with *mgu* σ. Then, we let $s = \sigma(\ell[r']_p), t = \sigma(r)$, and $c = \sigma(d), \sigma(d')$.
   - If p is the topmost position Λ, then π is called an *overlay*.
   - If π is an overlay, and α and α' are renamed versions of the same rule, then π is called *improper*. Otherwise, π is called *proper*.
2. For TRSs, where rewrite rules have no conditional part, conditional critical pairs boil down into the usual *critical pairs* $\langle s,t \rangle$.
3. For CS-TRSs we only use critical pairs whose critical position p is *active* in the left-hand side ℓ of the first rule, i.e., $p \in \mathscr{P}os^{\mu}(\ell)$. These are called *$\mu$-critical pairs*. However, in order to fully capture confluence of *CSR*, we need to consider *extended μ-critical pairs*, including μ-critical pairs but also *conditional* pairs of the form $\langle \ell[x']_p, r \rangle \Leftarrow x \hookrightarrow x'$, where x' is a fresh variable and x is a variable of ℓ such that $\ell|_p = x$ is active (i.e., $p \in \mathscr{P}os^{\mu}(\ell)$), but x is frozen somewhere else in ℓ or in r.[2]

---

[2] These are called LH_{μ}-critical pairs, see [21, Section 4.3] for further motivation.

In the following we consider *conditional pairs* $\langle s,t \rangle \Leftarrow c$ with a conditional part c that can be either of the form (a) $s_1 \approx t_1, \ldots, s_n \approx t_n$ for some terms s_i, t_i, $1 \leq i \leq n$ (for conditional critical pairs) or (b) $x \hookrightarrow x'$ for some variables x and x' (for extended μ-critical pairs). The following definitions from [3,16,23,27] are used below.

- A TRS is normalizing if every term can be rewritten into an irreducible term.
- A system $\mathcal{R}$ is *left-linear* if the left-hand side ℓ of all rules in $\mathcal{R}$ are linear terms.
- A left-linear TRS all whose critical pairs $\langle s,t \rangle$ satisfy $s = t$ is *weakly orthogonal*.
- A CS-TRS $(\mathcal{R}, \mu)$ is *level-decreasing* if for all rules $\ell \to r$ in $\mathcal{R}$, the level of each variable in r does not exceed its level in ℓ; the *level* $lv_\mu(t,x)$ of a variable x in a term t is obtained by adding the number of frozen arguments that are traversed from the root to the variable.
- A left-linear CTRS is *orthogonal* if it contains no *proper* conditional critical pairs.
- A CTRS $\mathcal{R}$ is of type 3 (3-CTRS) if for all rules $\ell \to r \Leftarrow c \in \mathcal{R}$, $\mathcal{V}ar(r) \subseteq \mathcal{V}ar(\ell) \cup \mathcal{V}ar(c)$. It is *deterministic* (DCTRS) if every rule $\ell \to r \Leftarrow s_1 \approx t_1, \ldots, s_n \approx t_n$ satisfies $\mathcal{V}ar(t_i) \subseteq \mathcal{V}ar(\ell) \cup \bigcup_{j=1}^{i-1} \mathcal{V}ar(t_j)$ for all $1 \leq i \leq n$. It is *properly oriented* if every rule $\ell \to r \Leftarrow s_1 \approx t_1, \ldots, s_n \approx t_n$ satisfies: if $\mathcal{V}ar(r) \not\subseteq \mathcal{V}ar(\ell)$, then $Var(s_i) \subseteq \mathcal{V}ar(\ell) \cup \bigcup_{j=1}^{i} -1\mathcal{V}ar(t_j)$ for all $1 \leq i \leq n$.
- A CTRS is *right-stable* if every rule $\ell \to r \Leftarrow s_1 \approx t_1, \ldots, s_n \approx t_n$ satisfies the following conditions: for all $1 \leq i \leq n$, (a) $(\mathcal{V}ar(\ell) \cup \bigcup_{j=1}^{i-1} \mathcal{V}ar(s_j \approx t_j) \cup \mathcal{V}ar(s_i)) \cap \mathcal{V}ar(t_i) = \varnothing$, and (b) t_i is either a linear constructor term or a ground $\mathcal{R}_u$-irreducible term, where $\mathcal{R}_u$ is obtained from the rules of $\mathcal{R}$ by just dropping the conditional part: $\mathcal{R}_u = \{\ell \to r \mid \ell \to r \Leftarrow c \in \mathcal{R}\}$.
- A CTRS is *normal* if for all rules $\ell \to r \Leftarrow c$ and conditions $s \approx t$ in c, term t is an irreducible ground terms [3, Definition 2].[3]

3.3 Running Examples

The following example introduces a CS-TRS which is used to illustrate our developments in the subsequent sections. The presentation follows the quite intuitive COPS format, which is the input format of CONFident (see Sect. 8 below for more details).

Example 1. In the following CS-TRS (corresponding to Ex14_AEGL02 in TPDB[4])

```
(VAR x y)
(REPLACEMENT-MAP
  (cons 1)
  (length)
  (length1)
)
(RULES
```

---

[3] The expression *normal form* is used in [3, Definition 2]. Although 'normal form' is not formally defined anywhere in [3], from the discussion in page 32 preceding [3, Definition 1], it is clear that 'normal form' means *irreducible term*. See [19] for a discussion about *normal forms* vs. *irreducible terms* in conditional rewriting.

[4] Termination Problems Data Base, see https://www.lri.fr/~marche/tpdb/.

```
from(x) -> cons(x,from(s(x)))
length(nil) -> 0
length(cons(x,y)) -> s(length1(y))
length1(x) -> length(x)
)
```

the replacement map specified in the REPLACEMENT-MAP section disallows rewritings at *frozen* (i.e., *non-active*) positions. For instance, no rewriting is allowed in the second argument of cons or in the argument of length and length1. Missing symbols in the section are given no replacement restriction.

The following example displays an *oriented* CTRS, again using COPS format.

Example 2. The following example (#409 in COPS[5]) displays an *oriented* CTRS.

```
(CONDITIONTYPE ORIENTED)
(VAR x y)
(RULES
f(x,y) -> g(s(x)) | c(g(x)) == c(a)
f(x,y) -> h(s(x)) | c(h(x)) == c(a)
g(s(x)) -> x
h(s(x)) -> x
b -> b
)
```

Note the use of '==' instead of '≈' in the conditional part of conditional rules. Section CONDITIONTYPE indicates the semantics of conditions as explained above.

4   Confluence Framework

In this section, we present a general framework for proving confluence of rewrite systems based on the combination of different techniques encapsulated as processors. We first define the kind of *problems* we deal with. Below we often use τ to refer them when no confusion arises.

Definition 3 (Confluence Problems).

– Let $\mathscr{R}$ be a CTRS (TRSs are included). A confluence problem, *denoted $CR(\mathscr{R})$, is* positive *if $\mathscr{R}$ is confluent; otherwise, it is* negative.
– Let $\mathscr{R}$ be a TRS and μ be a replacement map. A μ-confluence problem, *denoted* $CR(\mathscr{R},\mu)$, is positive *if $\mathscr{R}$ is μ-confluent; otherwise, it is* negative.

Definition 4 (Joinability Problems).

– Let $\mathscr{R}$ be a CTRS and π be a conditional pair *where the conditional part has no occurrence of $\hookrightarrow$. A joinability problem, denoted $JO(\mathscr{R},\pi)$, is* positive *if π is joinable in $\mathscr{R}$; otherwise, it is* negative.

---

[5] Confluence Problems database, see https://cops.uibk.ac.at/.

– *Let $\mathcal{R}$ be a TRS, μ be a replacement map, and π be a* conditional pair *where the conditional part contains at most an occurrence of* $\hookrightarrow$. *A* μ-joinability *problem, denoted* $JO(\mathcal{R}, \mu, \pi)$, *is* positive *if* π *is* μ-joinable *in* $\mathcal{R}$; *otherwise, it is* negative.

Proofs of properties represented by a problem τ can be recast as proofs of other *problems*, hopefully, easier to (dis)prove. *Processors* are in charge of such transformations.

Definition 5. *A* processor P *is a partial function from problems into sets of problems; alternatively it can return "no". The* domain *of* P *(i.e., the set of problems on which* P *is defined) is denoted* $\mathcal{D}om(\mathsf{P})$. *We say that* P *is*

– sound *if for all* $\tau \in \mathcal{D}om(\mathsf{P})$, τ *is positive whenever* $\mathsf{P}(\tau) \neq$ *"no" and all* $\tau' \in \mathsf{P}(\tau)$ *are positive.*
– complete *if for all* $\tau \in \mathcal{D}om(\mathsf{P})$, τ *is negative whenever* $\mathsf{P}(\tau) = $ *"no" or* τ' *is negative for some* $\tau' \in \mathsf{P}(\tau)$.

5   List of Processors

CONFident implements several processors. By lack of space, in our presentation we cannot explicitly define all auxiliary notions that are used to describe them. Instead, short descriptions and/or appropriate references are given.

Simplification. Before attempting a proof of confluence of a system $\mathcal{R}$, some simplifications are often possible:

1. *Removing or transforming rules (CS-TRSs and CTRSs).* All rules $t \rightarrow t$ or $t \rightarrow t \Leftarrow c$ for some term t are removed.
2. *Removing infeasible rules (CTRSs only).* Rules $\ell \rightarrow r \Leftarrow c$ with an infeasible condition c are removed. We use infChecker [11] for that purpose.
3. *Inlining conditional rules (CTRSs only).* As explained in [32], we can often reduce the number of conditions of a rule, by using *inlining*, see [32, Definition 4].

These are applied as much as possible (to each rule in the input system) by means of a *simplifying processor* P_{Simp}:

$$\mathsf{P}_{Simp}(CR(\mathcal{R})) = \{CR(\mathcal{R}')\}$$

where $\mathcal{R}'$ is obtained by using the previous transformations. Note that $\mathcal{R}'$ can become a TRS even for CTRSs $\mathcal{R}$ containing (proper) conditional rules. Since these transformations do not affect (μ-)confluence of $\mathcal{R}$ (because the one-step (context-sensitive) rewriting relation of $\mathcal{R}$ and the *reflexive closure* of the one-step (context-sensitive) rewriting relation of $\mathcal{R}'$ coincide), P_{Simp} is *sound* and *complete*.

Modular Decomposition. For TRSs $\mathcal{R}$, processor P_{MD} tries to find a *decomposition* of $\mathcal{R}$ into two TRSs $\mathcal{R}_1$ and $\mathcal{R}_2$.

$$\mathsf{P}_{MD}(CR(\mathcal{R})) = \{CR(\mathcal{R}_1), CR(\mathcal{R}_2)\}$$

iff $\mathscr{R} = \mathscr{R}_1 \cup \mathscr{R}_2$ and some of the *modularity conditions for confluence* is achieved: disjoint TRSs [34]; or constructor-sharing and left-linear TRSs [28]; or constructor-sharing and layer-preserving TRSs [26]. In all these papers, confluence is called *modular* with respect to a given combination (disjoint, constructor-sharing and left-linear, or constructor-sharing and layer preserving) whenever for all TRSs $\mathscr{R}_1$ and $\mathscr{R}_2$, the union $\mathscr{R}_1 \cup \mathscr{R}_2$ is confluent *iff* both $\mathscr{R}_1$ and $\mathscr{R}_2$ are. Accordingly, P_{MD} is *sound* and *complete*.

Orthogonality. For TRSs $\mathscr{R}$, processor P_{HL} implements Huet-Levy's Theorem (*weakly orthogonal TRSs are confluent*, see [27, Sect. 4.3]):

$$\mathsf{P}_{HL}(CR(\mathscr{R})) = \varnothing$$

iff $\mathscr{R}$ is weakly orthogonal. For CS-TRSs $(\mathscr{R}, \mu)$, by relying on [21, Coro. 36], we have:

$$\mathsf{P}_{HL}(CR(\mathscr{R}, \mu)) = \varnothing$$

iff $\mathscr{R}$ is left-linear and has no extended μ-critical pairs.[6] For 3-CTRSs $\mathscr{R}$, by relying on [27, Theorem 7.4.14][7]

$$\mathsf{P}_{HL}(CR(\mathscr{R})) = \varnothing$$

iff $\mathscr{R}$ is orthogonal, properly oriented, and right-stable. In all these uses, P_{HL} is *sound* and (trivially) *complete*.

Extended Huet Processor. For CTRSs $\mathscr{R}$, P_{Huet} checks joinability of (conditional) critical pairs.

$$\mathsf{P}_{Huet}(CR(\mathscr{R})) = \{JO(\mathscr{R}, \pi_1), \ldots, JO(\mathscr{R}, \pi_n)\}$$

for $\pi_1, \ldots, \pi_n$ the (possibly conditional) critical pairs of $\mathscr{R}$ [27, Def. 7.1.8]. For CS-TRSs $(\mathscr{R}, \mu)$,

$$\mathsf{P}_{Huet}(CR(\mathscr{R}, \mu)) = \{JO(\mathscr{R}, \mu, \pi_1), \ldots, JO(\mathscr{R}, \mu, \pi_n)\}$$

if $\pi_1, \ldots, \pi_n$ are the extended μ-critical pairs of $\mathscr{R}$. For both uses, P_{Huet} is *not* sound (joinability of critical pairs, alone, does not imply confluence), although it is *complete* ([27, Lemma 4.2.3] for TRSs and [21, Theorem 30] for CS-TRSs). In practice, this processor is used when proving confluence is not possible and we try to find a possible counterexample. As for CTRSs, by definition of conditional critical pair, the existence of non-joinable conditional critical pairs implies non-confluence of the CTRS.

Extended Huet-Newman Processor. For TRSs $\mathscr{R}$ with critical pairs $\pi_1, \ldots, \pi_n$, by relying on [2, Corollary 6.2.6],

$$\mathsf{P}_{HN}(CR(\mathscr{R})) = \{JO(\mathscr{R}, \pi_1), \ldots, JO(\mathscr{R}, \pi_n)\}$$

iff $\mathscr{R}$ is terminating. For CS-TRSs $(\mathscr{R}, \mu)$, with extended μ-critical pairs $\pi_1, \ldots, \pi_n$, by relying on [21, Theorem 32],

$$\mathsf{P}_{HN}(CR(\mathscr{R}, \mu)) = \{JO(\mathscr{R}, \mu, \pi_1), \ldots, JO(\mathscr{R}, \mu, \pi_n))\}$$

---

[6] Such CS-TRSs are called μ-orthogonal in [21, Definition 35].

[7] Originally in [33, Theorem 4.6], this result concerns *level-confluence*, which implies confluence. We also implement [27, Theorem 7.4.11] as part of P_{HL}.

iff $\mathscr{R}$ is μ-terminating. For *normal* CTRSs $\mathscr{R}$ with conditional critical pairs $\pi_1, \ldots, \pi_n$, by relying on [3, Theorem 2],

$$\mathsf{P}_{HN}(CR(\mathscr{R})) = \{JO(\mathscr{R}, \pi_1), \ldots, JO(\mathscr{R}, \pi_n)\}$$

iff $\mathscr{R}$ is left-linear, terminating, and $\pi_1, \ldots, \pi_n$ are joinable overlays. In all these uses, P_{HN} is *sound* and *complete*.

Confluence as Canonical Joinability of μ-Critical Pairs. The *canonical replacement map* $\mu_{\mathscr{R}}^{can}$ for a TRS $\mathscr{R}$ is *the most restrictive replacement map ensuring that the non-variable subterms of the left-hand sides of the rules of $\mathscr{R}$ are all active* [16, Section 5]. Replacement maps that are *less restrictive* than $\mu_{\mathscr{R}}^{can}$ (i.e., such that $\mu_{\mathscr{R}}^{can}(f) \subseteq \mu(f)$ for all symbols f in the signature) are collected in the set $CM_{\mathscr{R}}$. By relying on [10, Theorem 2],

$$\mathsf{P}_{CanJ}(CR(\mathscr{R})) = \{JO(\mathscr{R}, \mu, \pi_1), \ldots, JO(\mathscr{R}, \mu, \pi_n)\}$$

iff $\mathscr{R}$ is a left-linear and level-decreasing TRS, $\mu \in CM_{\mathscr{R}}$, $\pi_1, \ldots, \pi_n$ are the μ-critical pairs of $\mathscr{R}$, and $\mathscr{R}$ is μ-terminating. P_{CanJ} is *sound* but *not* complete.

Confluence as Canonical μ-Confluence. By relying on [16, Corollary 8.23],

$$\mathsf{P}_{CanCR}(CR(\mathscr{R})) = \{CR(\mathscr{R}, \mu)\}$$

iff $\mathscr{R}$ is left-linear and normalizing TRS, and $\mu \in CM_{\mathscr{R}}$. P_{CanCR} is *sound* but *not* complete.

Confluence of CTRSs as Confluence of TRSs. Processor $\mathsf{P}_{\mathscr{U}}$ transforms a confluence problem for a 3-CTRS $\mathscr{R}$ into a confluence problem for a TRS $\mathscr{U}(\mathscr{R})$ where $\mathscr{U}$ is the transformation from deterministic 3-CTRSs to TRSs in [27, Definition 7.2.48]. Then,

$$\mathsf{P}_{\mathscr{U}}(CR(\mathscr{R})) = \{CR(\mathscr{U}(\mathscr{R}))\}$$

iff $\mathscr{R}$ is a terminating and deterministic 3-CTRS [17, Theorem 8].[8] $\mathsf{P}_{\mathscr{U}}$ is *sound* but *not* complete. Processor $\mathsf{P}_{\mathscr{U}_{conf}}$ transforms a confluence problem for a deterministic 3-CTRS $\mathscr{R}$ into a confluence problem for a TRS $\mathscr{U}_{conf}(\mathscr{R})$, where $\mathscr{U}_{conf}$ is the transformation in [8, Definition 6]:

$$\mathsf{P}_{\mathscr{U}_{conf}}(CR(\mathscr{R})) = \{CR(\mathscr{U}_{conf}(\mathscr{R}))\}$$

iff $\mathscr{R}$ is a weakly left-linear[9] deterministic 3-CTRS. $\mathsf{P}_{\mathscr{U}_{conf}}$ is sound (see [8, Theorem 9]) but not complete.

Joinability Processor. For CTRSs $\mathscr{R}$ and conditional pairs π:

$$\mathsf{P}_{JO}(JO(\mathscr{R}, \pi)) = \begin{cases} \varnothing & \text{if } \pi \text{ is joinable w.r.t. } \mathscr{R} \\ \text{no} & \text{if } \pi \text{ is not joinable w.r.t. } \mathscr{R} \end{cases}$$

---

[8] Theorem 8 in [17] concerns transformation $\mathscr{U}$ and the optimized variant $\mathscr{U}_{opt}$ in [4]. Although the proof for $\mathscr{U}_{opt}$ is flawed due to a misuse of a result in [4], it holds for $\mathscr{U}$, though.

[9] Roughly speaking, a DCTRS is *weakly left-linear* if "variables that occur more than once in the lhs of a conditional rule and the rhs's of conditions should not occur at all in lhs's of conditions or the rhs of the conditional rule" [7, Definition 3.17].

Methods for proving and disproving joinability of conditional pairs are described in [13, Section 6]. For CS-TRSs $(\mathscr{R}, \mu)$,

$$P_{JO}(JO(\mathscr{R}, \mu, \pi)) = \begin{cases} \varnothing & \text{if } \pi \text{ is } \mu\text{-joinable w.r.t. } \mathscr{R} \\ \text{no} & \text{if } \pi \text{ is not } \mu\text{-joinable w.r.t. } \mathscr{R} \end{cases}$$

Methods for proving and disproving μ-joinability of conditional pairs are described in [21, Section 6]. For both uses P_{JO} is *sound* and *complete*.

Table 1 summarizes the main characteristics (domain of application, possibly requiring additional restrictions, see above; and soundness/completeness) of the enumerated processors.

Table 1. Processors in the confluence framework

	P_{Simp}	P_{MD}	P_{Huet}	P_{HL}	P_{HN}	P_{CanJ}	P_{CanCR}	$P_{\mathscr{U}}$	$P_{\mathscr{U}_{conf}}$	P_{JO}
TRSs	✓	✓	✓	✓	✓	✓	✓	✗	✗	✓
CS-TRSs	✓	✗	✓	✓	✓	✗	✗	✗	✗	✓
CTRSs	✓	✗	✓	✓	✓	✗	✗	✓	✓	✓
Sound	✓	✓	✗	✓	✓	✓	✓	✓	✓	✓
Complete	✓	✓	✓	✓	✓	✗	✗	✗	✗	✓

6 Proofs in the Confluence Framework

Confluence problems can be proved positive or negative by using a proof tree as follows. The following definition is given for CTRSs $\mathscr{R}$. For CS-TRSs it is similar.

Definition 6 (Confluence Proof Tree). *Let $\mathscr{R}$ be a CTRS. A confluence proof tree $\mathscr{T}$ for $\mathscr{R}$ is a tree whose root label is $CR(\mathscr{R})$, whose inner nodes are labeled with problems, and whose leaves are labeled either with problems, "yes" or "no". For every inner node* n *labeled with τ, there is a processor* P *such that $\tau \in \mathscr{D}om(P)$ and:*

1. *if* $P(\tau) = $ *"no" then* n *has just one child, labeled with "no".*
2. *if* $P(\tau) = \varnothing$ *then* n *has just one child, labeled with "yes".*
3. *if* $P(\tau) = \{\tau_1, \ldots, \tau_m\}$ *with $m > 0$, then* n *has m children labeled with the problems* $\tau_1, \ldots, \tau_m$.

In this way, a confluence proof tree is obtained by the combination of different processors. Examples can be seen in Fig. 1 below. The proof of the following result can be found in [35].

Theorem 1 (Confluence Framework). *Let $\mathscr{R}$ be a CTRS and $\mathscr{T}$ be a confluence proof tree for $\mathscr{R}$. Then:*

1. *if all leaves in $\mathscr{T}$ are labeled with "yes" and all involved processors are sound for the problems they are applied to, then $\mathscr{R}$ is confluent.*
2. *if $\mathscr{T}$ has a leaf labeled with "no" and all processors in the path from the root to such a leaf are complete for the problems they are applied to, then $\mathscr{R}$ is non-confluent.*

In the following, we show how processors are used to obtain a proof.

Example 3 (continuing Example 1). We start with the problem $CR(\mathscr{R},\mu)$ for the CS-TRS $(\mathscr{R},\mu)$ in Example 1. No preprocessing is possible. We only have the following extended μ-critical pair:

$$\pi: \langle \text{from(x')}, \text{cons(x,from(s(x)))} \rangle \Leftarrow x \hookrightarrow x'$$

Thus, $\mathsf{P}_{Huet}(CR(\mathscr{R},\mu)) = \{JO(\mathscr{R},\mu,\pi)\}$. By using the results in [21, Section 6.2], we can prove that π is not joinable. In particular, according to [21, Proposition 54], π is not joinable if the sequence

$$x \hookrightarrow x', \text{from(x')} \hookrightarrow^* z, \text{cons(x,from(s(x)))} \hookrightarrow^* z \qquad (1)$$

where z is a fresh variable, is *infeasible*. The infeasibility of (1) can be automatically verified using infChecker. Thus, $\mathsf{P}_{JO}(JO(\mathscr{R},\mu,\pi)) = $ "no". The proof tree is shown in Fig. 1 (left). Since P_{Huet} and P_{JO} are complete, $\mathscr{R}$ is not μ-confluent.

Example 4 (continuing Example 2). We proceed as follows:

1. We remove rule b -> b from $\mathscr{R}$ in Example 2 to obtain $\mathscr{R}' = \mathscr{R} - \{b \to b\}$. Hence, $\mathsf{P}_{Simp}(CR(\mathscr{R})) = \{CR(\mathscr{R}')\}$.
2. Since $\mathscr{R}'$ can be proved terminating (use MU-TERM [12]) we apply P_{HN} to $CR(\mathscr{R}')$. The CTRS $\mathscr{R}'$ has a single conditional critical pair:

$$\pi: \langle \text{g(s(x))}, \text{h(s(x))} \rangle \Leftarrow \text{c(h(x))} \;==\; \text{c(a)}, \; \text{c(g(x))} \;==\; \text{c(a)}$$

Therefore, $\mathsf{P}_{HN}(CR(\mathscr{R}')) = \{JO(\mathscr{R}',\pi)\}$.
3. Finally, we apply P_{JO} to $JO(\mathscr{R}',\pi)$. By, e.g., a simple exploration of the possible reducts of g(s(x)) and h(s(x)), we see that both terms rewrite to x by using the unconditional rules of $\mathscr{R}'$. Hence all instances of g(s(x)) and h(s(x)) by a substitution σ are also joinable. Thus, $\mathsf{P}_{JO}(JO(\mathscr{R}',\pi)) = \varnothing$.

The proof tree is shown in Fig. 1 (right). Since all processors used in the proof tree are sound, we conclude confluence of $\mathscr{R}$.

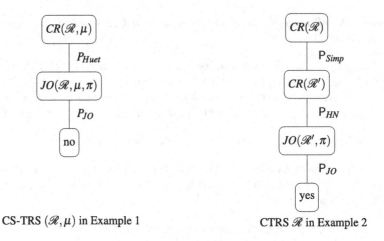

CS-TRS $(\mathscr{R},\mu)$ in Example 1   CTRS $\mathscr{R}$ in Example 2

Fig. 1. Proof trees in the confluence framework.

7 Strategy

Given a rewrite system $\mathscr{R}$, the processors enumerated in Sect. 5 are used to build a proof tree with root $CR(\mathscr{R})$ or $CR(\mathscr{R},\mu)$ to hopefully conclude $(\mu\text{-})$confluence or non-$(\mu\text{-})$confluence of $\mathscr{R}$ (Theorem 1). The selection and combination of processors to generate such a proof tree is usually encoded as a fixed *proof strategy* which is applied to the initial confluence problem $CR(\mathscr{R})$. Choosing the appropriate proof strategy for an input problem is not a trivial task. The strategy must take into account that many problems involved in the implementation of processors are *undecidable*. For instance, joinability of conditional pairs (required, e.g., by P_{Huet}) is, in general, undecidable. Also, calls to external tools trying to check undecidable properties like termination (as required, e.g., by P_{HN}) may fail or succeed proving the *opposite* property, i.e., non-termination. For these reasons, the application of processors is usually constrained by a *timeout* so that after a predefined amount of time, the strategy may try a different processor hopefully succeeding on the considered problem, or even *backtrack* to a previous problem in the proof tree. Typically, a thorough experimental analysis is needed to obtain a suitable strategy.

In our proof strategy, we use two strategy combinators, the *sequential* combinator and the *alternative* combinator. The strategies used in an alternative combinator can be executed in parallel. The proof strategy used in CONFident is as follows: (i) it tries to apply P_{Simp} to simplify the input system or its rules; then (ii) it tries to decompose the problem using P_{MD}; (iii) at this point, there is an alternative with the identity processors (that returns the same input system), P_{CanCR}, $\mathsf{P}_{\mathscr{U}}$, and $\mathsf{P}_{\mathscr{U}_{conf}}$; (iv) for each branch, there is an alternative of P_{HL}, P_{HN}, and P_{Huet}; and (v) it tries P_{JO} on each joinability problem.

8   Structure of CONFident

CONFident is written in Haskell and it has more than 100 Haskell files with almost 15000 lines of code (blanks and comments not included). The tool is used online through its web interface in:

http://zenon.dsic.upv.es/confident/

The main input format to introduce rewrite systems in CONFident is COPS format,[10] the official input format of the Confluence Competition (CoCo[11]). Examples 1 and 2 show the main features of COPS input format.[12] COPS format organizes the information about the rewrite system in several blocks: variable declaration; replacement map specification; type of CTRS according to the evaluation of conditions; rule description, etc.

CONFident uses specialized tools to solve auxiliary proof obligations. For instance,

- infChecker is used by P_{Simp} to prove infeasibility of conditional rules which are then discarded from the analysis. It is also used by P_{Huet}, P_{HL}, P_{HN} to remove infeasible conditional critical pairs. Finally, infChecker is also used to implement the tests of joinability and μ-joinability of (conditional) pairs required by P_{JO}.
- MU-TERM is used by P_{HN} and P_{CanJ} to check termination of CTRSs and μ-termination of TRSs.
- Prover9 [22] is used by P_{JO} to prove joinability of conditional pairs.
- Fort [29] is used by P_{CanCR} to check whether a TRS is normalizing.

Tools like MU-TERM or infChecker are connected as Haskell libraries that are directly used by CONFident, the rest of the tools are used by capturing external calls.

9   Experimental Results

CONFident participated in the 2021 International Confluence Competition (CoCo)[13] in the categories TRS, SRS, and CTRS, obtaining the first place in the CTRS category. Figure 2 (left) summarizes our benchmarks on the COPS collection of CTRSs used in the CoCo 2021 *full-run* (August 2021) which we use below to provide an analysis of use of our processors.

With respect to context-sensitive rewriting, our experimental evaluation on the CoCo 2021 collection of 100 TRSs $\mathscr{R}$ was as follows: we automatically associated the canonical replacement map $\mu_{\mathscr{R}}^{can}$ to each of the examples to obtain a benchmark suite for confluence of *CSR*. The results are summarized in Fig. 2 (right). Complete details can be found here:

---

[10] http://project-coco.uibk.ac.at/problems/.

[11] http://project-coco.uibk.ac.at/.

[12] The TPDB format, see https://www.lri.fr/~marche/tpdb/format.html, introduced in 2003 for use in the International Termination Competition (TermComp https://termination-portal.org/wiki/Termination_Competition) can also be used in CONFident.

[13] http://project-coco.uibk.ac.at/2021/.

Yes	No	TO	Maybe	Solved	Total
63	38	22	27	101	150

CTRSs: CoCo 2021 full run

Yes	No	TO	Maybe	Solved	Total
14	52	13	23	66	100

CS-TRSs: CoCo 2021 TRSs $\mathscr{R}$ plus $\mu_{\mathscr{R}}^{can}$

Fig. 2. Experimental results on examples from CoCo 2021

http://zenon.dsic.upv.es/confident/benchmarks/lopstr22/benchmarks.html

Table 2 summarizes the use of processors in our experiments. Processors P_{CanJ} and P_{CanCR} are not displayed as they do not apply to CS-TRSs or CTRSs. We display the *number of uses* of each processor along the whole benchmark set. Remind that some processors are used several times to solve a single example.

Table 2. Use of processors in the experiments

	P_{Simp}	P_{MD}	P_{Huet}	P_{HL}	P_{HN}	$P_{\mathscr{U}}$	$P_{\mathscr{U}_{conf}}$	P_{JO}
CS-TRS	5	2	52	11	4	–	–	53
CTRS	36	7	38	43	24	1	15	60

Some clarifications are in order. Regarding the CS-TRS benchmarks:

- P_{MD} is used in examples 653 and 662. In those TRSs $\mathscr{R}$, its canonical replacement map $\mu_{\mathscr{R}}^{can}$ imposes no restriction. Thus, $(\mathscr{R}, \mu_{\mathscr{R}}^{can})$ can be treated as a TRS and modular decomposition proceeds accordingly.
- Two of the 11 uses of P_{HL} correspond to the proof of confluence of the two modules obtained for example 662. This explains the mismatch between the 14 positive results (Fig. 2 right) and the $11 + 4 = 15$ joint uses of P_{HL} and P_{HN} which are the ones that are able to qualify confluence problems as positive.
- On the other hand, the answer for example 653 is negative. After decomposition, the first module is immediately proved non-confluent using P_{Huet} and P_{JO}.

Regarding the CTRS benchmarks:

- Many of the 36 uses of P_{Simp} transform CTRSs into TRSs by inlining conditions and/or removing infeasible conditional rules.
- The 7 uses of P_{MD} correspond to such TRSs obtained after using P_{Simp}: examples 271, 288, 334, 341, 360, 382, and 495. Examples 271, 360, and 382 go through this process and then are proved non-confluent using P_{Huet} and P_{JO}. Examples 288, 334, 341, and 495 are similarly treated and then proved confluent by two applications of P_{HL}. This explains the mismatch between the uses of P_{HL} and P_{HN} ($43 + 24 = 67$) and the number of positive proofs (63, see Fig. 2 left).

In order to compare CONFident with state-of-the-art tools in the field, we refer the reader to the recently obtained results in the 2022 edition of CoCo:

status	ACP	CO3	CONFident	CONFident_2021
YES	27	28	44	31
NO	16	19	28	25
MAYBE	57	53	28	44
total	100	100	100	100

Fig. 3. Results of the CTRS category of CoCo 2022

http://project-coco.uibk.ac.at/2022/results.php

Each year, the benchmark examples are randomly selected from the whole collection of COPS (oriented) CTRSs. Thus, the 2022 benchmarks set does not need to coincide with the 2021 benchmarks set. CONFident participated in the confluence subcategories (oriented) CTRS, SRS, and TRS. CONFident also participated in the new 'demo' category for confluence of context-sensitive rewriting (labeled CSR). In general, our results have been good in all aforementioned categories.

As for the CTRS category, Fig. 3 shows a snapshot of the results obtained by the participating tools, ACP, CO3, and CONFident, in the live competition of CoCo 2022 (the winner of the previous edition is automatically included, hence CONFident 2021). All examples solved by the other participating tools were also solved by CONFident. And there were proofs of confluence (e.g., example COPS/349) and proofs of non-confluence (e.g., example COPS/263) which were obtained by CONFident only. With 72% of success in the input examples, CONFident won the competition in this category and got one of the five FLoC 2022 Olympic Games gold medals granted to CoCo 2022.

10   Related Work

There are several tools that are able of automatically proving and disproving confluence of TRSs and oriented CTRSs. ACP (Automated Confluence Prover) [1] implements a divide-and-conquer approach in two steps: first, a decomposition step is applied (based on modularity results); then, direct techniques are applied to each decomposition. ConCon [31] first tries to simplify rules and remove infeasible rules from the input system, then it employs a number of confluence criteria for (oriented) 3-CTRSs. ConCon uses several confluence criteria, and tree automata techniques on reachability to prove (in)feasibility of conditional parts. In parallel, ConCon tries to show non-confluence using conditional narrowing (and some other heuristics). CSI [24] uses a set of techniques (Knuth and Bendix' criterion, non-confluence criterion, order-sorted decomposition, development closed criterion, decreasing diagrams and extended rules) and a strategy language to combine them. CoLL-Saigawa [30] is the combination of two tools: CoLL and Saigawa. If the input system is left-linear, it uses CoLL; otherwise, it uses

Saigawa. Among the techniques used by these tools are Hindley's commutation theorem together with the three commutation criteria, almost development closeness, rule labeling with weight function, Church-Rosser modulo AC, criteria based on different kinds of critical pairs, rule labeling, parallel closedness based on parallel critical pairs, simultaneous closedness, parallel-upside closedness, and outside closedness. CO3 [25] uses confluence (and termination) of $U(\mathscr{R})$ and $U_{opt}(\mathscr{R})$, in addition to narrowing trees for checking infeasibility of conditional parts in proofs of confluence of CTRSs.

Although the previous tools also use combinations of different techniques to obtain proofs of confluence, to the best of our knowledge, none of them formalize such a combination as done in this paper. As far as we know, an important difference between CONFident and all previous tools is the encoding of (non-)joinability of (conditional) pairs as combinations of *(in)feasibility* problems [11]. As explained in [15, 16] and further developed in [13, 21], this is possible due to the logic-based treatment of rewrite systems as first-order theories. This is also the key for CONFident to be able to smoothly handle join, oriented, and semi-equational CTRSs, something which is also a novel feature of the tool in comparison with the aforementioned tools. Furthermore, as far as we know, CONFident is the only tool implementing confluence criteria depending on *termination* of CTRSs (see the description of P_{HN} and $P_{\mathscr{U}}$) rather than more restrictive termination properties like quasi-decreasingness [27, Def. 7.2.39], which is equivalent to *operational termination* [18].

Remark 1 (Termination vs. operational termination of CTRSs). We refer the reader to [20] for a discussion about the relationship between termination and operational termination of (oriented) CTRSs. See also the URL

http://zenon.dsic.upv.es/muterm/benchmarks/ot-vs-t-20220721/benchmarks.html

for a collection of benchmarks making such differences explicit in practice.

The following example illustrates this point.

Example 5. Consider the following CTRS [13, Example 33]

```
(CONDITIONTYPE ORIENTED)
(VAR x)
(RULES
  c -> b
  d -> b
  f(a,x) -> c | x == a
  f(x,x) -> d | x == a
  g(x) -> d   | g(x) == b
  g(a) -> f(a,a)
)
```

which is *not* operationally terminating due to the third conditional rule (this can be automatically proved by MU-TERM, after small changes to fit into the TPDB format: remove (CONDITIONTYPE ORIENTED) and replace == by -> in the conditional rules). However, *termination* of $\mathscr{R}$ can also be proved by MU-TERM: we only need to add the header (CHECK-TERMINATION) before the input. We can exploit this fact to prove confluence of $\mathscr{R}$, see [13, Example 33] for details. CONFident is also able to prove confluence of this system.

11 Conclusions and Future Work

CONFident is a tool which is able to automatically prove and disprove confluence of variants of rewrite systems: TRSs, CS-TRSs, and Join, Oriented, and Semi-Equational CTRSs. The proofs are obtained by combining different techniques in what we call *Confluence Framework*, which we have introduced here, where *confluence* and *joinability* problems are handled (simplified, transformed, etc.) by means of *processors*, which can be freely combined to obtain the proofs which are displayed as a *proof tree*. In this paper, we have introduced 10 processors which can be used in the Confluence Framework. We have shown how to prove and disprove confluence of the aforementioned kinds of systems by using the Confluence Framework (Definition 6 and Theorem 1). CONFident has proved to be a powerful tool for proving confluence of CTRSs. This is witnessed by the first position obtained in the CTRS category of CoCo 2021 and 2022.

Regarding future work, many things remain to be done. For instance, as far as we know, modularity of μ-confluence has not been investigated yet. And no result concerning modularity of confluence of CTRSs (see, e.g., [26, Table 8.4]) has been implemented in CONFident yet. Also, being able to analyze confluence of conditional context-sensitive term rewriting systems [17, Section 8.1] appears as a natural goal. Also considering confluence of order-sorted rewrite systems [9] and rewrite systems with axioms [14] could be an interesting task for future work.

References

1. Aoto, T., Yoshida, J., Toyama, Y.: Proving confluence of term rewriting systems automatically. In: Treinen, R. (ed.) RTA 2009. LNCS, vol. 5595, pp. 93–102. Springer, Heidelberg (2009). https://doi.org/10.1007/978-3-642-02348-4_7
2. Baader, F., Nipkow, T.: Term Rewriting and All That. Cambridge University Press, Cambridge (1998)
3. Dershowitz, N., Okada, M., Sivakumar, G.: Confluence of conditional rewrite systems. In: Kaplan, S., Jouannaud, J.-P. (eds.) CTRS 1987. LNCS, vol. 308, pp. 31–44. Springer, Heidelberg (1988). https://doi.org/10.1007/3-540-19242-5_3
4. Durán, F., Lucas, S., Meseguer, J., Marché, C., Urbain, X.: Proving termination of membership equational programs. In: Heintze, N., Sestoft, P. (eds.) Proceedings of the 2004 ACM SIGPLAN Workshop on Partial Evaluation and Semantics-Based Program Manipulation 2004, Verona, Italy, 24–25 August 2004, pp. 147–158. ACM (2004). https://doi.org/10.1145/1014007.1014022
5. Giesl, J., Thiemann, R., Schneider-Kamp, P.: The dependency pair framework: combining techniques for automated termination proofs. In: Baader, F., Voronkov, A. (eds.) LPAR 2005. LNCS (LNAI), vol. 3452, pp. 301–331. Springer, Heidelberg (2005). https://doi.org/10.1007/978-3-540-32275-7_21
6. Giesl, J., Thiemann, R., Schneider-Kamp, P., Falke, S.: Mechanizing and improving dependency pairs. J. Autom. Reasoning **37**(3), 155–203 (2006). https://doi.org/10.1007/s10817-006-9057-7
7. Gmeiner, K., Gramlich, B., Schernhammer, F.: On soundness conditions for unraveling deterministic conditional rewrite systems. In: Tiwari, A. (ed.) 23rd International Conference on Rewriting Techniques and Applications (RTA 2012), RTA 2012, Nagoya, Japan, 28 May–2 June 2012. LIPIcs, vol. 15, pp. 193–208. Schloss Dagstuhl - Leibniz-Zentrum für Informatik (2012). https://doi.org/10.4230/LIPIcs.RTA.2012.193

8. Gmeiner, K., Nishida, N., Gramlich, B.: Proving confluence of conditional term rewriting systems via unravelings. In: 2nd International Workshop on Confluence, IWC 2013, pp. 35–39 (2013)
9. Goguen, J.A., Meseguer, J.: Order-sorted algebra I: equational deduction for multiple inheritance, overloading, exceptions and partial operations. Theor. Comput. Sci. **105**(2), 217–273 (1992). https://doi.org/10.1016/0304-3975(92)90302-V
10. Gramlich, B., Lucas, S.: Generalizing Newman's lemma for left-linear rewrite systems. In: Pfenning, F. (ed.) RTA 2006. LNCS, vol. 4098, pp. 66–80. Springer, Heidelberg (2006). https://doi.org/10.1007/11805618_6
11. Gutiérrez, R., Lucas, S.: Automatically proving and disproving feasibility conditions. In: Peltier, N., Sofronie-Stokkermans, V. (eds.) IJCAR 2020. LNCS (LNAI), vol. 12167, pp. 416–435. Springer, Cham (2020). https://doi.org/10.1007/978-3-030-51054-1_27
12. Gutiérrez, R., Lucas, S.: MU-TERM: verify termination properties automatically (system description). In: Peltier, N., Sofronie-Stokkermans, V. (eds.) IJCAR 2020. LNCS (LNAI), vol. 12167, pp. 436–447. Springer, Cham (2020). https://doi.org/10.1007/978-3-030-51054-1_28
13. Gutiérrez, R., Lucas, S., Vítores, M.: Confluence of conditional rewriting in logic form. In: Bojańczy, M., Chekuri, C. (eds.) 41st IARCS Annual Conference on Foundations of Software Technology and Theoretical Computer Science (FSTTCS 2021). Leibniz International Proceedings in Informatics (LIPIcs), vol. 213, pp. 44:1–44:18. Schloss Dagstuhl - Leibniz-Zentrum für Informatik, Dagstuhl, Germany (2021). https://doi.org/10.4230/LIPIcs.FSTTCS.2021.44
14. Kirchner, C., Kirchner, H.: Equational logic and rewriting. In: Siekmann, J.H. (ed.) Computational Logic, Handbook of the History of Logic, vol. 9, pp. 255–282. Elsevier (2014). https://doi.org/10.1016/B978-0-444-51624-4.50006-X
15. Lucas, S.: Proving semantic properties as first-order satisfiability. Artif. Intell. **277** (2019). https://doi.org/10.1016/j.artint.2019.103174
16. Lucas, S.: Context-sensitive rewriting. ACM Comput. Surv. **53**(4), 78:1–78:36 (2020). https://doi.org/10.1145/3397677
17. Lucas, S.: Applications and extensions of context-sensitive rewriting. J. Log. Algebr. Meth. Program. **121**, 100680 (2021). https://doi.org/10.1016/j.jlamp.2021.100680
18. Lucas, S., Marché, C., Meseguer, J.: Operational termination of conditional term rewriting systems. Inf. Process. Lett. **95**(4), 446–453 (2005)
19. Lucas, S., Meseguer, J.: Normal forms and normal theories in conditional rewriting. J. Log. Algebr. Meth. Program. **85**(1), 67–97 (2016). https://doi.org/10.1016/j.jlamp.2015.06.001
20. Lucas, S., Meseguer, J.: Dependency pairs for proving termination properties of conditional term rewriting systems. J. Log. Algebr. Meth. Program. **86**(1), 236–268 (2017). https://doi.org/10.1016/j.jlamp.2016.03.003
21. Lucas, S., Vítores, M., Gutiérrez, R.: Proving and disproving confluence of context-sensitive rewriting. J. Log. Algebr. Meth. Program. **126**, 100749 (2022). https://doi.org/10.1016/j.jlamp.2022.100749
22. McCune, W.: Prover9 & Mace4. Technical report (2005–2010). http://www.cs.unm.edu/~mccune/prover9/
23. Middeldorp, A., Hamoen, E.: Completeness results for basic narrowing. Appl. Algebra Eng. Commun. Comput. **5**, 213–253 (1994). https://doi.org/10.1007/BF01190830
24. Nagele, J., Felgenhauer, B., Middeldorp, A.: CSI: new evidence – a progress report. In: de Moura, L. (ed.) CADE 2017. LNCS (LNAI), vol. 10395, pp. 385–397. Springer, Cham (2017). https://doi.org/10.1007/978-3-319-63046-5_24
25. Nishida, N.: CO3 (Version 2.2). In: Mirmram, S., Rocha, C. (eds.) Proceedings of the 10th International Workshop on Confluence, IWC 2021, p. 51 (2021)

26. Ohlebusch, E.: On the modularity of confluence of constructor-sharing term rewriting systems. In: Tison, S. (ed.) CAAP 1994. LNCS, vol. 787, pp. 261–275. Springer, Heidelberg (1994). https://doi.org/10.1007/BFb0017487
27. Ohlebusch, E.: Advanced Topics in Term Rewriting. Springer, New York (2002). https://doi.org/10.1007/978-1-4757-3661-8
28. Raoult, J., Vuillemin, J.: Operational and semantic equivalence between recursive programs. J. ACM **27**(4), 772–796 (1980). https://doi.org/10.1145/322217.322229
29. Rapp, F., Middeldorp, A.: FORT 2.0. In: Galmiche, D., Schulz, S., Sebastiani, R. (eds.) IJCAR 2018. LNCS (LNAI), vol. 10900, pp. 81–88. Springer, Cham (2018). https://doi.org/10.1007/978-3-319-94205-6_6
30. Shintani, K., Hirokawa, N.: CoLL-Saigawa 1.6: a joint confluence tool. In: Mirmram, S., Rocha, C. (eds.) Proceedings of the 10th International Workshop on Confluence, IWC 2021, p. 51 (2021)
31. Sternagel, C.: CoCo 2020 participant: ConCon 1.10. In: Ayala-Rincón, M., Mirmram, S. (eds.) Proceedings of the 9th International Workshop on Confluence, IWC 2020, p. 65 (2020)
32. Sternagel, T.: Reliable confluence analysis of conditional term rewrite systems. Ph.D. thesis, Faculty of Mathematics, Computer Science and Physics, University of Innsbruck, August 2017
33. Suzuki, T., Middeldorp, A., Ida, T.: Level-confluence of conditional rewrite systems with extra variables in right-hand sides. In: Hsiang, J. (ed.) RTA 1995. LNCS, vol. 914, pp. 179–193. Springer, Heidelberg (1995). https://doi.org/10.1007/3-540-59200-8_56
34. Toyama, Y.: On the Church-Rosser property for the direct sum of term rewriting systems. J. ACM **34**(1), 128–143 (1987). https://doi.org/10.1145/7531.7534
35. Vítores, M.: CONFident: a tool for confluence analysis of rewriting systems (master thesis). Master's thesis, Departamento de Sistemas Informáticos y Computación. Universitat Politècnica de València, Spain, April 2022

Variant-Based Equational Anti-unification

María Alpuente[1], Demis Ballis[2], Santiago Escobar[1],
and Julia Sapiña[1(✉)]

[1] VRAIN, Universitat Politècnica de València,
Camino de Vera s/n, Apdo 22012, 46071 Valencia, Spain
{alpuente,sescobar,jsapina}@upv.es
[2] DMIF, University of Udine, Via delle Scienze, 206, 33100 Udine, Italy
demis.ballis@uniud.it

Abstract. The dual of most general equational unifiers is that of least general equational anti-unifiers, i.e., most specific anti-instances modulo equations. This work aims to provide a general mechanism for equational anti-unification that leverages the recent advances in variant-based symbolic computation in Maude. Symbolic computation in Maude equational theories is based on folding variant narrowing (FVN), a narrowing strategy that efficiently computes the equational variants of a term (i.e., the irreducible forms of all of its substitution instances). By relying on FVN, we provide an equational anti-unification algorithm that computes the least general anti-unifiers of a term in any equational theory E where the number of least general E-variants is finite for any given term.

1 Introduction

The concept of anti-unification (also known as generalization) was independently introduced by Plotkin [20] and Reynolds [21]. Anti-unification is relevant in a wide spectrum of automated reasoning techniques and applications where analogical reasoning and inductive inference are needed, such as ontology learning, analogy making, case-based reasoning, web and data mining, theorem proving, machine learning, program derivation, and inductive logic programming, among others [3,18,19]. For instance, the anti-unification algorithm of [14] has been recently used in the generation of fix patterns for automated program repair in Bloomberg's Fixie-learn [13] and Facebook's Getafix [4].

In the purely syntactic and untyped setting of [20,21], the syntactic generalization problem for two or more expressions consists in finding their *least general generalizer (lgg)*, i.e., the least general expression t such that all of the given expressions are instances of t under appropriate substitutions. For instance, consider an alphabet with three constants a, b, and c; three function symbols f, g and h; and variables x, y and z. Also consider the two terms

This work was partially supported by TAILOR, a project funded by EU Horizon 2020 research and innovation programme under GA No. 952215, grant PID2021-122830OB-C42 funded by MCIN/AEI/10.13039/501100011033 and by "ERDF A way of making Europe", and by Generalitat Valenciana under grant PROMETEO/2019/098.

$u = f(b, g(b, b))$ and $v = f(g(z, a), g(g(z, a), b))$. The expression $f(x, g(x, b))$ is the syntactic (and unique) least general generalizer of u and v since both $f(b, g(b, b))$ and $f(g(z, a), g(g(z, a), b))$ are substitution instances of $f(x, g(x, b))$. However, if the function symbol g is given a definition by means of an equational theory E consisting of the equation $g(x, y) = b$, then $g(b, b)$, $g(z, a)$, $g(x, y)$ and b are "la même chose" (more formally, they are equal modulo E) and so are $u = f(b, g(b, b))$ and $v = f(g(z, a), g(g(z, a), b))$, hence the least general generalizer of u and v is $f(b, b)$. Note that the syntactic generalizer $f(x, g(x, b))$ of u and v, and its E-equivalent term $f(x, b)$, are more general modulo E than the least general generalizer $f(b, b)$.

Given a set E of equations and two terms u and v to be generalized modulo E, we say that the term t is an E-generalizer of u and v if there are two terms t_1 and t_2, which are substitution instances of t, such that t_1 is equal (modulo E) to u and t_2 is equal (modulo E) to v. An E-generalizer of u and v that is less general than or incomparable to (modulo E) any other E-generalizer of the two terms is called a least general generalizer. The computation of equational least general generalizers is much more involved than syntactic generalization as it may require guessing the less general term pattern t and substitutions σ_1 and σ_2 that, when independently applied to t, get two terms $t_1 = t\sigma_1$ and $t_2 = t\sigma_2$ that are equal (modulo E) to two corresponding arguments in u and v. This guessing cannot be done by simple equational reasoning but requires logic-style, symbolic computation. For instance, if the theory E contains the equations $h(x, a) = f(g(x, a), g(g(x, a), b))$ and $h(x, b) = f(b, g(b, b))$ (with g obeying no equation), then $h(x, y)$ is a least general generalizer modulo E of $u = f(b, g(b, b))$ and $v = f(g(z, a), g(g(z, a), b))$. This is because there are two instances of $h(x, y)$ which are equal (modulo E) to u and v, respectively (namely, $\sigma_1 = \{y \mapsto b\}$ and $\sigma_2 = \{x \mapsto z, y \mapsto a\}$).

Similarly to the dual problem of E-unification of two terms, where there may be a set of incomparable, most general E-unifiers, the set of least general anti-unifiers of two terms is not generally singleton. For instance, the syntactic generalizer $f(x, g(x, b))$ of $u = f(b, g(b, b))$ and $v = f(g(z, a), g(g(z, a), b))$ above is still valid with the two equations for h and it is incomparable to $h(x, y)$, so both are least general generalizers. The anti-unification type of a theory can be defined similarly (but dually) to the unification types, i.e., based on the existence and cardinality of a minimal and complete set of least general generalizers [7].

In this work, we address the problem of least general anti-unification in order-sorted equational theories where function symbols are endowed with an equational definition. The intuition behind our least general generalization algorithm is that substitutions σ_1 and σ_2 mentioned above can be computed by narrowing most general terms $f(x_1, \cdots, x_n)$ in E, with f being an n-ary function symbol in the theory. Narrowing is a symbolic execution mechanism that generalizes term rewriting by allowing free variables in terms (as in logic programming) and handles them by using unification (instead of pattern matching) to non-deterministically reduce these terms. For instance, given $E = \{h(x, b) = f(b, g(b, b)), h(x, a) = f(g(x, a), g(g(x, a), b))\}$, there are two narrowing steps stemming from the term $h(x, y)$: 1) the term $h(x, y)$ narrows to $f(b, g(b, b))$ with computed narrowing substitution $\sigma_1 = \{y \mapsto b\}$; and 2) the term narrows to $f(g(x, a), g(g(x, a), b))$ with computed narrowing substitution $\sigma_2 = \{y \mapsto a\}$. In the last few years, there has been a resurgence of narrowing in many application areas such as equational unification, state space exploration, protocol analysis, termination analysis, theorem proving, deductive verification, model transformation, testing, constraint solving, and model checking.

Maude [8] is a language and a system that efficiently implements Rewriting Logic (RWL) [15]. Equational theories in Maude may include ordinary equations and algebraic axioms, i.e., distinguished equations expressing algebraic laws such as associativity (A), commutativity (C), and identity (i.e., unity) (U) of function symbols. Algebraic axioms are efficiently handled in Maude in a built-in way. For the sake of simplicity, the equational theories considered in this work do not contain algebraic axioms.

Maude provides quite sophisticated narrowing-based features that rely on built-in generation of the set of *variants* of a term t [10]. Essentially, a *variant* of a term t in the theory E is the canonical (i.e., irreducible in E) form of $t\sigma$ for a given substitution σ. Variants are computed in Maude by using the *folding variant narrowing strategy* [11]. When the theory satisfies the *finite variant property* (i.e., there is a finite number of most general variants for every term in the theory), folding variant narrowing computes a minimal and complete set of most general variants in a finite amount of time. Many theories of interest have the FVP, including theories that give algebraic axiomatizations of cryptographic functions used in communication protocols, where FVP is omni-present.

As far as we know, this is the first general, theory-independent algorithm for computing least general anti-unifiers modulo equational theories in *Plotkin's style*. A theory-agnostic E-generalization algorithm based on regular tree grammars is formalized by Burghardt in [5] that computes a finite representation of E-generalization sets. However, Burghardt's algorithm is restricted to equational theories E that induce regular congruence classes (i.e., the theory E is the deductive closure of finitely many ground equations). We establish that the novel algorithm that we propose in this paper is minimal, correct and complete (i.e., it computes a complete and minimal set of least general generalizers for any anti-unification problem). A prototype implementation in Maude [CDE+07] is currently under development.

In [1,2], we extended the classical untyped anti-unification algorithm of [20] to work: (1) modulo any combination of associativity, commutativity, and identity axioms (including the empty set of such axioms); (2) with typed structures that involve sorts, subsorts, and subtype polymorphism; and (3) under any combination of both, which results in a modular, order-sorted, least general anti-unification algorithm modulo algebraic axioms. The algorithm in [1,2] only applies to modular combinations of A, C, and U equational axioms. It cannot be used to solve anti-unification problems in the general, user-defined equational theories considered in this paper.

After some preliminaries in Sect. 2, in Sect. 3 we address the problem of generalizing two (typed) expressions modulo an equational theory, we formulate our least general generalization algorithm, and we illustrate it by means of a representative example. Section 4 proves the formal properties of our algorithm. In Sect. 5, we discuss further work and we conclude. A simple representative application of equational generalization to a biological domain is described in Appendix A.

2 Preliminaries

We follow the classical notation and terminology from [23] for term rewriting and from [12,16] for order-sorted equational logic.

We assume an *order-sorted signature* $\Sigma = (S, F, \leq)$ that consists of a finite poset of sorts $(S, \leq)$ and a family F of function symbols of the form $f : s_1 \times \cdots \times s_n \rightarrow s$, with $s_1, \cdots, s_n, s \in S$. Two sorts s and s' belong to the same connected component if either $s \leq s'$ or $s' \leq s$. We assume a *kind-completed signature* such that: (i) each connected component in the poset ordering has a top sort, and, for each $s \in S$, we denote by $[s]$ the top sort in the connected component of s (*i.e.,* if s and s' are sorts in the same connected component, then $[s] = [s']$); and (ii) for each operator declaration $f : s_1 \times \cdots \times s_n \rightarrow s$ in Σ, there is also a declaration $f : [s_1] \times \cdots \times [s_n] \rightarrow [s]$ in Σ. A given term t in an order-sorted term algebra can have many different sorts. Specifically, if t has sort s, then it also has sort s' for any $s' \geq s$; and because a function symbol f can have different sort declarations $f : s_1 \times \cdots \times s_n \rightarrow s$, a term $f(t_1, .., t_n)$ can have sorts that are not directly comparable [12].

We assume a fixed S-sorted family $\mathcal{V} = \{\mathcal{V}_s\}_{s \in S}$ of pairwise disjoint variable sets (*i.e.,* $\forall s, s' \in S : \mathcal{V}_s \cap \mathcal{V}_{s'} = \emptyset$), with each $\mathcal{V}_s$ being countably infinite. We write the sort associated to a variable explicitly with a colon and the sort, *i.e.,* x:Nat. A *fresh* variable is a variable that appears nowhere else. The set $\mathcal{T}_\Sigma(\mathcal{V})_s$ denotes all Σ-terms of sort s defined by $\mathcal{V}_s \subseteq \mathcal{T}_\Sigma(\mathcal{V})_s$ and $f(t_1, \cdots, t_n) \in \mathcal{T}_\Sigma(\mathcal{V})_s$ if $f : s_1 \times \cdots \times s_n \rightarrow s \in \Sigma$, $n \geq 0$ and $t_1 \in \mathcal{T}_\Sigma(\mathcal{V})_{s_1}, \cdots, t_n \in \mathcal{T}_\Sigma(\mathcal{V})_{s_n}$. Furthermore, if $t \in \mathcal{T}_\Sigma(\mathcal{V})_s$ and $s \leq s'$, then $t \in \mathcal{T}_\Sigma(\mathcal{V})_{s'}$. For a term t, we write $Var(t)$ for the set of all variables in t. $\mathcal{T}(\Sigma)_s$ is the set of ground terms of sort s, *i.e.,* t is a Σ-term of sort s and $Var(t) = \emptyset$. We write $\mathcal{T}(\Sigma, \mathcal{V}) = \bigcup_{s \in S} \mathcal{T}_\Sigma(\mathcal{V})_s$ and $\mathcal{T}(\Sigma) = \bigcup_{s \in S} \mathcal{T}(\Sigma)_s$ for the corresponding term algebras. We assume that $\mathcal{T}(\Sigma)_s \neq \emptyset$ for every sort s.

We assume *pre-regularity* of the signature Σ: for each operator declaration $f : s_1 \times \cdots \times s_n \rightarrow s$, and for the set S_f containing all sorts s' that appear in operator declarations of the form $f : s'_1, \cdots, s'_n \rightarrow s'$ in Σ such that $s_i \leq s'_i$ for $1 \leq i \leq n$, the set S_f has a least sort. Thanks to pre-regularity of Σ, each Σ-term t has a *unique least sort* that is denoted by $LS(t)$. The top sort in the connected component of $LS(t)$ is denoted by $[LS(t)]$. Since the poset $(S, \leq)$ is finite and each connected component has a top sort, given any two sorts s and s' in the same connected component, the set of least upper bound sorts of s and s' always exists (although it might not be a singleton set) and is denoted by $LUBS(s, s')$.

Throughout this paper, we assume that Σ has no *ad-hoc operator overloading*, *i.e.*, any two operator declarations for the same symbol f with equal number of arguments, $f : s_1 \times \cdots \times s_n \to s$ and $f : s'_1 \times \cdots \times s'_n \to s'$, must necessarily have $[s_1] = [s'_1], \cdots, [s_n] = [s'_n], [s] = [s']$.

The set of positions of a term t, written $Pos(t)$, is represented as a sequence of natural numbers referring to a subterm of t, *e.g.*, the subterm of $f(g(x, h(c)))$ occurring at position 1.2.1 is c. The set of non-variable positions is written $Pos_\Sigma(t)$. The root position of a term is Λ. The subterm of t at position p is $t|_p$, and $t[u]_p$ is the term obtained from t by replacing $t|_p$ by u. By $root(t)$, we denote the symbol occurring at the root position of t.

A *substitution* $\sigma = \{x_1 \mapsto t_1, \cdots, x_n \mapsto t_n\}$ is a mapping from variables to terms which is almost everywhere equal to the identity except over a finite set of variables $\{x_1, \cdots, x_n\}$, written $Dom(\sigma) = \{x \in \mathcal{V} \mid x\sigma \neq x\}$. Substitutions are *sort-preserving*, *i.e.*, for any substitution σ, if $x \in \mathcal{V}_s$, then $x\sigma \in \mathcal{T}_\Sigma(\mathcal{V})_s$. We assume substitutions are idempotent, *i.e.*, $x\sigma = (x\sigma)\sigma$ for any variable x. The set of variables introduced by σ is $VRan(\sigma) = \bigcup\{Var(x\sigma) \mid x\sigma \neq x\}$. The identity substitution is *id*. Substitutions are homomorphically extended to $\mathcal{T}(\Sigma, \mathcal{V})$. Substitutions are written in suffix notation (*i.e.*, $t\sigma$ instead of $\sigma(t)$), and, consequently, the composition of substitutions must be read from left to right, formally denoted by juxtaposition, *i.e.*, $x(\sigma\sigma') = (x\sigma)\sigma'$ for any variable x. The restriction of σ to a set of variables V is $\sigma|_V$. We call a substitution σ a *renaming* if there is another substitution σ^{-1} such that $(\sigma\sigma^{-1})|_{Dom(\sigma)} = id$.

A Σ-*equation* is an unoriented pair $t \doteq t'$, where t and t' are Σ-terms for which there are sorts s, s' with $t \in \mathcal{T}_\Sigma(\mathcal{V})_s$, $t' \in \mathcal{T}_\Sigma(\mathcal{V})_{s'}$, and s, s' are in the same connected component of the poset of sorts $(S, \leq)$. An *equational theory* (Σ, E) is a set E of Σ-equations. An *equational theory* (Σ, E) over a kind-completed, pre-regular, and order-sorted signature $\Sigma = (S, F, \leq)$ is called kind-completed, pre-regular, and order-sorted equational theory. Given an equational theory (Σ, E), order-sorted equational logic induces a congruence relation $=_E$ on terms $t, t' \in \mathcal{T}(\Sigma, \mathcal{V})$, see [12,16].

The relative generality E-*subsumption preorder* $\leq_E$ (simply $\leq$ when E is empty) holds between $t, t' \in \mathcal{T}(\Sigma, \mathcal{V})$, denoted $t \leq_E t'$ (meaning that t is more general than t' modulo E), if there is a substitution σ such that $t\sigma =_E t'$. The substitution σ is said to be a E-*matcher* for t' in t. The equivalence relation $\equiv_E$ (or $\equiv$ if E is empty) induced by $\leq_E$ is defined as $t \equiv_E t'$ if $t \leq_E t'$ and $t' \leq_E t$.

The E-*renaming equivalence* $t \simeq_E t'$ (or $\simeq$ if E is empty) holds if there is a renaming substitution θ such that $t\theta =_E t'$. In general, the relations $=_E$, $\equiv_E$ and $\simeq_E$ do not coincide; actually $=_E \subseteq \simeq_E \subseteq \equiv_E$. We can naturally extend $\leq_E$ to substitutions as follows: a substitution θ is more general than σ modulo E, denoted by $\theta \leq_E \sigma$, if there is a substitution γ such that $\sigma =_E \theta\gamma$, i.e., for all $x \in \mathcal{X}, x\sigma =_E x\theta\gamma$.

Given a set of equations E, $\overrightarrow{E}$ is a set of rewrite rules that result from orienting the equations of E from left to right. We call $(\Sigma, \overrightarrow{E})$ a *decomposition* of an equational theory (Σ, E) if $\overrightarrow{E}$ is *convergent*, i.e., confluent, terminating, and strictly coherent [17], and sort-decreasing. Under these conditions, the equations in E can be safely interpreted as simplification rules that can be used to compute a unique E-*canonical form* $t\downarrow_E$ for every term $t \in \mathcal{T}(\Sigma, \mathcal{V})$.

Given a decomposition $(\Sigma, \overrightarrow{E})$ of an equational theory and a substitution $\theta = \{x_1 \mapsto t_1, \cdots, x_n \mapsto t_n\}$, we let $\theta\downarrow_{\overrightarrow{E}} = \{x_1 \mapsto t_1\downarrow_{\overrightarrow{E}}, \cdots, x_n \mapsto t_n\downarrow_{\overrightarrow{E}}\}$. We say that (t', θ') is an E-*variant* [9,11] (or just a variant) of term t if for some substitution θ, $t' = (t\theta)\downarrow_{\overrightarrow{E}}$ and $\theta' = \theta\downarrow_{\overrightarrow{E}}$. A *complete set of most general E-variants* [11] (up to renaming) of a term t is a subset, denoted by $[\![t]\!]_E$, of the set of all E-variants of t such that, for each E-variant (t', σ') of t, there is an E-variant $(t'', \sigma'') \in [\![t]\!]_E$ such that $t'' \leq_E t'$ and $\sigma'' \leq_E \sigma'$. A decomposition $(\Sigma, \overrightarrow{E})$ has the *finite variant property* (FVP) [11] (also called a *FVP theory*) iff for each Σ-term t, a complete set $[\![t]\!]_E$ of its most general variants is finite.

Finally, we also consider a natural partition of the rewrite theory signature as $\Sigma = \mathcal{D} \uplus \Omega$, where Ω are the *constructor* symbols, which are used to define (irreducible) data values, and $\mathcal{D} = \Sigma \setminus \Omega$ are the *defined* symbols, which are evaluated away via equational simplification. Terms in $\tau(\Omega, \mathcal{V})$ are called *constructor* terms.

3   Least General Anti-unification Modulo Equational Theories via Variant Computation

In the following, we recall the order-sorted syntactic generalization algorithm as formalized in [1,2].

3.1   Syntactic Anti-unification

A term t is a syntactic generalizer of t_1 and t_2 if there are two substitutions σ_1 and σ_2 such that $t\sigma_1 = t_1$ and $t\sigma_2 = t_2$.

We represent a generalization problem between terms t and t' as a *constraint* $t \overset{x}{\triangleq} t'$, where x is a fresh variable that stands for a generalizer of t and t', that becomes more and more instantiated as the computation proceeds until becoming a least general generalizer. Given a constraint $t \overset{x}{\triangleq} t'$, any generalizer w of t and t' is given by a suitable substitution θ such that $x\theta = w$.

A set of constraints is represented by $s_1 \overset{x_1}{\triangleq} t_1 \wedge \cdots \wedge s_n \overset{x_n}{\triangleq} t_n$, or $\emptyset$ for the empty set. Given a constraint $t \overset{x}{\triangleq} t'$, we call x a *generalization variable*. We define the set of generalization variables of a set C of constraints as $GVs(C) = \{y \in \mathcal{V} \mid \exists u \overset{y}{\triangleq} v \in C\}$.

Note that, although it is natural to consider that a constraint $t \overset{x}{\triangleq} t'$ is commutative, the inference rules that are described do not admit that commutativity property for $\triangleq$ since we need to keep track of the origin of new generated generalization subproblems. However, the constructor symbol $\wedge$ that we use to build a set (conjunction) of constraints is *associative* and *commutative* in the inference rules described in this paper. Note that there are no defined symbols in the syntactic case, i.e. $\Sigma = \Omega$.

Definition 1. *A configuration* $\langle C \mid S \mid \theta \rangle$ *consists of three components: (i) the* constraint component C, *which represents the* set of unsolved constraints; *(ii) the* store component S, *which records the* set of already solved constraints, *and (iii)* the substitution component θ, *which binds some of the generalization variables previously met during the computation.*

Decompose
$$\frac{f \in (\Omega \cup \mathcal{V}) \wedge f : [\mathsf{s_1}] \times \cdots \times [\mathsf{s_n}] \to [\mathsf{s}]}{\langle f(t_1, \cdots, t_n) \overset{x:[\mathsf{s}]}{\triangleq} f(t'_1, \cdots, t'_n) \wedge C \mid S \mid \theta \rangle \to}$$
$$\langle t_1 \overset{x_1:[\mathsf{s_1}]}{\triangleq} t'_1 \wedge \cdots \wedge t_n \overset{x_n:[\mathsf{s_n}]}{\triangleq} t'_n \wedge C \mid S \mid \theta\sigma \rangle$$
where $\sigma = \{x:[\mathsf{s}] \mapsto f(x_1:[\mathsf{s_1}], \cdots, x_n:[\mathsf{s_n}])\}$, $x_1:[\mathsf{s_1}], \cdots, x_n:[\mathsf{s_n}]$ are fresh variables, and $n \geq 0$

Solve
$$\frac{root(t) \neq root(t') \wedge \nexists y \nexists \mathsf{s}'' : t \overset{y:\mathsf{s}''}{\triangleq} t' \in S}{\langle t \overset{x:[\mathsf{s}]}{\triangleq} t' \wedge C \mid S \mid \theta \rangle \to \langle C \mid S \wedge t \overset{z:\mathsf{s}'}{\triangleq} t' \mid \theta\sigma \rangle}$$
where $\sigma = \{x:[\mathsf{s}] \mapsto z:\mathsf{s}'\}$, $z:\mathsf{s}'$ is a fresh variable, and $\mathsf{s}' \in LUBS(LS(t), LS(t'))$

Recover
$$\frac{root(t) \neq root(t') \wedge \exists y \exists \mathsf{s}' : t \overset{y:\mathsf{s}'}{\triangleq} t' \in S}{\langle t \overset{x:[\mathsf{s}]}{\triangleq} t' \wedge C \mid S \mid \theta \rangle \to \langle C \mid S \mid \theta\sigma \rangle}$$
where $\sigma = \{x:[\mathsf{s}] \mapsto y:\mathsf{s}'\}$

Fig. 1. Basic inference rules for order-sorted least general generalization [1]

In Fig. 1, we consider any two terms t and t' in a constraint $t \overset{x}{\triangleq} t'$ having the same top sort; otherwise, they are incomparable and no generalizer exists. Starting from the initial configuration $\langle t \overset{x:[\mathsf{s}]}{\triangleq} t' \mid \emptyset \mid id \rangle$ where $[\mathsf{s}] = [LS(t)] = [LS(t')]$, configurations are transformed until a terminal configuration $\langle \emptyset \mid S \mid \theta \rangle$ is reached. The transition relation $\to$ on configurations is given by the smallest relation satisfying all of the rules of Fig. 1. Due to order-sortedness, in general there can be more than one least general generalizer of two expressions [1].

In this paper, variables of terms t and t' in a generalization problem $t \overset{x}{\triangleq} t'$ are considered as constants, and are never instantiated. The meaning of the rules is as follows.

- The **Decompose** rule is the syntactic decomposition generating new constraints to be solved.
- The **Solve** rule checks that a constraint $t \overset{x}{\triangleq} t' \in C$, with $root(t) \neq root(t')$, is not already solved. If not already in the store S, then the solved constraint $t \overset{x}{\triangleq} t'$ is added to S. Note that the **Solve** rule causes branching due to different choices of s', hereby producing multiple least general generalizers.

- The **Recover** rule checks if a constraint $t \overset{x}{\triangleq} t' \in C$, with $root(t) \neq root(t')$, is already solved, *i.e.*, if there is already a constraint $t \overset{y}{\triangleq} t' \in S$ for the same pair of terms (t, t') with variable y. This is needed when the input terms of the generalization problem contain the same generalization subproblems more than once, *e.g.*, the lgg of $f(f(a,a),a)$ and $f(f(b,b),a)$ is $f(f(y,y),a)$.

We illustrate the syntactic generalization calculus by means of the following example, where we disregard of sorts for the sake of simplicity.

Example 1. Consider the terms $t = f(g(a), g(y), a)$ and $t' = f(g(b), g(y), b)$. In order to compute the least general generalizer of t and t', we apply the inference rules of Fig. 1. The substitution component in the final configuration obtained by the lgg algorithm is $\theta = \{x \mapsto f(g(x_4), g(y), x_4), x_1 \mapsto g(x_4), x_2 \mapsto g(y), x_5 \mapsto y, x_3 \mapsto x_4\}$, hence the computed lgg is $x\theta = f(g(x_4), g(y), x_4)$. The execution trace is showed in Fig. 2. Note that variable x_4 is repeated to ensure that the least general generalizer is obtained.

$$lgg(f(g(a), g(y), a), f(g(b), g(y), b))$$
$$\downarrow \text{ Initial Configuration}$$
$$\langle f(g(a), g(y), a) \overset{x}{\triangleq} f(g(b), g(y), b) \mid \emptyset \mid id \rangle$$
$$\downarrow \text{ Decompose}$$
$$\langle g(a) \overset{x_1}{\triangleq} g(b) \wedge g(y) \overset{x_2}{\triangleq} g(y) \wedge a \overset{x_3}{\triangleq} b \mid \emptyset \mid \{x \mapsto f(x_1, x_2, x_3)\} \rangle$$
$$\downarrow \text{ Decompose}$$
$$\langle a \overset{x_4}{\triangleq} b \wedge g(y) \overset{x_2}{\triangleq} g(y) \wedge a \overset{x_3}{\triangleq} b \mid \emptyset \mid \{x \mapsto f(g(x_4), x_2, x_3), x_1 \mapsto g(x_4)\} \rangle$$
$$\downarrow \text{ Solve}$$
$$\langle g(y) \overset{x_2}{\triangleq} g(y) \wedge a \overset{x_3}{\triangleq} b \mid a \overset{x_4}{\triangleq} b \mid \{x \mapsto f(g(x_4), x_2, x_3), x_1 \mapsto g(x_4)\} \rangle$$
$$\downarrow \text{ Decompose}$$
$$\langle y \overset{x_5}{\triangleq} y \wedge a \overset{x_3}{\triangleq} b \mid a \overset{x_4}{\triangleq} b \mid \{x \mapsto f(g(x_4), g(x_5), x_3), x_1 \mapsto g(x_4), x_2 \mapsto g(x_5)\} \rangle$$
$$\downarrow \text{ Decompose}$$
$$\langle a \overset{x_3}{\triangleq} b \mid a \overset{x_4}{\triangleq} b \mid \{x \mapsto f(g(x_4), g(y), x_3), x_1 \mapsto g(x_4), x_2 \mapsto g(y), x_5 \mapsto y\} \rangle$$
$$\downarrow \text{ Recover}$$
$$\langle \emptyset \mid a \overset{x_4}{\triangleq} b \mid \{x \mapsto f(g(x_4), g(y), x_4), x_1 \mapsto g(x_4), x_2 \mapsto g(y), x_5 \mapsto y, x_3 \mapsto x_4\} \rangle$$

Fig. 2. Computation trace for (syntactic) generalization of terms $f(g(a), g(y), a)$ and $f(g(b), g(y), b)$

3.2 Anti-unification Modulo an Equational Theory

Given an equational theory E, a complete set of least general generalizers modulo E of terms u and v can be computed by extending the syntactic least general generalization calculus of Fig. 1 with the new rule of Fig. 3. Note that the considered extension turns the equational generalization algorithm into a more non-deterministic calculus by independently applying **Solve** and the new rule **Variant** to the same configuration.

For the sake of optimality, we assume that both u and v are canonical forms with respect to $\vec{E}$; otherwise, we simplify them to canonical form before the E-lgg computation starts so that we ensure that the computed solutions are canonical representatives w.r.t. E of the set of least general equational generalizers.

$$
\textbf{Variant} \quad
\frac{
\begin{array}{c}
f : [\mathsf{s_1}] \times \cdots \times [\mathsf{s_n}] \to [\mathsf{s}] \in \mathcal{D} \,\wedge \\
(t_1,\sigma_1),(t_2,\sigma_2) \in [\![f(x_1{:}[\mathsf{s_1}],\cdots,x_n{:}[\mathsf{s_n}])]\!]_E \,\wedge \\
u = t_1\rho_1 \wedge v = t_2\rho_2
\end{array}
}{
\langle u \stackrel{x:[\mathsf{s}]}{\triangleq} v \wedge C \mid S \mid \theta \rangle \to \\
\langle w_1{\downarrow}_{\vec{E}} \stackrel{x_1:[\mathsf{s_1}]}{\triangleq} w'_1{\downarrow}_{\vec{E}} \wedge \cdots \wedge w_n{\downarrow}_{\vec{E}} \stackrel{x_n:[\mathsf{s_n}]}{\triangleq} w'_n{\downarrow}_{\vec{E}} \wedge C \mid S \mid \theta\sigma \rangle
}
$$

with $\sigma = \{x{:}[\mathsf{s}] \mapsto f(x_1{:}[\mathsf{s_1}],\cdots,x_n{:}[\mathsf{s_n}])\}$, where $x_1{:}[\mathsf{s_1}],\cdots,x_n{:}[\mathsf{s_n}]$ are fresh variables, $w_i = x_i\sigma_1\rho_1$, $w'_i = x_i\sigma_2\rho_2$, $1 \le i \le n$, and $n \ge 0$

Fig. 3. Inference rule for variant-based order-sorted equational least general generalization

The novel rule **Variant**, proceeds as follows. Given the equational theory E, we consider the set of most general variants for any "most general" term $f(x_1{:}[\mathsf{s_1}],\cdots,x_n{:}[\mathsf{s_n}])$, with $f : [\mathsf{s_1}] \times \cdots \times [\mathsf{s_n}] \to [\mathsf{s}]$ being any defined function symbol in the theory signature. Recall that this can be easily achieved in Maude by first deploying the finite computation trees of folding variant narrowing for the considered terms and then gathering all of the variants from the nodes of the tree. Then, given the generalization problem $u \stackrel{x}{\triangleq} v$, we look for two variants (t_1,σ_1) and (t_2,σ_2) in the tree such that u is an instance of t_1 and v is an instance of t_2, i.e. $t_1\rho_1 = u$ and $t_2\rho_2 = v$, since u and v are E-canonical forms. This means that $f(x_1,\cdots,x_n)$ is a generalizer of both u and v, yet it may be too general.

The main idea of the bottom part of the rule is that a less general generalizer of both u and v can be obtained by recursively computing the generalizers of the combined substitutions, $\sigma_1\rho_1$ and $\sigma_2\rho_2$. That is, for each variable $x' \in Dom(\sigma_1 \cup \sigma_2)$, the generalization problem $x\sigma_1\rho_1{\downarrow}_{\vec{E}} \stackrel{x'}{\triangleq} x\sigma_2\rho_2{\downarrow}_{\vec{E}}$ is recursively solved. More precisely, the newly generated anti-unification problems $w_1{\downarrow}_{\vec{E}} \stackrel{x_1:[\mathsf{s_1}]}{\triangleq} w'_1{\downarrow}_{\vec{E}} \wedge \cdots \wedge w_n{\downarrow}_{\vec{E}} \stackrel{x_n:[\mathsf{s_n}]}{\triangleq} w'_n{\downarrow}_{\vec{E}}$ are previously simplified to canonical form w.r.t. E. This implies that: 1) at any computation step, all of the anti-unification problems in the constraint component are in canonical form w.r.t E; 2) It is unnecessary to modify rules **Solve** and **Recover** to semantically ask the store modulo E-equality when checking whether the anti-unification problem at hand was already solved.

It is worth noting that the syntactic rule **Decompose** could be safely removed from the generalization calculus in exchange of considering, in rule **Variant**, any function symbol f of Σ instead of just the defined symbols of $\mathcal{D}$. This is because: 1) the narrowing tree for a constructor term $c(x_1, \cdots, x_n)$ boils down to the very root term; 2) both, u and v, are c-rooted terms and they are instances of the root term $c(x_1, \cdots, x_n)$; 3) the original anti-unification problem for u and v is then replaced by the anti-unification subproblems for the corresponding arguments of the two terms, thus perfectly mimicking the effect of applying rule **Decompose** in this case.

Finally, a minimization post-processing must be performed in order to filter out all of the candidate generalizers that are not least general according to the relative generality ordering $\leq_E$, thus delivering the set of least general order-sorted anti-unifiers in E of the input terms. This is done by choosing a set of maximal elements of the set of all E-generalizers with regard to the ordering $\leq_E$.

Note that it may be the case that the subsumption relation $t \leq_E t'$ is *undecidable*, so that the above set of least general E-generalizers, although definable at the mathematical level, might not be effectively computable. Nevertheless, when: (i) each E-equivalence class is *finite* and can be effectively generated, and (ii) there is an E-matching algorithm, then we also have an effective algorithm for computing $lgg_E(t, s)$, since the relation $\leq_E$ is precisely the E-matching relation.

3.3   An Equational Anti-unfication Example

In [2], we studied generalization modulo algebraic axioms for the modular combinations of associativity, commutativity and identity axioms. Other theories such as idempotence and identity have been studied in [6,7]. In the following, we show how the generic least general generalization algorithm in this paper can be used to solve least general generalization problems modulo identity without resorting to devoted algorithms such as the ones in [2]. It is worth noting that the equational theory of identity has the FVP [11].

Example 2. Given two binary function symbols f and g such that f has an identity element e (i.e., for all x, $f(x, e) = x$ and $f(e, x) = x$) three constants a, b, and c, and the generalization problem $g(f(a, c), a) \stackrel{w}{\triangleq} g(c, b)$, the (different) algorithms of [2] and [6] produce the least general generalizer given by $\{w \mapsto g(f(x, c), f(x, y))\}$, where x and y are new variables. Following the new algorithm of this paper with only the two equations for the identity of f, we compute the desired least general generalization $g(f(w_{11}, c), f(w_{11}, w_{22}))$. A detailed computation trace for this example is shown in Fig. 4.

In the following section, we formally establish the formal properties of our equational, order sorted, least general anti-unification algorithm.

$$\langle g(f(a,c),a) \overset{w}{\triangleq} g(c,b) \mid \emptyset \mid id \rangle$$

Apply **Decompose**

$$\langle f(a,c) \overset{w_1}{\triangleq} c \wedge a \overset{w_2}{\triangleq} b \mid \emptyset \mid \theta_1 \rangle \text{ with } \theta_1 = \{w \mapsto g(w_1, w_2)\}$$

Apply **Variant** $(w_{12}, \{w_{11} \mapsto e\}) \in [\![f(w_{11}, w_{12})]\!]_E$

$f(a,c)$ is an instance of $f(w_{11}, w_{12})$

c is an instance of w_{12}

$(f(a,c) \overset{w_1}{\triangleq} c) =_E (f(a,c) \overset{w_1}{\triangleq} f(e,c))$

$$\langle a \overset{w_{11}}{\triangleq} e \wedge c \overset{w_{12}}{\triangleq} c \wedge a \overset{w_2}{\triangleq} b \mid \emptyset \mid \theta_1\theta_2 \rangle \text{ with } \theta_2 = \{w_1 \mapsto f(w_{11}, w_{12})\}$$

Apply **Solve**

$$\langle c \overset{w_{12}}{\triangleq} c \wedge a \overset{w_2}{\triangleq} b \mid a \overset{w_{11}}{\triangleq} e \mid \theta_1\theta_2 \rangle$$

Apply **Decompose**

$$\langle a \overset{w_2}{\triangleq} b \mid a \overset{w_{11}}{\triangleq} e \mid \theta_1\theta_2\theta_3 \rangle \text{ with } \theta_3 = \{w_{12} \mapsto c\}$$

Apply **Variant**

$(w_{21}, \{w_{22} \mapsto e\}) \in [\![f(w_{21}, w_{22})]\!]_E$

a is an instance of w_{21}

$(w_{22}, \{w_{21} \mapsto e\}) \in [\![f(w_{21}, w_{22})]\!]_E$

b is an instance of w_{22}

$(a \overset{w_2}{\triangleq} b) =_E (f(a,e) \overset{w_2}{\triangleq} f(e,b))$

$$\langle a \overset{w_{21}}{\triangleq} e \wedge e \overset{w_{22}}{\triangleq} b \mid a \overset{w_{11}}{\triangleq} e \mid \theta_1\theta_2\theta_3\theta_4 \rangle \text{ with } \theta_4 = \{w_2 \mapsto f(w_{21}, w_{22})\}$$

Apply **Recover**

$$\langle e \overset{w_{22}}{\triangleq} b \mid a \overset{w_{11}}{\triangleq} e \mid \theta_1\theta_2\theta_3\theta_4\theta_5 \rangle \text{ with } \theta_5 = \{w_{21} \mapsto w_{11}\}$$

Apply **Solve**

$$\langle \emptyset \mid a \overset{w_{11}}{\triangleq} e \wedge e \overset{w_{22}}{\triangleq} b \mid \theta_1\theta_2\theta_3\theta_4\theta_5 \rangle \text{ with } \theta_1\theta_2\theta_3\theta_4\theta_5 =$$
$$\{w \mapsto g(f(w_{11}, c), f(w_{11}, w_{22}))\}$$

Fig. 4. Computation trace for equational generalization of terms $g(f(a,c),a)$ and $g(c,b)$.

4 Correctness and Completeness of the Equational Anti-unification Algorithm

We follow the proof scheme of [1,2] and provide the formal proof of the following auxiliary results, which extend the corresponding lemmas in [1,2] to generalization modulo an equational theory.

Lemma 1. *Given terms t and t' and a fresh variable x, if $\langle t \overset{x}{\triangleq} t' \mid \emptyset \mid id \rangle \rightarrow^*$ $\langle C \mid S \mid \theta \rangle$ using the inference rules of Figs. 1 and 3, then $x\theta$ is a generalizer of t and t' modulo E;*

Proof. By case analysis of each one of the inference rules. In the decompose rule, $x{:}[\mathsf{s}] \mapsto f(x_1{:}[\mathsf{s}_1], \cdots, x_n{:}[\mathsf{s}_n])$ is clearly a more instantiated generalizer than $x{:}[\mathsf{s}]$. In the solve rule, $x{:}[\mathsf{s}] \mapsto z{:}\mathsf{s}'$ for s' a common sort of t and t' is again a more instantiated generalizer than $x{:}[\mathsf{s}]$. In the recover rule, $x{:}[\mathsf{s}] \mapsto y{:}\mathsf{s}'$ for $y{:}\mathsf{s}'$ the variable of an already existing generalization problem is again a more instantiated generalizer than $x{:}[\mathsf{s}]$. In the variant rule, $x{:}[\mathsf{s}] \mapsto f(x_1{:}[\mathsf{s}_1], \cdots, x_n{:}[\mathsf{s}_n])$ is again a more instantiated generalizer than $x{:}[\mathsf{s}]$. □

Lemma 2. *Given terms t and t' and a fresh variable x, if u is a generalizer of t and t' modulo E, then there is a derivation $\langle t \overset{x}{\triangleq} t' \mid \emptyset \mid id \rangle \rightarrow^* \langle C \mid S \mid \theta \rangle$ using the inference rules of Figs. 1 and 3, such that u and $x\theta$ are equivalent modulo renaming and modulo E.*

Proof. By induction on the generalizer u. If u is a variable or a constant, the proof is straightforward. If $u = f(u_1, \cdots, u_k)$, $t = f(t_1, \cdots, t_k)$, and $t' = f(t'_1, \cdots, t'_k)$, then the conclusion follows by the induction hypothesis. In this case, if f is a constructor, then the decompose rule should have been applied. And if f is not a constructor symbol, then the variant rule should have been applied but without computing any variant, just the general term $z = f(x_1, \cdots, x_k)$ since both t and t' are instances of z. If $u = f(u_1, \cdots, u_k)$ and either t or t' are not rooted by f, then $\exists \sigma : u\sigma\!\downarrow_{\overrightarrow{E}} = t$ and $\exists \sigma' : u\sigma'\!\downarrow_{\overrightarrow{E}} = t'$ but, by induction hypothesis, for each $i \in \{1, \cdots, k\}$, u_i is a generalizer of $u_i\sigma\!\downarrow_{\overrightarrow{E}}$ and $u_i\sigma'\!\downarrow_{\overrightarrow{E}}$ such that there are derivations using the inference rules of Figs. 1 and 3. Since $w = f(u_1\sigma\!\downarrow_{\overrightarrow{E}}, \cdots, u_k\sigma\!\downarrow_{\overrightarrow{E}})$ and $w' = f(u_1\sigma'\!\downarrow_{\overrightarrow{E}}, \cdots, u_k\sigma'\!\downarrow_{\overrightarrow{E}})$ are instances of a very general term $z = f(x_1, \cdots, x_k)$, there are variants (v_1, θ_1) and (v_2, θ_2) as well as substitutions ρ_1 and ρ_2 such that $w = z\theta_1\rho_1\!\downarrow_{\overrightarrow{E}}$ and $w' = z\theta_2\rho_2\!\downarrow_{\overrightarrow{E}}$. But then, the variant inference rule can be applied and the conclusion follows from the derivations for each pair $u_i\sigma\!\downarrow_{\overrightarrow{E}}$ and $u_i\sigma'\!\downarrow_{\overrightarrow{E}}$. □

By using the above lemmata, correctness and completeness follow.

Theorem 1 (Correctness). *Given a kind-completed, order-sorted equational FVP theory (Σ, E) and a generalization problem $\Gamma = t \overset{x{:}[\mathsf{s}]}{\triangleq} t'$, with $[\mathsf{s}] = [LS(t)] = [LS(t')]$, such that t and t' are Σ-terms, if $\langle t \overset{x{:}[\mathsf{s}]}{\triangleq} t' \mid \emptyset \mid id \rangle \rightarrow^* \langle \emptyset \mid S \mid \theta \rangle$ using the inference rules of Figs. 1 and 3, then $(x{:}[\mathsf{s}])\theta$ is a generalizer of t and t' modulo E. By applying the minimization post-processing, only least general generalizers are delivered, which ensures correctness.*

Theorem 2 (Completeness). *Given a kind-completed, order-sorted equational FVP theory (Σ, E) and a generalization problem $\Gamma = t \overset{x{:}[\mathsf{s}]}{\triangleq} t'$, with $[\mathsf{s}] = [LS(t)] = [LS(t')]$, such that t and t' are Σ-terms, if u is a least general generalizer of t and t' modulo E, then there is a derivation $\langle t \overset{x{:}[\mathsf{s}]}{\triangleq} t' \mid \emptyset \mid id \rangle \rightarrow^* \langle C \mid S \mid \theta \rangle$ using the inference rules of Figs. 1 and 3, such that u and $(x{:}[\mathsf{s}])\theta$ are equivalent modulo renaming and modulo E.*

Our algorithm straightforwardly terminates for FVP theories whose generalization type is finitary, as illustrated in the following example.

Example 3. Consider an equational theory with one sort s and equations $f(a) = b$ and $f(c) = d$. For the generalization problem $b \overset{x:[\mathsf{s}]}{\triangleq} d$, the trivial generalizer x can be obtained by applying the **Solve** rule but the least general equational generalizer given by $\{x \mapsto f(y)\}$ comes from applying the **Variant** rule (which can be applied only once).

Obviously, termination does not generally hold for FVP theories as witnessed by

Example 4. Consider an equational theory with one sort s and equations $f(a) = a$ and $f(b) = b$. For the generalization problem $a \overset{x:[\mathsf{s}]}{\triangleq} b$, there is an infinite number of increasingly less general generalizers $x_1{:}\mathsf{s}$, $f(x_2{:}\mathsf{s})$, $f(f(x_3{:}\mathsf{s}))$, $\ldots$, which can be computed by nondeterministically choosing between the **Solve** and the **Variant** rules at each generalization step. We note that the considered theory is Type 0 (nullary) yet being FVP.

Provided the generalization algorithm terminates for a given problem, strong correctness and completeness directly follow after applying the minimization post-processing.

Theorem 3 (Strong correctness and completeness). *Given a kind-completed, order-sorted equational FVP theory (Σ, E) and a generalization problem $\Gamma = t \overset{x:[\mathsf{s}]}{\triangleq} t'$, with $[\mathsf{s}] = [LS(t)] = [LS(t')]$, such that t and t' are Σ-terms, If the equational generalization algorithm terminates, the minimization post-processing delivers a set of least general equational generalizers for (Σ, E) and Γ.*

5   Conclusion

Computing generalizers is relevant in a wide spectrum of automated reasoning areas where analogical reasoning and inductive inference are needed. We believe that the equational least general generalization algorithm in this paper opens up a wealth of new applications in many areas where symbolic reasoning modulo equations is convenient. Some key results of this paper can be summarized as follows: (i) anti-unification can be nullary for equational theories that satisfy FVP; (ii) consequently, our complete equational generalization procedure is not in general terminating; (iii) if the procedure stops for a given problem, then the problem has a finite (possibly singleton) minimal complete set of generalizers, and this set can be computed by the subsequent minimization step.

We have formally established the correctness and completeness of our algorithm, while thanks to the minimization post-processing, minimality follows by construction when the algorithm terminates. Similarly to the dual problem of most general E-unification, there are many theories for which least general generalization is nullary (see [7]) and termination is difficult to achieve without quite demanding conditions such as requiring that each E-equivalence class is finite. Actually, our algorithm does not terminate even for theories that satisfy the FVP, as witnessed by Example 4. As future work, we plan to ascertain suitable requirements that may ensure termination of our equational least general generalization algorithm for a wide class of theories.

We are currently developing a prototype implementation of our method, and we plan to develop suitable strategies to boost performance of the tool. We also plan to extend our generic algorithm in order to support equational theories that may contain algebraic axioms such as (A), (C), and (U) following the modular methodology we formalized in [1,2].

A   An Application of Equational Generalization to a Biological Domain

In this section, we show how our anti-unification methodology can be productively used to analyze biological systems, e.g., to extract similarities and pinpoint discrepancies between two cell models that express distinct cellular states. To illustrate our example, we consider cell states that appear in the MAPK (Mitogen-Activated Protein Kinase) metabolic pathway that regulates growth, survival, proliferation, and differentiation of mammalian cells.

Our cell formalization is inspired by and slightly modifies the data structures used in Pathway Logic (PL) [22] —a symbolic approach to the modeling and analysis of biological systems that is implemented in Maude. Specifically, a cell state can be specified as a typed term as follows.

We use sorts to classify cell entities. The main sorts are Chemical, Protein, and Complex, which are all subsorts of sort Thing, which specifies a generic entity. Cellular compartments are identified by sort Location, while Modifier is a sort that is used to identify post-transactional protein modifications, which are defined by the operator "[-]" (e.g., the term [EgfR - act] represents the Egf (epidermal growth factor) receptor in an active state). We use the following equations to model modifications of an element p of sort Thing. Modifications may involve relocation of a chemical, phosphorilation of a protein or the activation of a receptor.

```
eq phosphorilate(p:Thing, X:Modifier) = [ p:Thing - X:Modifier ] .
eq relocate(p:Thing, reloc) = [ p:Thing - reloc ] .
eq activate(p:Thing, act) = [ p:Thing - act ] .
```

A complex is a compound element that is specified by means of the operator "<=>", which combines generic entities together.

Now, a *cell state* is represented by a term of the form [cellType | locs], where cellType specifies the cell type[1] and locs is a list of cellular compartments (or locations). Each location is modeled by a term of the form { locName

---

[1] To simplify the exposition, we only consider mammalian cells denoted by the constant mcell.

| comp }, where locName is a name identifying the location (e.g., CLm represents the cell membrane location), and comp is a list that specifies the entities included in that location.

Example 5. The term c_1

```
[ mcell | { Clc | Gab1 relocate(Grb2,reloc) Plcg Sos1 },
          { CLm | EgfR PIP2},
          { CLi | [Src - Yphos] [Hras - GDP] } ]
```

models a cell state of the MAPK pathway with three locations: the cytoplasm (CLi) includes four proteins Gab1, Grb2 (which has been relocated), Plcg, and Sos1; the membrane (CLm) includes the receptor EgfR and the chemical PIP2; the membrane interior (CLi) includes the proteins Hras (modified by GDP) and the protein Src in a phosphorilated state generated by the Yphos modifier.

In this scenario, anti-unification can be used to compare two cell states, c_1 and c_2. Indeed, any solution for the problem of generalizing c_1 and c_2 is a term whose non-variable part represents the common cell structure shared by c_1 and c_2, while its variables highlight discrepancy points where the two cell states differ.

Example 6. Consider the problem of generalizing the cell state of Example 5 and the following MAPK cell state c_2

```
[ mcell | { CLc | Gab1 [Grb2 - reloc] Plcg Sos1 },
          { CLm | Egf <=> activate(EgfR, act) PIP2 },
          { CLi | [Src - Tphos] [Hras - GDP] } ]
```

For instance, we can compute the following least general generalizer

```
[ mcell | { CLc | Gab1 [Grb2 - reloc] Plcg Sos1 },
          { CLm | X1:Thing PIP2 },
          { CLi | phosphorilate(Src, X2:Modifier) [Hras - GDP] } ]
```

where X1:Thing and X2:Modifier are variables. Each variable in the computed lgg detects a discrepancy between the two cell states. The variable X1:Thing represents a generic entity that abstracts the status of the receptor EgfR in the membrane location CLm of the two cells. That is, c_1's membrane includes the (inactive) receptor EgfR, whereas c_2's membrane contains the complex Egf <=> [EgfR - act] that activates the receptor EgfR and binds it to the ligand Egf to start the metabolic process. The variable X2:NModifier generalizes two phosphorilated states (i.e., Yphos and Tphos) of the protein Src obtained by two distinct phosphorilation modifiers. Note that the computed genralization introduces the partially instantiated function call phosphorilate(Src, X2:Modifier) to represent a generic phosphorilation for the protein Src.

References

1. Alpuente, M., Escobar, S., Espert, J., Meseguer, J.: A modular order-sorted equational generalization algorithm. Inf. Comput. **235**, 98–136 (2014). https://doi.org/10.1016/j.ic.2014.01.006
2. Alpuente, M., Escobar, S., Meseguer, J., Sapiña, J.: Order-sorted equational generalization algorithm revisited. Ann. Math. Artif. Intell. **90**(5), 499–522 (2022). https://doi.org/10.1007/s10472-021-09771-1
3. Armengol, E.: Usages of generalization in case-based reasoning. In: Weber, R.O., Richter, M.M. (eds.) ICCBR 2007. LNCS (LNAI), vol. 4626, pp. 31–45. Springer, Heidelberg (2007). https://doi.org/10.1007/978-3-540-74141-1_3
4. Bader, J., Scott, A., Pradel, M., Chandra, S.: Getafix: learning to fix bugs automatically. In: Proceedings of the 34th Annual ACM SIGPLAN Conference on Object-Oriented Programming, Systems, Languages, and Applications (OOPSLA 2019), pp. 159:1–159:27. Association for Computing Machinery (2019). https://doi.org/10.1145/3360585
5. Burghardt, J.: E-generalization using grammars. Artif. Intell. **165**(1), 1–35 (2005). https://doi.org/10.1016/j.artint.2005.01.008
6. Cerna, D.M., Kutsia, T.: Idempotent anti-unification. ACM Trans. Comput. Logic **21**(2), 10:1–10:32 (2020). https://doi.org/10.1145/3359060
7. Cerna, D.M., Kutsia, T.: Unital anti-unification: type and algorithms. In: Proceedings of the 5th IARCS International Conference on Formal Structures for Computation and Deduction (FSCD 2020), Leibniz International Proceedings in Informatics (LIPIcs), vol. 167, pp. 26:1–26:20. Schloss Dagstuhl - Leibniz-Zentrum für Informatik (2020). https://doi.org/10.4230/LIPIcs.FSCD.2020.26
8. Clavel, M., et al.: Maude Manual (Version 3.2.1). Technical Report, SRI International Computer Science Laboratory (2022). http://maude.cs.illinois.edu
9. Comon-Lundh, H., Delaune, S.: The finite variant property: how to get rid of some algebraic properties. In: Giesl, J. (ed.) RTA 2005. LNCS, vol. 3467, pp. 294–307. Springer, Heidelberg (2005). https://doi.org/10.1007/978-3-540-32033-3_22
10. Durán, F., Eker, S., Escobar, S., Martí-Oliet, N., Meseguer, J., Talcott, C.: Built-in variant generation and unification, and their applications in maude 2.7. In: Olivetti, N., Tiwari, A. (eds.) IJCAR 2016. LNCS (LNAI), vol. 9706, pp. 183–192. Springer, Cham (2016). https://doi.org/10.1007/978-3-319-40229-1_13
11. Escobar, S., Sasse, R., Meseguer, J.: Folding variant narrowing and optimal variant termination. J. Logic Algebraic Program. **81**(7–8), 898–928 (2012). https://doi.org/10.1016/j.jlap.2012.01.002
12. Goguen, J.A., Meseguer, J.: Order-sorted algebra i: equational deduction for multiple inheritance, overloading, exceptions and partial operations. Theor. Comput. Sci. **105**, 217–273 (1992). https://doi.org/10.1016/0304-3975(92)90302-V
13. Kirbas, S., et al.: On the introduction of automatic program repair in bloomberg. IEEE Softw. **38**(4), 43–51 (2021). https://doi.org/10.1109/MS.2021.3071086
14. Kutsia, T., Levy, J., Villaret, M.: Anti-unification for unranked terms and hedges. J. Autom. Reasoning **52**(2), 155–190 (2013). https://doi.org/10.1007/s10817-013-9285-6
15. Meseguer, J.: Conditional rewriting logic as a unified model of concurrency. Theor. Comput. Sci. **96**(1), 73–155 (1992). https://doi.org/10.1016/0304-3975(92)90182-F
16. Meseguer, J.: Membership algebra as a logical framework for equational specification. In: Presicce, F.P. (ed.) WADT 1997. LNCS, vol. 1376, pp. 18–61. Springer, Heidelberg (1998). https://doi.org/10.1007/3-540-64299-4_26

17. Meseguer, J.: Strict coherence of conditional rewriting modulo axioms. Theor. Comput. Sci. **672**, 1–35 (2017). https://doi.org/10.1016/j.tcs.2016.12.026
18. Muggleton, S.: Inductive logic programming: issues, results and the challenge of learning language in logic. Artif. Intell. **114**(1), 283–296 (1999). https://doi.org/10.1016/S0004-3702(99)00067-3
19. Ontañón, S., Plaza, E.: Similarity measures over refinement graphs. Mach. Learn. **87**(1), 57–92 (2012). https://doi.org/10.1007/s10994-011-5274-3
20. Plotkin, G.D.: A note on inductive generalization. Mach. Intell. **5**, 153–163 (1970)
21. Reynolds, J.C.: Transformational systems and the algebraic structure of atomic formulas. Mach. Intell. **5**, 135–151 (1970)
22. Talcott, C.: Pathway logic. In: Bernardo, M., Degano, P., Zavattaro, G. (eds.) SFM 2008. LNCS, vol. 5016, pp. 21–53. Springer, Heidelberg (2008). https://doi.org/10.1007/978-3-540-68894-5_2
23. TeReSe: Term Rewriting Systems. Cambridge University Press, Cambridge (2003). https://doi.org/10.1017/S095679680400526X

Verification and Synthesis

Model Checking Meets Auto-Tuning of High-Performance Programs

Natalia Garanina[1,2]([✉]) [iD], Sergey Staroletov[1,3] [iD], and Sergei Gorlatch[4] [iD]

[1] On Visit at the University of Muenster, Münster, Germany
garanina@iis.nsk.su
[2] A.P. Ershov Institute of Informatics Systems, Novosibirsk, Russia
[3] Institute of Automation and Electrometry, Novosibirsk, Russia
[4] University of Muenster, Münster, Germany

Abstract. The paper aims at combining two research areas that traditionally have been disjoint: 1) model checking as used in formal verification, and 2) auto-tuning as used in high-performance computing. Our auto-tuning is an important use case of the general concept of automated algorithm configuration and parameter tuning: we optimize parallel programs by finding the optimal values of the performance-critical program parameters for a particular high-performance architecture and input data size. There are many parameters that influence a program's performance, such that finding the optimal configuration of these parameters is a hardly manageable task even for experts in high-performance computing. Auto-tuning helps to automate this process; however, it is usually very time-consuming. In this paper, we propose to apply model checking for accelerating auto-tuning by using a counter- example constructed during the verification of the optimality property of the program. We describe a proof-of-concept implementation of our approach for auto-tuning programs written in OpenCL – the standard for programming modern multi-core CPU (Central Processing Units) and many-core GPU (Graphics Processing Units) – using the popular SPIN verifier and its model representation language Promela.

Keywords: Model checking · Temporal logics · Counterexamples · High-performance computing · Auto-Tuning · SPIN · Promela

1 Motivation and Related Work

In this paper, we aim at bringing together two research areas that have been traditionally quite distinct or even disjoint: on the one hand, model checking used in program verification and, on the other hand, auto-tuning used in optimizing programs for modern high-performance architectures that comprise multi-core universal processors (CPU) and many-core Graphics Processing Units (GPU).

The general concept of *auto-tuning* [15] has become recently especially popular in developing parallel programs: it finds the values of the performance-critical

© The Author(s), under exclusive license to Springer Nature Switzerland AG 2022
A. Villanueva (Ed.): LOPSTR 2022, LNCS 13474, pp. 63–82, 2022.
https://doi.org/10.1007/978-3-031-16767-6_4

program parameters that ensure optimal performance of the program code on a particular target architecture and problem data size. Typical examples of tuning parameters for parallel programs are: number of threads, tile size, workgroup size, shared-memory block size, etc. The potentially high number of such parameters and their complicated interplay in influencing program performance makes it very difficult even for an expert to find a (near to) optimal combination of parameter values that ensures good performance on a particular machine and for a particular size of input data.

An auto-tuning framework (*auto-tuner*) automatically generates a search space of parameter configurations and examines it by running the program for chosen configurations on a real target high-performance system. The currently popular auto-tuners include OpenTuner [1], ATLAS [6], PATUS [3], FFTW [7], CLTune [21], ATF [23], etc. They use a variety of techniques to find the optimal solution, including simulated annealing, random search, genetic algorithms, machine learning, and dynamic programming. Only few auto-tuners offer exhaustive search, which guarantees to find the optimal result but implies extremely high time costs for checking all possible configurations: the search for a solution of high quality may take several hours or even days on a high-performance system.

In this paper, we aim to improve auto-tuning by using modern model checking tools. Our approach is designed to automatically find good tuning parameter values faster than existing auto-tuners, and without using real hardware. Model checking is widely used for formal program verification: it checks the satisfiability of a particular program property for all scenarios of a program model behavior. Both the model and the property are specified using formal languages. For example, a program model can be represented as a Kripke structure, and a property as an LTL temporal logic formula. If the property is not satisfied then the model checking method can find a *counterexample*, i.e., conditions and sequence of actions of the model that imply that the property is not satisfied.

Our auto-tuning approach is based on exhaustive or swarm search by using a counterexample constructed during the verification of the optimality property for a program to auto-tune. We have been inspired by research on using counterexamples for solving optimization problems and, in particular, compiling optimal schedules for reactive systems [2,19,24,25,28]. A special edition of Dagstuhl seminar [4] was devoted to the interrelation of automatic planning/optimization and model checking methods. Modern model checking tools examine each element of the search space using various shortcuts, such as symbolic encoding, partial order reduction, and abstraction [5]. These shortcuts facilitate exhaustive exploration of larger search spaces in a shorter time.

The main benefit that we expect of using model checking for auto-tuning is that the target high-performance architecture does not have to be available when searching for the optimal parameter values of a parallel program designed for this architecture. We are not aware of previous approaches to use model checking for auto-tuning programs designed for high-performance systems with modern multi- and many-core processors. The approach discussed at ICSE-2019 and presented as an invited work at SPIN-2019 Workshop [18] uses a custom model checker to obtain optimal parameters for multi-variable systems in the automotive industry, which can be considered similar to auto-tuning, but it does not use the counterexample method that we try in the present paper.

Our particular domain for auto-tuning in this paper are parallel programs written in OpenCL [16] which is an open standard for programming various architectures: multi-core CPU, many-core GPU, FPGA, etc. We focus on the abstract platform model of OpenCL as our target architecture, in order to ensure generality and flexibility of our approach. As our model checking tool, we use the SPIN verifier [12] with its modeling language Promela [20] whose semantics combines the CSP (Communicating Sequential Processes) [11] parallelism and the actor model [10]. We initially proposed our idea of using model checking for auto-tuning in the Russian-language paper [9] where we model the Nvidia's Fermi architecture as an abstract multiprocessor with a warp scheduling for processing elements. The current paper refines our initial ideas and extends them by developing a proof-of-concept implementation of auto-tuning for OpenCL programs using the SPIN model checker and conducting first experiments with it. Here, we abstract from a particular hardware architecture in favor of the OpenCL Platform model in order to develop a more flexible approach.

The main contributions and the structure of the paper are as follows. In Sect. 2, we present our adaptation of the counterexample technique in model checking to the auto-tuning problem. Section 3 introduces our abstract model of the OpenCL Platform Model and its representation in the Promela language. Section 4 describes our use of the SPIN model checker for auto-tuning, i.e., finding the optimal configuration of OpenCL program parameters. Section 5 offers adaptation of our general auto-tuning method for limited computation resources. Section 6 gives the experimental results. Section 7 summarizes our findings and provides an outline for future research.

2   Our Adaptation of Model Checking for Auto-Tuning

Our idea of using model checking for auto-tuning is based on the general counterexample-guided approach as described, e.g., in [2]. We consider parallel programs that transform some input data to output data in a parallel manner. The auto-tuning problem for such parallel programs is to find the values of performance-critical program parameters (we call them *tuning parameters*) that allow to obtain the result of the calculation in the shortest possible time.

Let us first briefly outline our approach. We formulate a general optimality property as *the over-time property* Φ_o for the impossibility of program termination within particular time as follows: "A parallel program *cannot* terminate within T units of time", i.e., it requires a longer run time than T. Then we use a temporal logic to formalize this property, such that the over-time property can be formally verified in the model which represents the execution of the parallel program on a particular target architecture, using some model checking tool. If the property is not satisfied, it means that the computation actually terminates within the model time T. In this case, the model checker constructs a counterexample that describes the conditions for program termination in a model time not longer than T, including the corresponding configuration of tuning parameters that are responsible for the program's performance. Next, we can gradually approximate the given termination model time T and check the over-time property again and again until we reach a *minimal* model time T_{min} of the program: if we decrease this time by one unit of time, the model checker will prove that the Φ_o property is satisfied, i.e., the program really cannot terminate within $T_{min} - 1$ units of time. This way, we find both the minimal model time of the parallel program and the corresponding values of tuning parameters to achieve this time; in other words, we have auto-tuned our program.

To implement our outlined idea of auto-tuning using model checking, we should choose a suitable initial time value T_{ini} and determine a procedure for moving from T_{ini} towards the minimal model time T_{min}. The initial value of the termination model time T_{ini} can be specified by simulating the program model: usually model checking tools allow for simulating model execution scenarios, such that it is possible to reveal the value of parallel program execution time in any of the scenarios. To find a minimal termination model time, we may use, for example, the following general bisection method in which predicate $C_{ex}(T)$ is true iff a model checker generates a counterexample for the model and Φ_o property with time T:

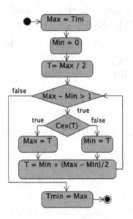

Fig. 1. The bisection method

So, our proposed method of using model checking with counterexamples for auto-tuning a parallel program proceeds in four steps, as follows:

1. Representing the parallel program with its tuning parameters and target architecture in the language of a model checking tool.
2. Formulating the over-time property Φ_o for the inability to terminate the program execution within time T in the language of a model checking tool.

3. Searching for the minimal program termination time T_{min} starting from an initial time T_{ini} given by a simulation of the model constructed in Step 1.
4. Extracting information about the optimal configuration of program tuning parameters from the counterexample found for the minimal time T_{min}.

3   Our Modeling Approach: From OpenCL to Promela

In this section, we describe how our auto-tuning method outlined in the previous section can be implemented for our particular use case – auto-tuning of OpenCL programs using the model checking tool SPIN and its modeling language Promela. We target OpenCL, because it covers programming for practically all currently used and emerging heterogeneous parallel architectures: multicore processors (CPU), Graphics Processing Units (GPU), FPGA, etc.

3.1   An Abstract OpenCL Platform Model

Figure 2 shows the architecture components of our Abstract Platform based on the platform model as defined in the OpenCL standard [16].

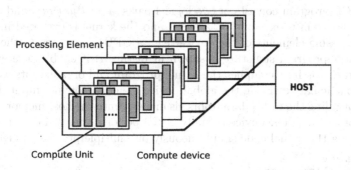

Fig. 2. Entities in OpenCL platform [16]

The abstract model in Fig. 2 corresponds to the currently most widespread use case of OpenCL: *compute devices* represent (possibly multiple) GPUs that are connected to the host CPU. The host is responsible for loading data to and from the *global memory* of devices. Every device includes *compute units* to process the data, while each unit contains *processing elements*. For example, the newest Ampere A100 architecture of Nvidia Corp. comprises in one device (GPU) altogether 108 compute units (called streaming processors in the Nvidia terminology) with a total number of 6192 processing elements (so-called CUDA cores). For simplicity of modeling, we assume in our model that every abstract unit includes 2^n abstract processing elements that are universal calculators.

A compute unit has fast *local memory*, to which all its processing elements have access. Data from global memory of a device can be loaded there. The ratio of the access speed to local memory and global memory is usually between $1/10$ and $1/100$ depending on a particular processor model.

For modeling in the Promela language, we represent all components of our abstract platform model – devices, units, processing elements, as well as the host process that distributes computations among devices – using different Promela processes. These processes are hierarchically linked: the host process starts devices; devices activate their units that regulate the work of their processing elements. To synchronize their work, they use handshake message channels for launch and finish commands, as well as for reporting about termination. The difference in the speed of access to local and global memory is modeled using constant values specifying the memory access time. To simulate the global time in the system, we use a special process that counts the number of active processing elements to determine the moment when the time has to be increased.

In this work, we do not take into account the communication time between platform components, which in the practice of GPU programming is significantly lower than other time delays. We describe the details of our Promela implementation of the abstract platform in Sect. 4.

3.2 An Abstract OpenCL Program

An OpenCL program consists of two logical parts: a *host program* and a *kernel*. The host program is executed on a CPU, and the kernel is executed in parallel by all processing elements of the device (e.g., a GPU) connected to the host.

The host program structure is shown in Listing 1; it enables the execution of the kernel: the host compiles the kernel program and organizes its work with data, in particular reserving the global device memory, copying input data into it, and uploading the result data from this memory into the host memory for subsequent processing. The device (usually GPU) performs parallel data processing by executing the kernel code simultaneously on multiple processing elements.

```
int main (void) {
  1. Initialize OpenCL
  2. Compile kernel source code
  3. Reserve global memory on the device and copy input data
     to the device
  4. Execute kernel (instances)
  5. Copy output data from the device
  6. Analyze and process output data
}
```

Listing 1. Host program in OpenCL: abstract structure

A typical OpenCL program processes input arrays and outputs the results of that processing. Therefore, as a rule, many kernels in parallel evaluate expressions based on the available data, depending on the array index, and assign the result of the calculation to a separate element of the output array. Note that arrays may be multidimensional, with corresponding multidimensional indices.

Listing 2 shows a typical structure of an OpenCL kernel; each instance of the OpenCL kernel is executed by a so-called *work item* that has an identifier corresponding to the array index. Thus, work items perform the same calculations for different array elements as is usual in the concept of data parallelism [27]. If the computations of an iteration of the loop as in Listing 2 depend on the computations of another iteration, i.e., on the array index, then OpenCL provides *barriers* for synchronizing computations. When executed on the underlying architecture, several work items are united in a *workgroup*, either explicitly by the programmer or automatically by a specific OpenCL implementation, such that all work items of a workgroup are executed on the same compute unit of the device.

```
__kernel void abstract_kernel (__global float* N_g, __global
    float* R_g, int size) {
1.  __local float N_l[TS];
2.  int idx_g = get_global_id(0);
3.  int idx_l = get_local_id(0);
4.  float result = 0;
5.  for (int i = 0; i < size / TS; ++i) {
        // access to global memory
6.      N_l[idx_l] = f(i, idx_l, size, N_g);
        // waiting for local co-workers
7.      barrier (CLK_LOCAL_MEM_FENCE);
8.      if b(idx_l) // access to local memory
9.          for (int k = 0; k < TS; ++k)
                result = g1(k, idx_l, N_l, result);
10.     else for (int k = 0; k < TS; ++k)
                result = g2(k, idx_l, N_l, result);
        // waiting for local co-workers
11.     barrier (CLK_LOCAL_MEM_FENCE);
    }
    // copy the result of this item to global memory
12. R_g[h(idx_g, size)] = result;
}
```

Listing 2. Typical scheme of an OpenCL kernel program

In OpenCL (which is based on the C programming language), there are four memory types: *global, constant, local, and private*. All work items and the host have access to global memory. Constant memory is an immutable part of global memory. Elements of one workgroup have access to local memory. Work items can use private memory. Since the access to local memory on the device is significantly faster than access to global memory, the kernel often specifies what chunks of data (*tiles*) and how are loaded into local memory.

In order to illustrate how we model the execution of OpenCL programs using the model checking tools in general and the Promela language in particular, we define the following abstract representation of an OpenCL kernel program. This program processes an input array to resulting output array by performing abstract computation with four abstract functions over integer and float variables.

In Listing 2, as is usually the case for data-parallel computations, elements of arrays are processed. For each index of the array, a separate work item calculates the local result of the kernel code execution. In our example program in the listing, the input data is array N_g of size size. The output (result) here are the elements of the R_g array. To reduce accesses to global memory, line 1 in the listing declares a local array N_1 of size TS whose elements depend on the input data. Each member of a workgroup that obtains the value of its index idx_1 in line 2, applies function f to calculate its value in parallel using local array N_1[idx_1] in line 6; this value can be used by all members of the workgroup, so in line 7 every workgroup member waits until the global data of all members of this workgroup are processed. This waiting is implemented by the synchronization operator barrier. Further in lines 9–10, the iterative calculation of the result depends only on the local data and the index of the group element. In addition, depending on the index, these calculations can be performed in different ways: in line 8, the Boolean function b(idx_1) controls the calculation options (function g1 or g2). In line 11, the work item waits for the completion of the calculations of all co-workers with the current local data, and at the next iteration of the loop in line 5, local data are updated based on the next portion of global data. When input global data are fully processed, the result of the work item is saved in global memory in array element R_g, the index of which depends on the size of the input data and on the idx_g global index received by the work item with index idx_1 in line 2.

Our example in Listing 2 is deliberately simplified. In general, arrays may be multidimensional; there may be several input arrays, and, in addition, there may be other input variables and constants located in global memory; the output can comprise multiple arrays; there are no changes in global memory that require synchronization of all processes in all workgroups. The pseudocode in Listing 2 can be easily enriched with these details without going beyond the scope of its functions and operators and, thus, our approach is applicable in the general case.

In our approach based on the Promela language, we exploit the fact that Promela, like OpenCL, is close to the C language. Hence, we can translate OpenCL programs into the Promela language taking into account the following restrictions. Since the SPIN verification framework assumes an abstraction from the computational aspects of programs and is intended to check the interaction, synchronization and coordination of parallel processes, all data in the Promela model must be of a finite type. Moreover, when modeling the abstract OpenCL kernel in Promela, we abstract from specific calculations. To find the optimal parameter values, we only take into account the time of these calculations, which depends on the number and ratio of accesses to the global and local memory. Therefore, computations in lines 6, 9, 10, and 12 of Listing 2 are replaced in the Promela model of the kernel by the code that implements time ticking required for these computations. For the same reason, we ignore the parameters and local variables of the kernel that specify the content of the data for calculations (lines 1–4). This abstraction can be refined for a particular program and hardware by estimating run time for every function used in the program by considering the time of all primitive operations in the function and the ratio of the global memory access time to the local memory access time (these characteristics are usually known from the hardware specifications). However, the amount of these calculations which depends on size must be taken into account. Hence, the code in Listing 2 is representative enough up to the number of loops and program control structures, because for modeling massive parallel computations, only the size of the input data matters.

An important aspect that we take into account in our Promela-based modeling is the synchronization of workgroup elements relative to changes in local and global memory. To provide local synchronization, our model introduces barrier processes that are responsible for separate workgroups, while for global synchronization we introduce a barrier process for all work items. In our example kernel, there is no global barrier, but its implementation in Promela is quite similar to the implementation of the local barrier. The role of the host program in our Promela modeling is reduced to the process of "compiling" the kernel, i.e., distribution of computations on a given device. We present more details of the Promela implementation of the execution of both OpenCL kernel and its host program in the next section, which also describes the application of model checking to optimize the performance of OpenCL programs.

4   Using SPIN for Auto-Tuning OpenCL Programs

In this section, we describe in detail how we implement the four steps of our counterexample-based approach (Sect. 2) to auto-tuning OpenCL programs using the model-checking tool SPIN and its language Promela. Our modeling of OpenCL programs execution is based on the standard OpenCL semantics [16].

According to the OpenCL semantics, the OpenCL compiler allocates a host (CPU) connected to a device (CPU, GPU, or FPGA) for the execution of the OpenCL program. We assume that the device integrates m units, and the work items of one workgroup are executed on one unit. Each work item in a workgroup is sequentially executed on one processing element of the unit: altogether 2^{mn} work items are executed simultaneously, with one instruction performed in one clock cycle. Since the Abstract OpenCL Platform Model does not care about *warps* (groups of work items for cooperative scheduling), our Promela model also does not consider warps. Our method can be customized for a particular hardware with its special warp policy by changing the orchestration of processing elements by their unit. Kernel code may contain conditional operators depending on the index of the work item. Without warp scheduling, different branches of such operators are simultaneously executed by the corresponding processing element performing the work item. Work items can use data from both local unit memory and global device memory, but local memory data is not available to the members of other workgroups running on other units.

We consider the following parameters that affect the performance of an OpenCL program. These parameters usually depend on size – the size of the program's input data; the number of work items also depends on the size of the data. The tuning parameters considered in this paper are as follows:

- *Workgroup size* WG (defined in the host program). With an optimally selected workgroup size, all processing elements of all units are fully and evenly loaded, which clearly leads to a reduction in the total computation time.

– *Tile size* TS (defined in the kernel): the optimal choice of the size of data
  blocks periodically loaded into fast local memory minimizes the number of
  calls to slow global memory, which also leads to faster execution.

In some parallel programs, there could be several tile sizes (e.g., when the
computation uses matrices of different size), but different sizes of workgroups
usually are not required. Our Promela model for computations chooses tuning
parameters in a non-deterministic manner by randomly selecting them in the
range depending on the input data size. Definitely, the more non-determinism is
in the model (in particular with an increase in the number of tuning parameters),
the more resources are necessary to perform the model checking.

So, we solve the problem of finding the optimal workgroup size WG and tile size
TS for the abstract kernel abstract_kernel (Listing 2) and its host program,
executed on the Abstract Platform described in Sect. 3.1.

Step 1 of the Counterexample Method

This step is the most time-consuming stage of our method as it is necessary to
take into account all details of executing an abstract parallel OpenCL program on
an abstract OpenCL platform. We define the following parallel Promela processes
in our model *PM* for modeling this execution:

– initial process main selects the values for the tuning parameters and starts
  the host and clock processes;
– process host activates several processes device;
– every process device launches its subordinate processes unit;
– every process unit starts processes implementing its processing elements pex
  and their local memory barrier;
– every process pex performs computations for the abstract_kernel;
– every process barrier locally synchronizes processing elements pex;
– service process clock implements global time counting.

In Fig. 3, we show the sequence and communication diagram for these processes. Pairs of processes form master-slave structures: (host, device), (device,
unit), (unit, pex), and (unit, barrier). The master starts (run), activates (go)
and stops (stop) its slave processes. Slave processes report about termination
(done). The processes communicate through handshake channels. In the diagram, we show only one instance for each process. Barrier synchronization is
implemented using messages, by waiting for them to be sent by a predefined
number of processes. Time is incremented in process clock after the completion
of a computation step by all processing elements. Next, we describe our modeling
design step-by-step in detail.

Listing 3 shows how process main selects the values for tuning parameters
WG and TS and starts processes host and clock. The number of devices ND, the
number of units NU per the device, and the number of processing elements NP
per unit are global constants declared at the beginning of the model description,
as well as factor GMT for the time of computations using the global memory in
process pex. In our model, the number of running Promela processes is made
up of one main process, one clock, one host, no more than ND devices, no more

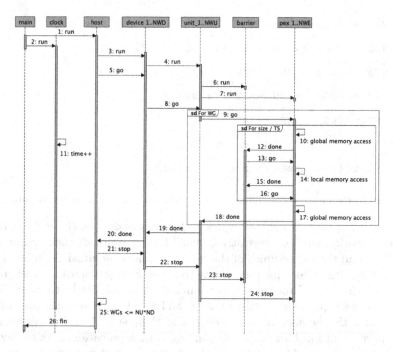

Fig. 3. Sequence diagram for the discussed promela model

than NU*ND units, no more than NU*ND barriers, and no more than NU*ND*NP processing elements. We assume for simplicity that data size `size` is a power of 2. Therefore, the numbers WG and TS are also some random powers of 2. These powers are chosen in lines 3 and 5. Since Promela does not support exponentiation, randomly selected numbers can be obtained by appropriate bitwise shift of `size`. The number NWD of devices that should be started by the host (lines 8, 9) and the number NWU of units that should be started by every device (line 10) both depend on the number WGs of workgroups. The number NWE of processing elements that should be started by every unit depend on the size WG of a workgroup (line 11). These assignments minimize the number of simultaneously executing processing elements (line 12). In this process, we specify the current value of computation time T (line 13). In line 14, the model of parallel computations starts.

```
active proctype main(){
byte d;
1.    byte n = 10;
2.    size = 1 << n; // size = 2^n
   // workgroup size selection
3.    select (d : 1 .. n-1);
4.    WG = size >> (n - d);
   // tile size selection
5.    select (d : 1 .. n-1);
6.    TS = size >> (n - d);
   // number of working groups
```

```
7.    WGs = size / WG;
      // number of working devices
8.    NWD = (WGs <= NU * ND -> (WGs / NU) : ND);
      // if WGs <= NU
9.    NWD = (WGs / NU -> NWD : 1);
      // number of working units
10.   NWU = (WGs <= NU -> WGs : NU);
      // number of working elements
11.   NWE = (WG <= NP -> WG : NP);
      // total number of working elements
12.   allNWE = NWE * NWU * NWD;
13.   T = 100;
14.   atomic{run host(); run clock();}
}
```

Listing 3. Promela-process for selecting parameters and launching computation

In Listing 4, process host activates NWD processes device (lines 2, 3). If the number of workgroups WGs is relatively small then it waits for their termination (lines 6, 7) and marks the finish of the target parallel computations in line 17 by variable FIN. Otherwise, this process reactivates the devices until all workgroups are served (line 12). Processes device and unit act similarly to host. They start their slave processes, activate them and await their termination, taking into account the number of workgroups and their size WG. After termination they report about finishing the corresponding master processes: unit to device, and device to host. After receiving the stopping signal from the master, the units and devices, in turn, stop all their slave processes. Promela implementation details for these processes as well as local synchronization process barrier and global time process clock are available in [8].

```
proctype host () {
  chan d_hst = [0] of {mtype : action};
  chan hst_d = [0] of {mtype : action};
1.   FIN = false;
2.   atomic{for(i : 0..NWD-1){run device(d_hst, hst_d)}}
3.   atomic{for(i : 0..NWD-1){hst_d ! go}}
4.   if
5.   :: WGs <= NU*ND ->
6.            atomic { for(i : 0..NWD-1) {
7.                      d_hst ? done; hst_d ! stop;} }
8.   :: else ->
9.            for(i : 0..(WGs/NU*ND)-ND) {
10.           atomic { d_hst ? done;
11.                    allNWE = allNWE + NWE*NWU;
12.                    hst_d ! go;} }
13.           for(i : 0..ND-1) {
14.           atomic { d_hst ? done;
15.                    hst_d ! stop;} }
16.  fi;
17.  FIN = true;
}
```

Listing 4. Promela-process for the host-program

Listing 5 shows in detail the work item process pex that performs computations of an instance of the kernel code abstract_kernel presented in Listing 2. The total number of these processes that are created in the Promela model depends on the size of the input data. The number of simultaneous `pex` processes depends on the number of units, which is significantly smaller than the total number of processes. Each of them is started by its own unit, whose Promela process is described in [8].

```
inline long_work (gt, tz) {
1. do
2. :: time > (start_time + gt * tz) -> break;
3. :: else -> atomic {
4.                cur_time = time;
5.                NRP_work++;
6.                time == cur_time + 1;//wait
7.                }
8. od;
}
proctype pex (byte me; chan pex_b; chan b_pex;
                        chan pex_u; chan u_pex){
1.   do
2.   :: u_pex ? go ->
3.             atomic {
4.                start_time = time;
5.                cur_time = time; }
6.             for (i : 0 .. size/TS-1) {
                // access to global memory
7.                long_work(GMT, TS)
8.                pex_b ! done;
                // waiting for local co-workers
9.                b_pex ? go;
10.               start_time = time;
11.               if // 'if' access to local memory
12.               :: me % 2 -> long_work(1, TS)
                     // 'else' access to local memory
13.               :: else -> long_work(1, TS)
14.               fi;
15.               pex_b ! done;
                // waiting for local co-workers
16.               b_pex ? go;
              }
              // copy the result to global memory
17.           start_time = time;
18.           long_work(GMT, 1)
19.           pex_u ! done;
20.  :: u_pex ? stop -> break;
21.  od;
}
```

Listing 5. Promela-process `pex` for a processing element

Process `pex` is connected by the handshake synchronization channels `pex_b` and `b_pex` with the local group barrier, and `pex_u` and `u_pex` with the master unit. In these channels, the work item receives start and stop commands, and also informs about the termination of computations. In our model, we abstract from the specific computations that the kernel performs, so we only use the computation time. We also assume that a computation in local memory takes one time unit, and a computation using global memory takes `GMT` units of time. This abstraction can be refined for a particular program and hardware.

Thus, in process `pex` we model only the number of computational steps performed by the kernel (the `for` loop in line 6), depending on the size of the input data and calls to global memory (lines 7 and 18) and to local memory (lines 12–13). Upon termination of the computation step, `pex` reports this event to the process that implements global time by increasing the counter of the currently running `NRP_work` processes (line 5 of inline macro `long_work`). Note that due to the blocking semantics of the Promela language, the process can proceed to the next stage of its computation only when the global time `time` is increased by 1 (line 6 of `long_work`). The "long work" modeling of computations of the abstract kernel function `f`, `g1`, `g2` and `h` finishes after `gt*tz` time units, depending on the type of memory accessed. Synchronization on the local barrier occurs twice, as in the original kernel: line 7 of the kernel (Listing 2) corresponds to line 9 of the model (Listing 5), and line 11 corresponds to line 16. Process `pex` terminates (line 19) after writing its result into global memory.

Step 2 of the Counterexample Method

In specializing the over-time property Φ_o for the auto-tuning problem, we use the value of variable `FIN` that marks the end of calculations, and the final value `time`. The over-time formula without superindex is used in the model checking approach to general auto-tuning problem, while this formula with superindex 'p' is specialized for our method which uses Promela model. The SPIN property specification language is temporal logic LTL, such that we can write:

$$\Phi_o^p = \mathbf{G}(\mathtt{FIN} \rightarrow (\mathtt{time} > T)),$$

which corresponds to the statement "Always when the parallel program terminates, its execution time is greater than T."

Step 3 of the Counterexample Method

The third step of our method finds the minimal time for which a parallel computation program can terminate. This step begins with launching the SPIN verifier with the constructed model PM and the formula Φ_o^p for some value of time T. We then decrease the value of T until the SPIN stops generating counterexamples, i.e., until it agrees that the program cannot be executed in a time shorter than the final T. In our approach, we find the execution path with minimal model time. This path may not be the shortest one due to many model steps which do not increase the value of variable `time`. We indeed came across such paths in our experiments. The initial value of T can be found using the simulation mode in SPIN. During simulation, SPIN reproduces one of the finite scenarios of the system behaviour, fixing the values of the variables used in the model at the end of the simulation. Therefore, we can use value `time` which corresponds to the end of the program in the simulated scenario. To decrease the value of T in the next SPIN runs, we may use the bisection method shown in Fig. 1. The final counterexample gives the minimal model time value.

Step 4 of the Counterexample Method

The final step of our approach is to analyze the last counterexample to extract the optimal configuration of tuning parameters. For counterexample analysis, SPIN provides running a simulation corresponding to the counterexample. In the auto-tuning problem, there is no need to search for the optimal computation path. Therefore, there is not necessary to analyze the transitions of the final counterexample. To solve our problem, we only need to extract the values of the tuning parameters WG and TS, which are known in the final counterexample simulation. The final values of the tuning parameters WG and TS form the optimal parameter configuration we are looking for.

5   Refining the Counterexample Method for Limited Computation Resources

Due to the nature of our solution with a large number of interactions through channels, with an increase in the size of the input data, the memory required for the verification process in Step 3 begins to grow and may exceed the physical memory of the computer. In our experiments, the memory sometimes exceeded the limit of 16 GB of RAM. We address this problem by using *the swarm model checking* method proposed by the SPIN author Holzmann [13, 14]. This method uses state hashes and therefore does not visit all possible states of the system. The swarm model checking starts several different verification tests checking the specified property during bounded time and with a bounded number of model steps. Similar to the standard model checking method, it generates counterexamples when one of the paths violates the property. The search of such a path can be parallelized across processor cores and even performed on different network nodes. In [26], we already applied this approach to the automatic solution of various puzzles and practical problems.

We use swarm model checking for alternative non-bisection searching for the minimal termination model time in the over-time property Φ_o^p. We can formulate *the non-termination property* Φ_t for the impossibility of program termination as follows: "A parallel program *cannot* terminate" (LTL formula $\Phi_t = \mathbf{G}(\neg\mathtt{FIN})$). We definitely know that our parallel programs that compute some output data must terminate. Hence, we expect that there is at least one counterexample which demonstrates that the program terminates and provides the termination model time. Swarm model checking produces several termination model times from several counterexamples, from which we can choose the minimal termination model time. To be sure that there is no smaller time, we launch successively swarm model checking with a decreasing model time and over-time property Φ_o^p in the following manner: we stop searching for the minimal termination model time if swarming with the current model time provides no results within the previous swarm execution time or this swarming finds no smaller times. In other words, the criterion for stopping the search for the optimal time is the ability of the SPIN swarm to find counterexamples, rather than the number of such findings. If the swarm does not find a counterexample as quickly as at the previous swarm launching, the counterexample with a smaller time value does not exist with very high probability. In future work, we plan to formally prove that the configuration of tuning parameters found by the swarm is really optimal.

Figure 4 shows our algorithm that implements this searching strategy with functions `Min_time_Swarm(F)` and `Exe_time_Swarm(F)` for the minimal model time found by the swarm for formula F and the execution time of this swarm, respectively. Predicate `Swarm(F, exe_time)` is true iff the swarming formula F finishes within `exe_time`. Formula `F_t` is for the non-termination property, and formula `F_o(T)` is for the over-time property with time T.

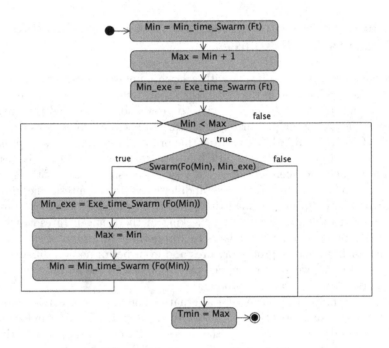

Fig. 4. The swarm search method

We have developed a script which simulates each counterexample found by the swarm and finds values of `time`, `TS` and `WG` in the output. We also provide a simple program which, after the script has finished, sorts these counterexample results by `time` values with corresponding tuning parameters `TS` and `WG`.

To make our approach more practical, we assume that every device and every unit of a device work in exactly the same manner, i.e., it takes exactly the same time (and other resources) to perform computation of the same complexity. Hence, to estimate the computation time, we can abstract from the number of devices and the number of units in these devices and consider just one device and one unit with all its processing elements. Note that we cannot consider just one processing element because, in general, they compute different functions of different complexity depending on their local identifiers while the devices and units synchronize their work independently on computation complexity. With this abstraction, the number of Promela processes is made up of one main process, one clock, one host, one device, one unit, one barrier and several processing elements. In the model used in our experiments [8], the total number of Promela processes is 10. Here, the only really large parameter is the input data size.

6   Experimental Results

Table 1 shows the results of a series of experiments conducted with SPIN model checker (version 6.5.1).

Table 1. Found parameter values and memory consumption during the experimental model checking process

N	Size	Model time	Steps	TS	WG	Memory usage (exhaustive mode)	Memory usage (swarm mode)	Verification time	1st trail in	1st trail optimality
1	8	44	1658	4	4	0.280 GB	–	2 s	1 s	84%
2	16	156	5673	4	8	2.081 GB	–	25 s	1 s	65%
3	32	584	21011	4	16	14.767 GB	115 MB	25 m/1h	7 s/1 s	79%/77%
4	64	2224	71495	8	32	–	128 MB	1h	1 s	83%
5	128	9344	267119	64	64	–	172 MB	1h	1 s	94%
6	256	36234	1300634	4	4	–	1.145 GB	2h	3 s	94%
7	512	142090	5099397	4	4	–	2.367 GB	2h	3 s	99%
8	1024	549912	15973533	32	16	–	16 GB	4h	3 m	99%

During the tests, we played with size of the input data for a platform architecture with the following parameters: one device, one unit and four processing elements. Up to input data size 32, exhaustive verification with over-time formula Φ_o^p was possible for our machine, which finds optimal values of parameters with the shortest simulation time (parameter which is also calculated in our model). For reference, we include model steps, shown in SPIN simulation mode for the best counterexample. When the data size is significantly larger, we may hit the 16 GB memory threshold. Therefore, we run the swarm verification with non-termination formula Φ_t on 1–8 cores for given maximum verification time threshold, and the swarm process is now able to find a large number of counterexamples with trails to the final state FIN for larger data sizes. We also developed a runner script to process all the trails found by SPIN. It simulates a particular trail, obtains the simulation time and TS/WG parameters from the simulation output, sorts them by time and required steps. Using such a script finally helps to obtain the minimal time and optimal parameters from a bunch of trails. Getting multiple trails is possible due to -e parameter (create trails for all errors) during the verification and swarm run. We also had to increase maximum search depth depending on the input size with the last one set to 2×10^8 by option -m.

In Table 1, "Model time" is the time that is calculated in the Promela model (variable time), and "Verification time" is the time spent by the SPIN verifier or its swarm processes. In the last two columns of the table, we show the time required to obtain the first counterexample with a trail – the quickest suboptimal solution of the problem (both using exhaustive and swarm methods) and its optimality as the ratio of the optimal solution modeling time to the time of the first counterexample (if the times coincide, we also take into account the number of steps spent).

7 Conclusion

Our long-term goal is the development of rigorous, formally-based auto-tuning methods for high-performance parallel programs by relying on the model checking approach, in particular using the technique of counterexample-guided search. The results of auto-tuning are the optimal values of tuning parameters that ensure the best possible performance of the given program on a particular parallel architecture for a particular input data size. We address programs written in OpenCL which is an emerging open standard for programming various kinds of parallel architectures including multi-core CPU, GPU, and FPGA. Our approach described in this paper is based on developing an abstract model of OpenCL computations and then expressing the model of program execution and optimality properties in the language Promela of the model checking tool SPIN.

In comparison to existing auto-tuners, our logic-based approach offers an important advantage. Our simulation of the execution of OpenCL programs in Promela abstracts from specific computations, keeping the logic of interaction and synchronization of parallel program processes in the target parallel architecture. Due to the formal semantics of the Promela language, the model of a given OpenCL program can be viewed as the formal operational semantics of interaction and synchronization of parallel program processes on a selected platform and device architecture. By varying the parameters and algorithms of interaction between the components of an abstract device, it is possible to define and study specific processor architectures. This makes it possible to search for optimal program settings in the absence of real target processors, while existing auto-tuning frameworks cannot provide such an opportunity.

In our future work, we plan to customize our general auto-tuning method for a specific program executed on a specific hardware, e.g., the case study with matrix multiplication on the most recent Ampere GPU architecture by Nvidia Corp. Knowing the Ampere specification, we can customize the ratio of the global memory access time to the local memory access time, and the performance time for every function used in the program by considering all primitive operations in the function. We also should take into account specific organisation of communication for Ampere units with their processing elements.

We also plan to add the communication time between processes to the model, as well as consider other settings, in particular, the number of work items. In addition, to improve our counterexample method, we are going to try using the never claim pruning from [22], and finding optimal values from [25], which avoids multiple runs of the SPIN verifier in the counterexample method. We also plan to improve the scalability of our counterexample method by modeling a warp-based scheduling [17], because due to warping, the number of simultaneously working processing elements becomes smaller, which implies reduction of interleaving non-determinism in the model. Finally, we will explore the scalability of our approach w.r.t. the size of input data. If we develop a method to construct the analytical dependence of the optimal parameters on the data size, we can prove the exact optimal parameters for small data and then scale them up to big data.

Acknowledgements. We are grateful to the anonymous referees for their great effort in helping us to improve the paper. Natalia Garanina was supported by the scholarship of DAAD (German Academic Exchange Service). Sergei Gorlatch was partially funded by the Deutsche Forschungsgemeinschaft (DFG, German Research Foundation) within the project Nr. 470527619 (PPP-DL) at the University of Muenster.

References

1. Ansel, J., Kamil, S., Veeramachaneni, K., et al.: Opentuner: an extensible framework for program autotuning. In: Proceedings of 2017 IEEE International Parallel and Distributed Processing Symposium (IPDPS), pp. 385–392. IEEE (2017)
2. Brinksma, E., Mader, A., Fehnker, A.: Verification and optimization of a PLC control schedule. Int. J. Softw. Tools Technol. Transf. **4**, 21–33 (2002)
3. Christen, M., Schenk, O., Burkhart, H.: PATUS: a code generation and autotuning framework for parallel iterative stencil computations on modern microarchitectures. In: Proceedings of 2011 IEEE International Parallel Distributed Processing Symposium, pp. 385–392. IEEE (2011)
4. Cimatti, A., Edelkamp, S., Fox, M., Magazzeni, D., Plaku, E.: Automated planning and model checking (Seminar 14482). Dagstuhl Rep. **4**(11), 227–245 (2015). https://doi.org/10.4230/DagRep.4.11.227
5. Clarke, E.M., Henzinger, T.A., Veith, H. (eds.) Handbook of Model Checking. Springer, Cham (2018). https://doi.org/10.1007/978-3-319-10575-8
6. Clint, W., Dongarra, J.: Automatically tuned linear algebra software. In: Proceedings of the ACM/IEEE Conference on Supercomputing, pp. 385–392. IEEE (1998)
7. Frigo, M., Johnson, S.G.: The design and implementation of FFTW3. IEEE **93**(2), 187–195 (2005)
8. Garanina, N., Staroletov, S.: Discussed models in Promela (2022). https://github.com/SergeyStaroletov/PromelaSamples/tree/master/autotune_opencl
9. Garanina, N.O., Gorlatch, S.P.: Autotuning parallel programs by model checking. Model. Anal. Inf. Syst. **28**(4), 338–355 (2021). in Russian
10. Gaspari, M., Zavattaro, G.: An Algebra of Actors. In: Ciancarini, P., Fantechi, A., Gorrieri, R. (eds.) FMOODS 1999. ITIFIP, vol. 10, pp. 3–18. Springer, Boston (1999). https://doi.org/10.1007/978-0-387-35562-7_2
11. Hoare, C.A.R.: Communicating Sequential Processes. Prentice-Hall, Hoboken (1985)
12. Holzmann, G.J.: The SPIN Model Checker: Primer and Reference Manual. Addison-Wesley Professional, Boston (2003)
13. Holzmann, G.J., Joshi, R., Groce, A.: Tackling large verification problems with the swarm tool. In: Havelund, K., Majumdar, R., Palsberg, J. (eds.) SPIN 2008. LNCS, vol. 5156, pp. 134–143. Springer, Heidelberg (2008). https://doi.org/10.1007/978-3-540-85114-1_11
14. Holzmann, G.J., Joshi, R., Groce, A.: Swarm verification techniques. IEEE Trans. Softw. Eng. **37**(6), 845–857 (2010)
15. Hoos, H.H.: Automated algorithm configuration and parameter tuning. In: Hamadi, Y., Monfroy, E., Saubion, F. (eds.) Autonomous Search, pp. 37–71. Springer, Heidelberg (2011). https://doi.org/10.1007/978-3-642-21434-9_3
16. Khronos: OpenCL specification by Khronos OpenCL working group 2021 (2021). https://www.khronos.org/registry/OpenCL/specs/3.0-unified/html/OpenCL_API.html

17. Lashgar, A., Baniasadi, A., Khonsari, A.: Warp size impact in GPUs: large or small? In: Proceedings of the 6th Workshop on General Purpose Processor Using Graphics Processing Units, pp. 146–152 (2013)
18. Lazreg, S., Cordy, M., Collet, P., Heymans, P., Mosser, S.: Multifaceted auto-mated analyses for variability-intensive embedded systems. In: 2019 IEEE/ACM 41st International Conference on Software Engineering (ICSE), pp. 854–865. IEEE (2019)
19. Malik, R., Pena, P.: Optimal task scheduling in a flexible manufacturing system using model checking. IFAC-PapersOnLine **51**(7), 230–235 (2018)
20. Nimble-code: Promela language grammar (2021). http://spinroot.com/spin/Man/grammar.html
21. Nugteren, C., Codreanu, V.: Cltune: a generic auto-tuner for OpenCL kernels. In: Proceedings of 9th International Symposium on Embedded Multicore/Many-core Systems-on-Chip, pp. 385–392. IEEE (2015)
22. Panizo, L., Salmerón, A., Gallardo, M.D.M., Merino, P.: Guided test case genera-tion for mobile apps in the TRIANGLE project: work in progress. In: Proceedings of the 24th ACM SIGSOFT International SPIN Symposium on Model Checking of Software, pp. 192–195 (2017)
23. Rasch, A., Gorlatch, S.: ATF: a generic directive-based auto-tuning framework. Concurrency Comput. Pract. Experience **31**(5), e4423 (2019). https://doi.org/10.1002/cpe.4423
24. Ruys, T.C., Brinksma, E.: Experience with literate programming in the modelling and validation of systems. In: Proceedings of the 4th International Conference on Tools and Algorithms for the Construction and Analysis of Systems (TACAS 1998), pp. 393–408 (1998)
25. Ruys, T.C.: Optimal scheduling using branch and bound with SPIN 4.0. In: Ball, T., Rajamani, S.K. (eds.) SPIN 2003. LNCS, vol. 2648, pp. 1–17. Springer, Hei-delberg (2003). https://doi.org/10.1007/3-540-44829-2_1
26. Staroletov, S.: Model checking games and a genome sequence search. In: Journal of Physics: Conference Series, vol. 1679, p. 032020. IOP Publishing (2020)
27. Subhlok, J., Stichnoth, J.M., O'hallaron, D.R., Gross, T.: Exploiting task and data parallelism on a multicomputer. In: Proceedings of the Fourth ACM SIGPLAN Symposium on Principles and Practice of Parallel Programming, pp. 13–22 (1993)
28. Wijs, A., Pol, J.V.D., Bortnik, E.M.: Solving scheduling problems by untimed model checking: the clinical chemical analyser case study. Int. J. Softw. Tools Technol. Transf. **11**(5), 375–392 (2016)

Building a Join Optimizer for Soufflé

Samuel Arch[1]([✉])[ID], Xiaowen Hu[1][ID], David Zhao[1][ID], Pavle Subotić[2][ID],
and Bernhard Scholz[1][ID]

[1] The University of Sydney, Sydney, Australia
{sarc9328,xihu5895,dzha3983}@uni.sydney.edu.au,
bernhard.scholz@sydney.edu.au
[2] Microsoft, Belgrade, Serbia
pavlesubotic@microsoft.com

Abstract. Datalog has grown in popularity as a domain-specific language (DSL) for real-world applications. Crucial to its resurgence has been the advent of high-performance Datalog compilers, including Soufflé. Yet this high performance is unobtainable for users unless they provide performance hints such as join orders for rules.

In this paper, we develop a join optimizer for Soufflé that automatically computes high-quality join orders using a *feedback-directed optimization* strategy: In a profiling stage, the compiler obtains join size estimates, and in a join ordering stage, an offline join optimizer derives cost-optimal join orders. The performance of the automatically optimized joins is demonstrated using complex real-world applications, including DOOP, DDISASM, and VPC, surpassing the performance of un-tuned join orders by a geometric mean speedup of 12.07×.

Keywords: Datalog · Query optimization · Compilers

1 Introduction

In recent years, Datalog [1,13] has evolved from a recursive database query language to a domain-specific language (DSL) for crafting complex industrial-strength applications, including static program analysis [11,29], network analysis [7], smart contract de-compilation [21], and binary disassembly [18]. Datalog can express complex algorithms with a collection of relations and recursive rules. These applications expressed in Datalog are performance-sensitive for real-world workloads. For example, a static analysis tool such as DOOP [11] may run on software projects with millions of lines of code. Hence, Datalog used as a DSL necessitates compilation techniques for efficient execution [35].

In a bottom-up Datalog system, logic rules can be executed more than once due to recursion and operate over very large data sets. Hence, the runtime of rules is paramount for efficiency. The task of a join optimizer is to find high-quality *join orders*, i.e., the order in which to join the relations in a rule. There are a factorial number of possible left-deep join orders in the number of atoms in the rule, and the performance gap between good and bad join orders can be several orders of magnitude [30].

While automatically finding join orders is well-studied [20,33,36] and known as query optimization in the database community, databases are different to Datalog compilers. For instance, databases normally make no assumptions about future workloads and thus find join orders on the fly at *run-time*, which incurs overheads. Moreover, database workloads rarely contain recursion. Thus, these techniques do not support recursive rules very well. As a result, the database community has little to offer for implementing Datalog compilers whose challenge lies in the repeated execution of *unchanging, recursive* rules on different inputs with small variations [44].

For this reason, high-performance Datalog compilers such as Soufflé [26] allow users to optimize join orders using manual annotations at design time. This approach eliminates the overhead of finding join orders at run-time, instead shifting the burden to the developer. However, for non-experts, finding the right join order for large, complex rules can be an insurmountable task. To illustrate the challenge of finding fast join orders, we present a Datalog rule from the DDIS-ASM [18] project, a binary dis-assembler written in Soufflé. DDISASM disassembles stripped binaries into re-assemblable assembly code in a series of analyses. The rule we select is from the Data Access Pattern (DAP) analysis where the atom `data_access_pattern(Address,Size,Multiplier,FromWhere)` represents a data access on an `Address` of size `Size` with multiplier `Multiplier` from address `FromWhere`. The rule derives new data accesses by propagating previous accesses, incrementing the address value by the multiplier to more accurately disassemble the binary.

For this rule there are 24 different join orders amongst the 4 positive atoms. We write the rule in two logically equivalent ways, with the order of the first 2 atoms swapped, illustrating 2 different join orders. In this rule, Soufflé joins the relations in the order in which they are written from left to right, but in general, the join order does not always coincide with the specified order of a rule[1].

```
propagated_data_access(EA+Mult,Mult,EA_ref) :-      propagated_data_access(EA+Mult,Mult,EA_ref) :-
  % Propagate previous access by multiplier           % Propagate previous access by multiplier
  data_byte(EA+Mult,_),                               propagated_data_access(EA,Mult,EA_ref),
  propagated_data_access(EA,Mult,EA_ref),             data_byte(EA+Mult,_),
  % No collision with next data access pattern        % No collision with next data access pattern
  !possible_data_limit(EA+Mult),                      !possible_data_limit(EA+Mult),
  % No collision with other data access pattern        % No collision with other data access pattern
  last_data_access(EA+Mult,Last),                     last_data_access(EA+Mult,Last),
  Last > EA,                                          Last > EA,
  % No direct collision with data access              % No direct collision with data access
  data_access_pattern(Last,Size,Mult,_),              data_access_pattern(Last,Size,Mult,_),
  Size+Last <= EA+Mult.                               Size+Last <= EA+Mult.
```

Fig. 1. A rule from DDISASM written in two ways

When executing the rule in DDISASM, during disassembly of the *gamess* binary from the SPECCPU 2006 suite of binaries [22], Soufflé executes the first

---

[1] Soufflé relies on a greedy heuristic [15] at compile-time, selecting the next atom to join one at a time with the largest fraction of bounded attributes.

join order in 120.9s and the second join order in 0.02s, opening a performance gap of over 6000×. An expert user may provide join orders manually by using `.plan` statements [16] to hand-tune rule execution. However, finding good join orders is a tedious and time-consuming process, and breaks performance declarativeness. Users are expected to have a deep understanding of the rule execution strategies in Soufflé, if performance is needed.

In this paper, we present an *offline* feedback-directed strategy [40] for join ordering in Datalog compilers. With our new strategy we can derive high-quality join orders automatically. The strategy consists of a profiling and a join ordering stage. The profiling stage produces estimates for the expected number of tuples for each candidate join [36] using a representative input. The estimates are later ingested in the join ordering stage to derive high-quality join orders.

Our approach has the following advantages. First, the rule-set is known ahead of time, so we can perform lightweight *program-specialized* profiling of the Datalog program collecting statistics only for the smallest set of necessary join size computations. Second, the join ordering is performed at compile-time, so that the compiler can search for the cost-optimal join order without incurring any run-time overheads. Third, our approach uses a *recursive rule cost model*, guaranteeing cost-optimal join orders for recursive rules by relying on per-iteration statistics from the instrumented execution. Fourth, our approach is robust; the join orders generated by a representative input tend to generalize over large changes to the input.

We have implemented our new join optimizer in Soufflé [26] as an open-source contribution included in Release 2.3 [17]. We have conducted experiments on industrial-strength applications including DOOP [11], DDISASM [18] and VPC [7] and our join optimizer derives join orders outperforming hand-tuned ones by a geometric mean speedup of 1.09× and un-tuned orders by 12.07×. The contributions of this work are summarized as follows:

1. A novel adaptation of the *feedback-directed optimization strategy* for the join ordering problem.
2. A *program-specialized profiling strategy* for instrumenting Datalog programs to collect accurate join size estimations with automatic index selection.
3. A join optimizer with a *recursive rule cost-model* that finds minimum cost join orders for both recursive and non-recursive rules.

2 Background and Motivating Example

Optimizing joins in compiling Datalog engines is challenging and highly dependent on the rule evaluation strategy. Modern engines, such as Soufflé, frequently use a stratified bottom-up evaluation [1]. For stratified Datalog, an extended dependency graph is built for which the nodes are relations, and edges emanate from the head atoms to the body atoms of rules. The program can be stratified if and only if the dependency graph is free of cycles containing negated atoms. A stratum is a strongly connected component that may contain multiple mutually recursive relations (and their rules). Each stratum is computed by evaluating the rule-set in a fixpoint loop, terminating when the rules fail to produce new facts and the strata are ordered according to their topological number. Datalog engines adopt semi-naïve evaluation [8] for computing the facts of each stratum. Semi-naïve evaluation has a fixpoint loop for each stratum and finds newly derived facts by considering only the new facts from the previous iteration of the fixpoint loop. As a result, recursive relations in the body of rules can be replaced by *delta relations* where a delta relation only contains the new facts derived from the last iteration. Therefore, a recursive rule $A_{n+1}(X_{n+1})$:− $A_1(X_1), ..., A_n(X_n)$ with n mutually recursive relations in the body, results in n *versions* of the recursive rule with semi-naive evaluation as follows:

$$\texttt{new\_}A_{n+1}(X_{n+1}) \text{ :− } \texttt{delta\_}A_1(X_1), A_2(X_2), ..., A_n(X_n).$$
$$\texttt{new\_}A_{n+1}(X_{n+1}) \text{ :− } A_1(X_1), \texttt{delta\_}A_2(X_2), ..., A_n(X_n).$$
$$...$$
$$\texttt{new\_}A_{n+1}(X_{n+1}) \text{ :− } A_1(X_1), A_2(X_2), ..., \texttt{delta\_}A_n(X_n).$$

For the motivating example in Fig. 1, Soufflé places each semi-naïve rule-version into the same stratum, evaluating them in a fixpoint loop until no new fact is found. Since this rule has only one mutually recursive relation in the body, it has only one rule-version to compute. Hence the rule will be evaluated as shown in Fig. 2 with the semi-naïve rule-version evaluated inside the fixpoint loop.

```
delta_propagated = propagated
while delta_propagated ≠ ∅ do

    Eval(new_propagated(EA+Mult,Mult,EA_ref) :-
            delta_propagated(EA,Mult,EA_ref),
            data_byte(EA+Mult,_),
            ...)

    delta_propagated = new_propagated
    propagated = propagated ∪ new_propagated
    new_propagated = ∅
```

Fig. 2.   Semi-naïve   evaluation   for   the   motivating   example   with propagated_data_access abbreviated as propagated

To evaluate each semi-naïve rule-version in the fixpoint loop, Soufflé uses indexed nested loop joins due to runtime and memory efficiency [41]. To evaluate each rule-version, the join order determines the loop-nest, placing the first relation in the outer-loop, the next relation in the next loop and so forth, continuing in this order until the entire loop-nest is unrolled. Finally, optimizations are applied to the loop-nest, i.e., rewriting scans over relations with filters into indexed scans. The join order is also known as a left-deep one since the result of each join is pipelined directly as input into the next join operator. For the two formulations of the Datalog rule, Soufflé uses the order of relations as they are written in the rule resulting in the loop-nests shown in Fig. 3.

Examining the loop-nests in Fig. 3, the first join order iterates the cross-product of data_byte and delta_propagated_data_access (abbreviated as delta_propagated), filtering for tuples where the address accessed on data_byte is that of delta_propagated with the added multiplier, i.e., NextEA = EA+Mult. Hence, the complexity of the two outer loops of the loop-nest is of the order $\mathcal{O}(|\text{data\_byte}| \times |\text{delta\_propagated}|)$ excluding logarithmic factors. By comparison, using the second join order, delta_propagated is iterated in the outer loop grounding EA and Mult. Then, an efficient index scan can be performed on data_byte to quickly check if there exist any tuples with address EA+Mult. Thus, the corresponding complexity of the two outer loops of the loop-nest is $\mathcal{O}(|\text{delta\_propagated}|)$.

We generated a profile for the *gamess* input from the SPECCPU2006 benchmark suite for DDISASM. From the profile, we observe that this rule produces only 53 tuples. However, despite producing almost no output, the first join order takes 120.9s to complete, iterating for each of the 1.5 million tuples of the data_byte relation through (on average) 567 tuples in the delta_propagated relation. On the other hand, the second join order only iterates through delta_propagated before using an index to check if a matching tuple exists in data_byte. As a result, the join order terminates in only 0.02s, a difference of over 6000×. Therefore, the above example demonstrates the utmost importance of good join orders for the performance in Soufflé.

Due to the complex semi-naive rule versions with constantly changing delta relations and the factorial number of possible left-deep join orders, manually finding high-quality join orders is tedious and time-consuming, as shown in the example. As a result, users require a deep understanding of the engine's internal rule execution strategies to find good join orders. Even then, an (expert) user only has a limited time budget for experimentation since there are too many potential join orders to explore. Therefore, users typically move on when they find a sufficiently fast join order and do not fully explore the solution space. Given that the performance gap is so vast between low-quality and high-quality join orders, it is paramount from a usability and a performance viewpoint that Datalog engines such as Soufflé find high-quality join orders automatically without user intervention.

```
for all t₁ ∈ data_byte do                for all t₁ ∈ delta_propagated do
  for all t₂ ∈ delta_propagated do          /* EA+Mult */
    /* NextEA = EA+Mult */                  if (t₁(1) + t₁(2), _) ∈ data_byte do
    if t₁(1) = t₂(1) + t₂(2) do             ...
      ...                                     insert (...) into new_propagated
      insert (...) into new_propagated
```

Fig. 3. Indexed loop-nests for the two formulations of the motivating example

3   A Join Optimizer for Soufflé

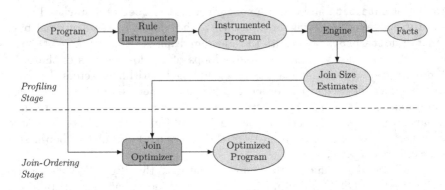

Fig. 4. The FDO Strategy for Join Optimization in Soufflé

To automatically derive join orders for the user, we propose an adapted *Feedback-Directed Optimization* (FDO) strategy [40] for join ordering. For our join optimizer, the FDO strategy has two stages (shown in Fig. 4), a *profiling stage* and a *join-ordering stage*. The profiling stage compiles and runs the Datalog program, using a representative input. As a side-effect of the run, statistics about the execution are produced. The join-ordering stage uses these statistics (the feedback) as input for its compilation. The statistics provide the join optimizer with estimates of the size of each candidate join and the join optimizer then uses these join size estimates and its cost model to derive *cost-optimal* left-deep join orders for all rules in the program using Selinger's algorithm [36]. The key challenges that we address with our join optimizer are:

(1) *Efficiently collecting a potentially exponential number of join size estimates.*
(2) *Developing a cost-model for recursive (and non-recursive) rules.*

We address Challenge (1) with a *program-specialized profiling strategy* that efficiently collects only the necessary statistics. We address Challenge (2) by introducing a *recursive rule cost model* for selecting join orders that computes join size estimates on an iteration-by-iteration basis. Note that for our approach, a representative input (i.e., a training data set) must be chosen in the profiling stage so that the produced join orders do not degrade the application's performance with normally occurring inputs. We demonstrate in Sect. 4 that our approach can generalize well (i.e. a representative input performs within 10% of the optimal for DOOP and DDISASM), and most inputs are representative.

3.1   The Profiling Stage

The profiling stage's task is to efficiently collect join size estimates for the join ordering stage. The join size estimate of an atom depends on its position in a join order. For example, recall the loop-nest of Fig. 3 for the motivating example. The join size estimates for atoms `data_byte` and `delta_propagated` can change depending on whether they are placed in the first or second loop in the join order. The cost differences stem from the join attributes of the atoms, which are bound by values from outer loops and/or constants. In the example, the join uses the attributes `EA` and `Mult` bound by `delta_propagated` in the outer loop to join `data_byte` using the value `EA+Mult`. The first column of relation `data_byte` becomes a join attribute with value `EA+Mult`, and we want to estimate the number of tuples in `data_byte` that have this value.

The database literature [12,19] introduced the concept of selectivity, which measures the degree to which a predicate filters tuples. An accurate measure for selectivity can be found by projecting the set of tuples on the join attributes and counting the number of projected tuples. Then, the join size can be estimated by dividing the relation size by the number of projected tuples. More generally, the join size estimate can be expressed for an atom as,

$$f_{a_1,\dots,a_k}(R) = \frac{|R|}{|\pi_{a_1,\dots,a_k}(R)|} \tag{1}$$

using relational algebra [14] notation where $a_1,\dots,a_k$ are join attributes[2] of the atom with relation R, where $\pi_{a_1,\dots,a_k}(R)$ is the set of tuples in R projected on the join attributes and where $|R|$ is the cardinality of relation R. Note that the formula can be refined for constant attributes filtering out tuples that whose constants do not match.

According to Eq. 1, the join size estimate depends on which of the relation's attributes become join attributes, i.e., $a_1,\dots,a_k$. When relations appear later in the join order, more attributes are bound; hence, the join size estimate becomes smaller. Note that there could be 2^m different join size estimates where m is the number of attributes of relation R (and even more considering constant attributes as well). However, only a small number of join size estimates are necessary to cover all possible join orders of a rule that may occur for a concrete rule. Since the rule set is given in a Datalog compiler, our program-specialized profiling strategy can compute the collection of potential join attributes ahead of time.

The algorithm for determining the collection of join size computations employs a variation of the *sideways information passing (SIP) graph* [1,9]. The graph G_ρ is constructed for a rule ρ of the shape $A_0(X_0) :- A_1(X_1),\dots,A_n(X_n)$. The vertices of the graph are the body atoms $A_i(X_i)$ for all i, $1 \le i \le n$. By abuse of notation, we assume that the arguments X_i are sets of variables (ignoring constants) that occur as arguments. There is a directed edge from one atom A_i to another A_j if its arguments X_i bind at least one argument in X_j. The set of incoming edges is denoted by function *in*, i.e., $A_j \in in(A_i)$. We denote the bindings variables themselves by $bvars(A_j, A_i)$ between two atoms A_i and A_j. We depict the SIP graph for the motivating example in Fig. 5.

---

[2] Not necessarily all attributes are join attributes.

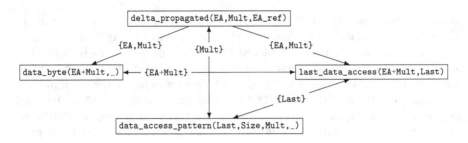

Fig. 5. The SIP graph for the motivating example

Only an atom's neighbours with incoming edges in the sideways information passing graph control the join attributes. From this observation, we can construct a simple algorithm that determines the collection of join attributes. Algorithm 1 computes for each relation the possible join attributes that can be bound in the SIP graph for a rule, i.e., the candidate joins on that relation. The algorithm considers for each rule ρ in the program P, its SIP graph G_ρ. Each atom A_i in the SIP graph finds its corresponding relation. Set B represents a collection of sets of variable bindings for all potential atoms A_j that could be placed before A_i. We perform a power-set construction for all possible subsets of set B. We make the union U of all p_i and compute J the join attributes in A_i bound by U. Finally, we add the join attribute set to the result set S_R.

Algorithm 1 ComputeUniqueJoins(P)

1: Let S be empty for all relations R in P, i.e., $S_R = \emptyset$
2: **for all** $\rho \in P$ **do**
3:    **for all** $A_i \in G_\rho$ **do**
4:       Let R be the relation for A_i
5:       Let $B = \{bvars(A_j, A_i) \mid A_j \in in(A_i)\}$ be the possible bindings passed to A_i
6:       **for all** $p_i \in \mathcal{P}(B)$ **do**
7:          Let $U = \bigcup p_i$ be all bindings from a subset of incoming edges
8:          Let J be the attributes in A_i bound by U
9:             $S_R = S_R \cup J$
10: **return** S

We illustrate the execution of Algorithm 1 on the motivating example when it encounters the atom `data_access_pattern(Last,Size,Mult,_)`. For this atom, there are two incoming edges, from `delta_propagated(EA,Mult,EA_ref)` and `last_data_access(EA+Mult,Last)`. Therefore, the set of all possible bindings B in the algorithm will hold $\{\{Mult\}, \{Last\}\}$. Any combination of these bindings can be possible (considering whether these atoms appear before or after `data_access_pattern` in the join order). Therefore, the power-set of B is enumerated $\{\{\{Mult\}\}, \{\{Last\}\}, \{\{Mult\}, \{Last\}\}\}$. Then for each subset, the bindings are collected with a set union operation to produce the set U. Set U

will take on the values $\{Mult\}, \{Last\}, \{Mult, Last\}$ for each subset. Since $Last$ corresponds to the first attribute, and $Mult$ corresponds to the third attribute, each binding will correspond to the join attributes $\{3\}, \{1\}, \{1, 3\}$. The set S_R then contains for the relation last_data_access, these sets of join attributes. The process continues for the remaining atoms, producing sets of join attributes (and hence candidate joins) for each relation.

We use the solution set S of Algorithm 1 to instrument the Datalog program at compile time. The instrumentation injects join size computations into the execution that will be evaluated during run-time to produce each join size estimate. The instrumentation of the program differentiates between recursive and non-recursive relations. For recursive relations, the join size computations are placed inside the fixpoint loop of the stratum (as determined by the semi-naive evaluation algorithm [8] explained in Sect. 2). Figure 6 shows the instrumented semi-naïve evaluation of the Datalog compiler. The join size computations on delta_propagated are placed in the fixpoint loop and the join size computations for other non-recursive relations, e.g., data_byte are placed in earlier strata as soon as they are fully computed.

```
delta_propagated = propagated
while delta_propagated ≠ ∅ do
    EstimateJoinSize(delta_propagated, { })
    EstimateJoinSize(delta_propagated, {2})

    Eval(new_propagated(EA+Mult,Mult,EA_ref) :-
            delta_propagated(EA,Mult,EA_ref),
            data_byte(EA+Mult,_),
            ...)

    delta_propagated = new_propagated
    propagated = propagated ∪ new_propagated
    new_propagated = ∅
```

Fig. 6. The instrumented semi-naïve evaluation for the motivating example

Computing Join Size Estimates. The join size computations are evaluated at run-time in the profiling stage to derive the join size estimates. Each join size estimate is found by counting the number of tuples in R and counting the unique tuples after the projection of R onto the join attributes (cf. Eq. 1). A naive way to compute the number of unique keys comprises the following steps: (1) projecting every tuple in the relation onto the join attributes, (2) sorting the projected tuples, and (3) iterating and counting the number of duplicates (and hence unique tuples). Note that the sorting step can be avoided by assuming that the tuples are already sorted on the join attributes ahead of time.

However, Soufflé's machinery facilitates a more efficient approach. Soufflé represents each relation R as a collection of multiple in-memory B-Tree indices [27]. Each index for a relation totally orders the tuples in R using a lexicographical ordering ℓ, i.e., $\ell = 1 \prec 2$ would order tuples by attribute 1 then break ties using attribute 2. For each join size estimate, we would like to find an index for R where its lex-order ℓ has the set of join attributes as a prefix, ensuring that the tuples projected on the join attributes will be traversed in sorted order. When the attributes for a join size form a prefix in the lex-order, we say that the join size estimate is covered by the index. To ensure every join size estimate is covered by an index, we can rely on Soufflé's automatic index selection algorithm [41]. The algorithm inspects the joins on each relation (called *primitive searches*) and ensures that each can be covered by an index, using the minimum total number of indexes for each relation. To achieve the same result with join size estimates, we represent each estimate as a primitive search with the same set of attributes, which guarantees that an index will cover it, eliminating the sorting step entirely.

Algorithm 2 EstimateJoinSize(R, J)

1: Let J be the set of join attributes.
2: Let $Dup = 0$ be the number of duplicates.
3: Let $R_\ell = LookupIndex(R, J)$
4:
5: **for all** $Curr \in R_\ell$ **do**
6:    **if** $\pi_{a_i \in J}(Prev) = \pi_{a_i \in J}(Curr)$ **then**
7:       $++Dup$
8:    $Prev = Curr$
9: **return** $\frac{|R_\ell|}{|R_\ell| - Dup}$.

An outline of the join size computation is shown in Algorithm 2. To extend the algorithm for constant join attributes, R_ℓ is first filtered for the tuples satisfying the constant attributes. Considering EstimateJoinSize(`delta_propagated`, $\{2\}$), Algorithm 2 will execute as follows. Firstly, an index R_ℓ will be found with the set of join attributes $\{2\}$ as a prefix. Since the relation has arity 3, the possible index orders are: $\ell = 2 \prec 1 \prec 3$ or $\ell = 2 \prec 3 \prec 1$ over the attributes of the relation. Next, the index is traversed in order, comparing the attribute in position 2 with the previous tuple. Since the index is sorted on attribute 2 first, duplicate values will appear in sequence. Finally, the relation size divided by the number of unique values on attribute 2 is retrieved as the estimated join size. For the *gamess* fact-set, on the first iteration, $|R_\ell| = 31,615$ tuples and $|R_\ell| - Dup = 23$ unique keys. Hence the expected size of the join for the first iteration on attribute 2 is $\frac{31,615}{23} = 1375$ tuples (rounding up). These join size estimates for each candidate join order can then be used to guide the cost model in the join ordering stage to find high-performance join orders.

Note that multiple join size computations can be covered by the same index. For instance, `data_access_pattern(Last,Size,Mult,_)` has the join size computations $\emptyset, \{3\}, \{1\}, \{1,3\}$. Instead of sorting 4 times (creating 4 distinct indexes), the 2 indexes $\ell = 3 \prec \ldots$ and $\ell = 1 \prec 3 \prec \ldots$ can cover them. Hence, our indexing technique for join size estimates creates little overhead for the profiling stage, producing the necessary statistics for the join ordering stage.

3.2   The Join Ordering Stage

The problem of finding join orders is well-known in the database literature [24, 25, 30, 33, 37] as part of query optimization. A query optimizer's task is finding the fastest query plan (i.e. the fastest way of executing a query) efficiently using a cost-model [36]. The challenge is that each query has $n!$ possible left deep joins when there are n relations to join. In addition, for each possible join order, each relation can be accessed using different methods, i.e., a hash-join, sort-merge join, nested-loop join or a scan of the entire relation. In the context of Soufflé, every relation is accessed using indexed nested loop joins, and, therefore, each join order corresponds to exactly one query plan. However, there are still $n!$ possible left-deep join orders to consider.

Fig. 7. An illustration of Selinger's algorithm which maps sets of atoms to minimum cost join orders

Selinger [36] observed that finding a minimum cost left-deep join order can be achieved without explicitly considering all $n!$ possible candidates. The insight is that if a join order for a subset of relations is sub-optimal, it can never appear in the optimal join order. Hence, the optimal join order can be found inductively through dynamic programming by considering the optimal join order for every subset of relations. The process is shown in Fig. 7 to join 2 relations. First, each subset of size 1 corresponds to a single minimum cost join order. Next, for the subset $\{1, 2\}$, the algorithm considers removal of one relation i.e. the sets $\{1\}$ and $\{2\}$. For each of these subsets, it considers the minimum cost join order found for them, i.e. [1] and [2], and adds this to the cost of extending the join order to include the removed relation, i.e. $[1 \rightarrow 2]$ or $[2 \rightarrow 1]$. In this example, the cost of $[2 \rightarrow 1]$ is cheaper and is saved, with $[1 \rightarrow 2]$ never being considered further. This process continues up the lattice until the minimum cost join order for all relations is found, and the algorithm terminates. The algorithm has a complexity of $\mathcal{O}(n \times 2^n)$ since there are 2^n subsets to consider, and each subset must consider $\mathcal{O}(n)$ join orders from one level below. Hence, Selinger's algorithm substantially improves upon the brute-force approach of considering all $n!$ left-deep join orders.

Selinger's algorithm (and other query optimization strategies) are designed for queries without recursion. Hence the literature offers little guidance for finding join orders for recursive rules. One approach would be to treat each recursive rule as if it were non-recursive, i.e. by taking the average size of a delta relation across all of the iterations of a given rule and using this average to drive the cost model. The disadvantage of this approach is that Selinger's algorithm would no longer guarantee high-quality join orders. For instance, a delta relation may be very large for the first iteration of the rule and then very small for subsequent iterations (as less new knowledge is derived). If the rule is executed for many iterations, placing the delta relation at the beginning of the join order is usually the most efficient. However, since the initial size of the delta relation is very high, its average might still be very high, and the join order chosen won't place the delta relation first, leading to worse performance. Although more sophisticated aggregate statistics could be used (for example, taking the geometric mean), any aggregate would fail to capture the costs for rules with multiple recursive relations that grow and shrink throughout different iterations.

To address this challenge, we develop a *recursive rule cost model* for Selinger's algorithm, which maintains accurate statistics for each candidate join on an *iteration-by-iteration* basis. Our approach relies on the fact that join size estimates are computed per iteration during the profiling stage as join size computations are placed inside the fix-point loop for each stratum. Under our cost model, the tuples for a particular candidate join are represented by a *vector* of length I where I is the number of iterations of the rule. Under our model, the cost of executing any particular join order is calculated as follows:

$$
\begin{aligned}
\mathrm{CostToJoin}(\{R_1,\ldots,R_k\}, S) = {} & \mathrm{CostToJoin}(\{R_1,\ldots,R_k\}) \\
& + \mathrm{Arity}(S) \\
& \times \sum_{i=1}^{I} \mathrm{TuplesFromJoin}_i(\{R_1,\ldots,R_k\}) \\
& \times \mathrm{ExpectedJoinSize}_i(S, J)
\end{aligned}
$$

The cost to join relations $\{R_1,\ldots,R_k\}$ with a new relation S is the cost to compute the previous join added to the new join cost. The new join cost is then calculated as the arity of the new relation S multiplied by the sum of tuple accesses across all i iterations from 1 to I by the join. For each iteration i, the number of tuples is calculated as the number of tuples from the previous join (the number of tuples from the outer loop) multiplied by the expected join size of S for this iteration, using join attributes J grounded by the previously joined relations.

To illustrate our approach, consider joining the first two atoms in the motivating example in Fig. 1. The algorithm estimates the cost of each choice between candidate join orders, as shown in Fig. 8. The cost of $(1, 2)$ (the left path shown

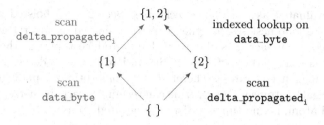

Fig. 8. The possible paths (and hence join orders) for the motivating example (Color figure online)

in red) with the cost model described previously is:

$$\text{Arity}(\texttt{data\_byte}) \times \sum_{i=1}^{I} |\texttt{data\_byte}|$$

$$+ \text{Arity}(\texttt{delta\_propagated}) \times \sum_{i=1}^{I} |\texttt{data\_byte}| \times |\texttt{delta\_propagated}_i|$$

For the right path up the lattice (shown in blue) for order $(2, 1)$, the cost is:

$$\text{Arity}(\texttt{delta\_propagated}) \times \sum_{i=1}^{I} |\texttt{delta\_propagated}_i|$$

$$+ \text{Arity}(\texttt{data\_byte}) \times \sum_{i=1}^{I} |\texttt{delta\_propagated}_i| \times 1$$

Since the indexed lookup using the second join order only accesses a single tuple, the join order $[2 \rightarrow 1]$ is cheaper than $[1 \rightarrow 2]$ and saved. For the remaining atoms in the rule, the process continues up the lattice using dynamic programming, finding join orders for larger subsets of atoms by using the minimum cost join orders previously computed for each smaller subset. Eventually, the cheapest path up the lattice is found, corresponding to the minimum cost join order.

Overall, our adapted usage of Selinger's algorithm increases its time complexity from $\mathcal{O}(n \times 2^n)$ where n is the number of positive atoms to $\mathcal{O}(n \times 2^n \times I)$ where I is the number of iterations. However, the advantage of this approach is that the join sizes (and hence costs) for each iteration are considered separately, and the total cost is minimized, allowing the optimizer to select the cost-optimal join order for recursive rules.

Note that our join optimizer still finds high-quality join orders for rules that contain negated atoms, even though they are not considered explicitly in the algorithm. First, the join optimizer finds the join order considering only the positive atoms and unrolls the rule into a loop-nest. Then, the negated atoms, which are evaluated as existence checks (see Sect. 2), are hoisted as high as possible in the loop-nest so that they can be evaluated as eagerly as possible. Since negated atoms act as sinks, they don't produce tuples in the loop-nest and hence don't affect the cost of a candidate join (which is determined by the number of tuples it generates). Therefore, our join optimizer performs well for rules with negated atoms unless the rule can terminate early by better placement of a negated atom, i.e. no tuples satisfy the negated atom.

4   Experimental Evaluation

We have conducted several experiments to understand the quality of the proposed join optimizer for Soufflé. Specifically, we aim to answer the following questions:

1. What is the performance of the join optimizer in comparison with current join ordering heuristics in Soufflé?
2. Are the orders that the join optimizer produces on given training data sets robust for different inputs?
3. What is the overhead of the profiling and join ordering stages?

Experiments are run without virtualization using an AMD Ryzen Threadripper 2990WX (3GHz 32-Core Processor). The operating system is Ubuntu 20.10, with programs compiled using GCC 10.30. All performance-related benchmarks are run in single-threaded mode and executed three times for reliability.

We evaluate the join optimizer on the following industrial-strength Datalog applications consisting of hundreds of rules/relations. First, **DOOP** [11] is a framework supporting various types of static analysis of Java programs. We run the *context-insensitive* analysis on the Java programs present in the *DaCapo* [10] benchmark. Second, **DDISASM** [18] is a tool that transforms stripped binaries into re-assemblable assembly code through a series of analyses written in Datalog. We run DDISASM on the SPECCPU 2006 [22] suite of binaries. Third, **Virtual Private Cloud (VPC)** [7] is a benchmark taken from a real-world network security analysis framework deployed in Amazon Web Services.

Join Optimizer Performance. We compare the performance of Soufflé's heuristic join orders with the performance of the new join optimizer. Note that **DOOP** and **DDISASM** are hand-tuned Datalog implementations, whereas **VPC** is automatically generated Datalog code from a network model and is not hand-tuned. Figure 9 illustrates the speed-up achieved by the join optimizer for various input data sets of DOOP, DDISASM and VPC. The join optimizer delivers a performance speedup of up to 1.13× for DOOP. For DDISASM, we observe improved performance with the join optimizer on 11 out of 17 fact sets of up to 1.35× and a geometric mean speedup of 1.069× overall. For 6 out of 17 data sets, performance degrades (in the worst case on *GemsFDTD* by 0.85×). The slowdown is due to the join optimizer selecting new join orders that result in

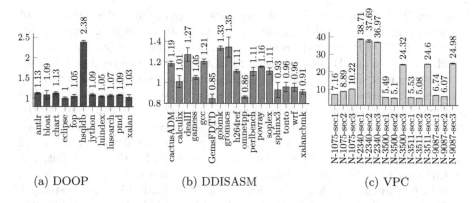

(a) DOOP   (b) DDISASM   (c) VPC

Fig. 9. Runtime Speed-up of the Join Orders Produced by the Join Optimizer.

extra indexes on relations, slowing down fact-sets that are write-heavy for certain relations.

For VPC, the join optimizer provides better speedups because the join orders for rules are not manually tuned. The speedup ranges from 5.08× up to 38.71× with a geometric mean of 12.07×. These experiments show that the join optimizer finds orders that, on average, perform well for DOOP and DDISASM even in comparison with hand-tuned join orders and delivers outstanding performance in the absence of hand-tuned joins such as VPC.

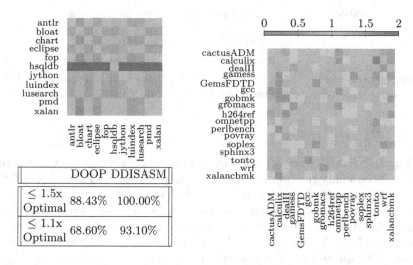

	DOOP	DDISASM
≤ 1.5x Optimal	88.43%	100.00%
≤ 1.1x Optimal	68.60%	93.10%

Fig. 10. A heat map representing the relative slowdown when optimizing on input A and evaluating on input B compared to optimizing on B and evaluating on B.

Training Data Robustness. For this experiment, we evaluate the robustness of the join optimizer using different data sets as training sets. For this experiment, we run DOOP with context-insensitive points-to analysis using the DaCapo benchmark suite and DDISASM using SPECCPU 2006. The results are shown in Fig. 10 as heat maps. A point in the heat map is a combination of a *training* input (on the x-axis) and a *test* input (on the y-axis). We generate the join orders for the *training* input using our join optimizer and use the same join orders for the *test* input. To evaluate the robustness of the training, we compute the slowdown for each combination. A ratio exceeding 1 is a performance slowdown indicating that the *training* input fails to generalize join orders for the *test* input. For DOOP, only 68.6% of the benchmarks have a slowdown ratio of 1.1× or lower, with 14 benchmarks having a slowdown ratio of at least 1.5×. The test input *hsqldb* is an outlier that generalizes poorly with a slowdown ratio of 3.68× to 6.10×. However, the join optimizer is quite robust for DDISASM's training data, with 93.1% of the runs having a slowdown ratio of less than 1.1×.

For both benchmarks, when a representative training input is selected (e.g., *pmd* for DOOP and *GemsFDTD* for DDISASM), the performance of the chosen join orders can generalize across the benchmark, staying within 10% of the optimal case. This shows that the join optimizer generalizes effectively when trained on a representative input. In any case, our experiments show that new join orders do not need to be re-derived for every new input, given the inputs have a similar structure. We conjecture that in most domains, the structure e.g., relative join sizes for different candidate join orders, would remain largely invariant.

Table 1. The overhead of the join optimizer at each stage

	DOOP			DDISASM			VPC		
	min	avg	max	min	avg	max	min	avg	max
Profiling Stage Slowdown	1.62×	2.61×	4.66×	1.05×	1.18×	1.20×	1.00×	1.18×	1.60×
Join Ordering Stage Time	1m28s	1m33s	1m37s	51s	1m	1m57s		< 1s	

Profiling and Join Ordering Overheads. For our next experiment, we are interested in determining the overhead of our program-specialized profiling and the overhead of running the join optimizer in the join ordering stage. From Table 1, the maximum overall slowdown is 4.66× for DOOP, the largest since there is complex mutual recursion, executing for many iterations. By comparison, the slowdown for DDISASM and VPC is 1.18× on average since they are mostly non-recursive. Overall, the slowdowns for the profiling stage are acceptable, ranging on average from 1.18× to 2.61×.

As shown from Table 1, the maximum time to run the join ordering stage is 1m37s for DOOP, 1m57s for DDISASM and less than 1 second for VPC. DOOP has a large overhead due to rules with larger bodies and rule iterations. DDISASM takes the longest due to some rules with much larger rule bodies than in DOOP. Finally, since VPC has few iterations due to less mutual recursion, the join ordering stage finishes in less than 1 second. Overall, the join ordering stage of the join optimizer only takes a few minutes for complex industrial strength applications and occurs at compile-time, not run-time, which is acceptable.

5 Related Work

Evaluating Datalog as a DSL. LogicBlox [5] employs worst-case optimal joins, requiring users to manually rewrite and duplicate relations with different attribute orders to achieve satisfactory performance. BDDBDDB [42] uses binary decision diagrams to store relations, but high-performance relies on finding variable orderings, which is an NP-Hard problem [32]. Socialite [38] requires users to provide execution plans that enforce a join order. Other engines such as μZ [23], Flix [31], and PADatalog [4] also require the user to manual tune and provide performance hints that are no longer necessary when using Soufflé with the join optimizer. The technique in [39] provides cost estimates statically before execution.

Database Systems. Relational database management systems rely on cost-based optimization with both bottom-up [6,36] or top-down [20] approaches searching for a low-cost join order by estimating the actual execution cost of each candidate. Since the latency for each request is the sum of the optimization time and run-time, optimizers terminate after finding a sufficiently good join order. By comparison, Soufflé exhaustively runs its join optimizer at compile-time resulting in cost-optimal join orders, including for recursive rules. Additionally, Soufflé knows the rules apriori, allowing the join optimizer to collect only the necessary statistics, leading to a lightweight join optimization process that consistently produces high-quality join orders.

Auto-Scheduling for DSLs. There have been several compiling DSLs such as Halide [34], GraphIt [43], and TACO [28]. These DSLs separate the algorithm (what to compute) from the schedule (how to compute it). For instance, Halide allows users to provide schedules that control the degree of parallelization, vectorization, loop tiling and loop fusion. Auto-schedulers for these DSLs use sophisticated techniques [2,3] such as generating hundreds of thousands of random programs and schedules and training a machine-learned cost model for unseen schedules. Soufflé exposes only join-orders for optimization that are less sensitive to architectural details, allowing for simple cost models that rely on relational selectivities alone to achieve high-performance.

6 Conclusion

This paper presents an FDO strategy for join ordering targeting Datalog compilers. We have demonstrated that our optimizer is competitive with hand-tuned join orders while outperforming un-tuned orders by 12.07× on average. Our optimizer is lightweight, incurring an average slowdown of 2.61× for the slowest application during statistics collection. The join orders are also robust when given a well-chosen, representative input. Overall, our join optimizer can save significant human effort spent manually tuning and enables users to achieve high-performance automatically without breaking declarativeness.

Acknowledgements. This work was generously supported by Fantom Foundation and by the Australian Government through the ARC Discovery Project funding scheme (DP210101984).

References

1. Abiteboul, S., Hull, R., Vianu, V.: Foundations of Databases, vol. 8. Addison-Wesley Reading (1995)
2. Adams, A., et al.: Learning to optimize halide with tree search and random programs. ACM Trans. Graph. **38**(4), 1–12 (2019)
3. Anderson, L., Adams, A., Ma, K., Li, T.M., Jin, T., Ragan-Kelley, J.: Efficient automatic scheduling of imaging and vision pipelines for the GPU. In: Proceedings of the ACM on Programming Languages 5(OOPSLA), pp. 1–28 (2021)
4. Antoniadis, T., Triantafyllou, K., Smaragdakis, Y.: Porting doop to soufflé: a tale of inter-engine portability for datalog-based analyses. In: Proceedings of the 6th ACM SIGPLAN International Workshop on State Of the Art in Program Analysis, pp. 25–30 (2017)
5. Aref, M., et al.: Design and implementation of the logicblox system. In: Proceedings of the 2015 ACM SIGMOD International Conference on Management of Data, pp. 1371–1382 (2015)
6. Astrahan, M.M., et al.: System R: relational approach to database management. ACM Trans. Graph. **1**(2), 97–137 (1976)
7. Backes, J., et al.: Reachability analysis for AWS-based networks. In: Dillig, Isil, Tasiran, Serdar (eds.) CAV 2019. LNCS, vol. 11562, pp. 231–241. Springer, Cham (2019). https://doi.org/10.1007/978-3-030-25543-5_14
8. Bancilhon, F.: Naive evaluation of recursively defined relations. In: Brodie, M.L., Mylopoulos, J. (eds) On Knowledge Base Management Systems. Topics in Information Systems. Springer, NY (1986). https://doi.org/10.1007/978-1-4612-4980-1_17
9. Beeri, C., Ramakrishnan, R.: On the power of magic. In: Proceedings of the Sixth ACM SIGACT-SIGMOD-SIGART Symposium on Principles of Database Systems, pp. 269–284 (1987)
10. Blackburn, S.M., et al.: The DaCapo benchmarks: Java benchmarking development and analysis. In: Proceedings of the 21st Annual ACM SIGPLAN Conference on Object-Oriented Programming Systems, Languages, and Applications, pp. 169–190 (2006)
11. Bravenboer, M., Smaragdakis, Y.: Strictly declarative specification of sophisticated points-to analyses. In: Proceedings of the 24th ACM SIGPLAN Conference on Object Oriented Programming Systems Languages and Applications, pp. 243–262 (2009)
12. Bruno, N.: Automated Physical Database Design and Tuning, 1st edn. CRC Press Inc., Boca Raton (2011)
13. Ceri, S., Gottlob, G., Tanca, L., et al.: What you always wanted to know about datalog (and never dared to ask). IEEE Trans. Knowl. Data Eng. **1**(1), 146–166 (1989)

14. Codd, E.. F..: A relational model of data for large shared data banks. In: Broy, Manfred, Denert, Ernst (eds.) Software Pioneers, pp. 263–294. Springer, Heidelberg (2002). https://doi.org/10.1007/978-3-642-59412-0_16
15. Developers, S.: Soufflé documentation (2016). https://souffle-lang.github.io/pdf/abdulthesis.pdf
16. Developers, S.: Soufflé documentation (2016). https://souffle-lang.github.io/handtuning#profiler
17. Developers, S.: Soufflé release 2.3 (2022). https://github.com/souffle-lang/souffle/releases/tag/2.3
18. Flores-Montoya, A., Schulte, E.: Datalog disassembly. In: 29th USENIX Security Symposium (USENIX Security 2020), pp. 1075–1092 (2020)
19. Garcia-Molina, H., Widom, J., Ullman, J.D.: Database System Implementation. Prentice-Hall Inc., USA (1999)
20. Graefe, G.: The cascades framework for query optimization. IEEE Data Eng. Bull. **18**(3), 19–29 (1995)
21. Grech, N., Brent, L., Scholz, B., Smaragdakis, Y.: Gigahorse: thorough, declarative decompilation of smart contracts. In: 2019 IEEE/ACM 41st International Conference on Software Engineering (ICSE), pp. 1176–1186. IEEE (2019)
22. Henning, J.L.: SPEC CPU2006 benchmark descriptions. ACM SIGARCH Comput. Archit. News **34**(4), 1–17 (2006)
23. Hoder, Kryštof, Bjørner, Nikolaj, de Moura, Leonardo: μZ– an efficient engine for fixed points with constraints. In: Gopalakrishnan, Ganesh, Qadeer, Shaz (eds.) CAV 2011. LNCS, vol. 6806, pp. 457–462. Springer, Heidelberg (2011). https://doi.org/10.1007/978-3-642-22110-1_36
24. Ioannidis, Y.E.: Query optimization. ACM Comput. Surv. **28**(1), 121–123 (1996)
25. Jarke, M., Koch, J.: Query optimization in database systems. ACM Comput. Surv. **16**(2), 111–152 (1984)
26. Jordan, Herbert, Scholz, Bernhard, Subotić, Pavle: SOUFFLÉ: on synthesis of program analyzers. In: Chaudhuri, Swarat, Farzan, Azadeh (eds.) CAV 2016. LNCS, vol. 9780, pp. 422–430. Springer, Cham (2016). https://doi.org/10.1007/978-3-319-41540-6_23
27. Jordan, H., Subotić, P., Zhao, D., Scholz, B.: A specialized b-tree for concurrent datalog evaluation. In: Proceedings of the 24th Symposium on Principles and Practice of Parallel Programming, pp. 327–339 (2019)
28. Kjolstad, F., Kamil, S., Chou, S., Lugato, D., Amarasinghe, S.: The tensor algebra compiler. In: Proceedings of the ACM on Programming Languages 1(OOPSLA), pp. 1–29 (2017)
29. Lagouvardos, S., Dolby, J., Grech, N., Antoniadis, A., Smaragdakis, Y.: Static analysis of shape in TensorFlow programs. In: Hirschfeld, R., Pape, T. (eds.) 34th European Conference on Object-Oriented Programming (ECOOP 2020). Leibniz International Proceedings in Informatics (LIPIcs), vol. 166, pp. 15:1–15:29. Schloss Dagstuhl-Leibniz-Zentrum für Informatik, Dagstuhl, Germany (2020)
30. Leis, V., et al.: Query optimization through the looking glass, and what we found running the Join Order Benchmark. VLDB J. **27**(5), 643–668 (2017). https://doi.org/10.1007/s00778-017-0480-7
31. Madsen, M., Yee, M.H., Lhoták, O.: From datalog to flix: a declarative language for fixed points on lattices. SIGPLAN Not. **51**(6), 194–208 (2016)
32. Meinel, C., Slobodová, A.: On the complexity of constructing optimal ordered binary decision diagrams. In: Prívara, I., Rovan, B., Ruzička, P. (eds.) MFCS 1994. LNCS, vol. 841, pp. 515–524. Springer, Heidelberg (1994). https://doi.org/10.1007/3-540-58338-6_98

33. Neumann, T., Radke, B.: Adaptive optimization of very large join queries. In: Proceedings of the 2018 International Conference on Management of Data, pp. 677–692 (2018)
34. Ragan-Kelley, J., Barnes, C., Adams, A., Paris, S., Durand, F., Amarasinghe, S.: Halide: a language and compiler for optimizing parallelism, locality, and recomputation in image processing pipelines. ACM SIGPLAN Not. **48**(6), 519–530 (2013)
35. Scholz, B., Jordan, H., Subotić, P., Westmann, T.: On fast large-scale program analysis in datalog. In: Proceedings of the 25th International Conference on Compiler Construction, pp. 196–206 (2016)
36. Selinger, P.G., Astrahan, M.M., Chamberlin, D.D., Lorie, R.A., Price, T.G.: Access path selection in a relational database management system. In: Readings in Artificial Intelligence and Databases, pp. 511–522. Elsevier (1989)
37. Sellis, T.K.: Multiple-query optimization. ACM Trans. Database Syst. **13**(1), 23–52 (1988)
38. Seo, J., Guo, S., Lam, M.S.: Socialite: datalog extensions for efficient social network analysis. In: 2013 IEEE 29th International Conference on Data Engineering (ICDE), pp. 278–289. IEEE (2013)
39. Sereni, D., Avgustinov, P., de Moor, O.: Adding magic to an optimising datalog compiler. In: Proceedings of the 2008 ACM SIGMOD International Conference on Management of Data, pp. 553–566. SIGMOD 2008, Association for Computing Machinery, NY (2008). https://doi.org/10.1145/1376616.1376673
40. Smith, M.D.: Overcoming the challenges to feedback-directed optimization (keynote talk). SIGPLAN Not. **35**(7), 1–11 (2000)
41. Subotić, P., Jordan, H., Chang, L., Fekete, A., Scholz, B.: Automatic index selection for large-scale datalog computation. Proc. VLDB Endow. **12**(2), 141–153 (2018)
42. Whaley, John, Avots, Dzintars, Carbin, Michael, Lam, Monica S..: Using datalog with binary decision diagrams for program analysis. In: Yi, Kwangkeun (ed.) APLAS 2005. LNCS, vol. 3780, pp. 97–118. Springer, Heidelberg (2005). https://doi.org/10.1007/11575467_8
43. Zhang, Y., Yang, M., Baghdadi, R., Kamil, S., Shun, J., Amarasinghe, S.: GraphIt: a high-performance graph DSL. In: Proceedings of the ACM on Programming Languages 2(OOPSLA), pp. 1–30 (2018)
44. Zhao, D., Subotic, P., Raghothaman, M., Scholz, B.: Towards elastic incrementalization for datalog. In: Veltri, N., Benton, N., Ghilezan, S. (eds.) PPDP 2021: 23rd International Symposium on Principles and Practice of Declarative Programming, Tallinn, Estonia, 6–8 September 2021, pp. 20:1–20:16. ACM (2021)

From Infinity to Choreographies
Extraction for Unbounded Systems

Bjørn Angel Kjær, Luís Cruz-Filipe(⊠) ⬤, and Fabrizio Montesi⬤

Department of Mathematics and Computer Science, University of Southern Denmark,
Campusvej 55, 5230 Odense M, Denmark
{lcfilipe,fmontesi}@imada.sdu.dk

Abstract. Choreographies are formal descriptions of distributed systems, which focus on the way in which participants communicate. While they are useful for analysing protocols, in practice systems are written directly by specifying each participant's behaviour. This created the need for *choreography extraction*: the process of obtaining a choreography that faithfully describes the collective behaviour of all participants in a distributed protocol.

Previous works have addressed this problem for systems with a predefined, finite number of participants. In this work, we show how to extract choreographies from system descriptions where the total number of participants is unknown and unbounded, due to the ability of spawning new processes at runtime. This extension is challenging, since previous algorithms relied heavily on the set of possible states of the network during execution being finite.

Keywords: Choreography · Extraction · Concurrency · Message passing

1 Introduction

Choreographies are coordination plans for concurrent and distributed systems, which describe the expected interactions that system participants should enact [5,14]. Languages for expressing choreographies (choreographic languages) are widely used for documentation and specification purposes, some notable examples being Message Sequence Charts [7], UML Sequence Diagrams [16], and choreographies in the Business Process Modelling Notation (BPMN) [15]. More recently, such languages have also been used for programming and verification, e.g., as in choreographic programming [13] and multiparty session types [6] respectively.

In practice, many system implementations do not come with a choreography yet. *Choreography extraction* (extraction for short) is the synthesis of a choreography that faithfully represents the specification of a system based on message passing (if it exists) [1,3,11,12]. Extraction is helpful because it gives developers

Partially supported by Villum Fonden, grant no. 29518.

a global overview of how the *processes* (abstractions of endpoints) of a system interact, making it easier to check that they collaborate as intended. In general, though, it is undecidable whether such a choreography exists, making extraction a challenging problem.

Current methods for extraction cannot analyse systems that spawn new processes at runtime: they can only deal with systems where the number of participants is finite and statically known. This is an important limitation, because many modern distributed systems dynamically create processes for several reasons, such as scalability. The aim of this article is to address this shortcoming.

As an example of a system that cannot be analysed by previous work, consider a simple implementation of a serverless architecture (Example 1).

Example 1. A simple serverless architecture, written in pseudocode (we will formalise this example later in the article). A client sends a request to an entry-point, which then spawns a temporary process to handle the client. The spawned process computes the response to the request. Then it offers the client to make another request, in which case a new process is spawned to handle that, since the new request may require a different service.

```
client:
    send init to server;
    loop {
        server presents worker; receive result from worker;
        if finished
            then request termination from worker; terminate;
            else request next from worker; server:=worker;
    }

server:
    receive init from client; Handle(server);

    procedure Handle(parent) {
        spawn worker with {
            parent presents client; ComputeResult();
            send result to client; receive request from client;
            switch request {
                next: Handle(worker);
                termination: terminate;
            }
        }
        introduce worker and client; terminate;
    }
```

Example 1 illustrates the usefulness of extraction: a human could manually go through the code and check that the two processes will interact as intended; however, despite it being a greatly simplified example, it is not immediately obvious whether the processes will communicate correctly or not.

Previous methods for extraction use graphs to represent the possible (symbolic) execution space of the system under consideration. The challenge presented by code as in Example 1 is that these graphs are not guaranteed to be finite anymore, because of the possibility of spawning new processes at runtime.

In this article we introduce the first method for extracting choreographies that supports process spawning, i.e., the capability of creating new processes at runtime. Our main contribution consists of a theory and implementation of extraction that use name substitutions to obtain finite representations of infinite symbolic execution graphs. Systems with process spawning have a dynamic topology, which further complicates extraction: new processes can appear at runtime, and can then be connected to other processes to enable communication. We extend the languages used for extraction in previous work with primitives for capturing these features, and show that our method can deal with them.

Structure of the paper. In Sect. 2, we recap the basic theory of extraction. In Sect. 3, we introduce the languages for representing systems (as networks of processes) and choreographies. Section 4 reports our method for extracting networks with an unbounded number of processes (due to spawning), its implementation and limitations. We conclude in Sect. 5.

Related work. We have already mentioned most of the relevant related work in this section. Choreography extraction has been explored for languages that include internal computation [3], process terms that correspond to proofs in linear logic [1], and session types (abstract terms without internal computation) [11,12]. Our method deals with the first case (the most general among those cited). Our primitives for modelling process spawning are inspired by [4].

2   Background

This section summarizes the framework for choreography extraction that we extend [2,3,8,17]. The remainder of the article expands upon this work to extend the capabilities of extraction, and to bring it closer to real systems.

2.1   Networks

Distributed systems are modelled as *networks*, which consist of several participants executing in parallel. Each participant is called a *process*, and the sequence of actions it executes is called a *behaviour*. Each process also includes a set of *procedures*, consisting of a name and associated behaviour.

Behaviours are formally defined by the grammar given below.

$$B ::= \mathbf{0} \mid X \mid \mathsf{p}!m; B \mid \mathsf{p}?; B \mid \mathsf{p} \oplus \ell; B \mid \mathsf{p\&}\{\ell_1 : B_1, \ldots, \ell_n : B_n\}$$
$$\mid \mathtt{if}\ e\ \mathtt{then}\ B_1\ \mathtt{else}\ B_2$$

Term $\mathbf{0}$ designates a terminated process. Term X invokes the procedure named X. Invoking a procedure must be the last action on a behaviour – in other words, we only allow tail recursion. Term $\mathsf{p}!m; B$ describes a behaviour where the executing process evaluates message m and sends the corresponding value to process p, then continues as B. The dual term $\mathsf{p}?; B$ describes receiving a message from p, storing it locally and continuing as B. Behaviour $\mathsf{p} \oplus \ell; B$ sends the selection of label ℓ to process p then continues as B, while the dual $\mathsf{p}\&\{\ell_1 : B_1, \ldots, \ell_n : B_n\}$ offers the behaviours $B_1, \ldots, B_n$ to p, which can be selected by the corresponding labels $\ell_1, \ldots, \ell_n$. Finally, $\mathtt{if}\ e\ \mathtt{then}\ B_1\ \mathtt{else}\ B_2$ is the conditional term: if the Boolean expression e evaluates to true, it continues as B_1, otherwise, it continues as B_2.

The syntax

```
p {
    def X₁ { B₁ }
    ⋮
    def Xₙ { Bₙ }
    main { B }
}
```

describes a process named p with local procedures $X_1, \ldots, X_n$ defined respectively as $B_1, \ldots, B_n$, intending to execute behaviour B.

A network is specified as a sequence of processes, all with distinct names, separated by vertical bars (|). Example 2 defines a valid network, which we use as running example throughout this section to explain the existing extraction algorithm.

Example 2. This network describes the protocol for an online store. The customer sends in items to purchase, then asks the store to proceed to checkout, or continue browsing.

Once the customer proceeds to checkout, they send their payment information to the store. The store then verifies that information, and either completes the transaction, or asks the client to re-send payment information if there where a problem.

```
customer {
    def browse{ store!item; if checkout
        then store⊕buy; purchase;
        else store⊕more; browse }
    def purchase{ store!payment; store&{accept: 0, reject: purchase} }
    main{ browse }
} |
store {
    def offer{ customer?; customer&{buy: payment, more: offer} }
    def payment{ customer?; if accepted
        then customer⊕accept; 0
        else customer⊕reject; payment }
    main { offer }
}
```

2.2 Choreographies

Global descriptions of distributed systems, specifying interactions between participants rather than their individual actions, are called *choreographies*. Similar to processes in networks, a choreography contains a set of procedure definitions, and a main body. The terms of choreography bodies are defined by the grammar below and closely correspond to the actions in process behaviours.

$$C ::= \mathbf{0} \mid X \mid \mathsf{p}.m \rightarrow \mathsf{q}; C \mid \mathsf{p} \rightarrow \mathsf{q}[\ell]; C \mid \texttt{if } \mathsf{p}.e \texttt{ then } C_1 \texttt{ else } C_2$$

Term $\mathbf{0}$ denotes a choreography body where all processes are terminated. Term X invokes the procedure with name X. In the communication $\mathsf{p}.m \rightarrow \mathsf{q}; C$, process p sends message m to q, which stores the result, and the system continues as described by choreography body C. Likewise, in label selection $\mathsf{p} \rightarrow \mathsf{q}[\ell]; C$, process p selects an action in q by sending the label ℓ, and the system continues as C. In the conditional $\texttt{if } \mathsf{p}.e \texttt{ then } C_1 \texttt{ else } C_2$, process p starts by evaluating the Boolean expression e; if this resolves to true, then the choreography continues as C_1, otherwise it continues as C_2.

Example 3. The protocol described by the network in Example 2 can be written as the following choreography.

```
def Buy {
    customer.item -> store; if customer.checkout
        then customer -> store[buy]; Pay
        else customer -> store[more]; Buy
}
def Pay {
    customer.payment -> store; if store.accepted
        then store -> customer[accept]; 0
        else store -> customer[reject]; Pay
}
main {Buy}
```

2.3 Extraction Algorithm

The extraction algorithm from [2,3] consists of two steps. The first step is building a graph that represents a symbolic execution of the network. The second is to traverse this graph, using its edges to build the extracted choreography.

Graph Generation. The first step in extracting a choreography from a network is building a *Symbolic Execution Graph* (SEG) from the network. A SEG is a directed graph representing an abstraction of the possible evolutions of the network over time. It abstracts from the concrete semantics by ignoring the concrete values being communicated and considering both possible outcomes for every conditional. Nodes contain possible states of the network, and edges connect nodes that are related by execution of one action (the label of the edge).[1]

Edges in the SEG are labeled by *transition labels*, which represent the possible actions executable by the network: value communications (matching a send action with the corresponding receive), label selection (matching selection and offer), and conditionals. For the last there are two labels, representing the two possible outcomes (the "then" and "else" branch, respectively).

$$\lambda ::= \mathsf{p}.e \rightarrow \mathsf{q} \mid \mathsf{p} \rightarrow \mathsf{q}[\ell] \mid \mathsf{p}.e \; \mathtt{then} \mid \mathsf{p}.e \; \mathtt{else}$$

As an example, we show how to build the SEG for the network in Example 2 (see Fig. 1). The main behaviours of the two processes are procedure invocations (node on top). Expanding the corresponding definitions, we find out that the first action by customer is sending to store, while store's first action is receiving from customer. These actions match, so the network can execute an action reducing both store and customer. This results in a new network, which is placed in a new node, and we connect both nodes by the transition label describing the executed action.

The next action by customer is receiving a label from store, but store needs to evaluate a conditional expression to decide which label to send. There are two possible outcomes for these evaluation, so we create two new nodes and label the edges towards them with the corresponding possibilities (then or else). Continuing to expand the else branch leads to a network that is already in the SEG, so we simply add an edge to the node containing that network. The then branch evolves in two steps into a second conditional, whose else branch again creates a loop, while its then branch evolves into a network where all processes has terminated. This concludes the construction of the SEG.

In this example SEG generation went flawlessly, but that is not always the case. We saw that a process trying to send a message must wait for the receiving process to be able to execute a matching receive; this can lead to situations where the network is *deadlocked* – no terms can be executed. In that case, the behaviour of the network cannot be described by a choreography, and the network cannot be extracted.

This algorithm also relies on the fact that network execution is confluent: the success of extraction does not depend on which action is chosen when constructing the SEG, in case several are possible. (This can affect the algorithm's performance, though.) Furthermore, guaranteeing that all possible evolutions of the network are captured requires some care when closing loops: all processes must reduce in every cycle in the SEG. This is achieved by marking processes in the network and checking that every loop contains a node where all processes are marked. These aspects are orthogonal to the current development, and we refer the interested reader to [3] for details.

---

[1] The formal details can be found in [2,3].

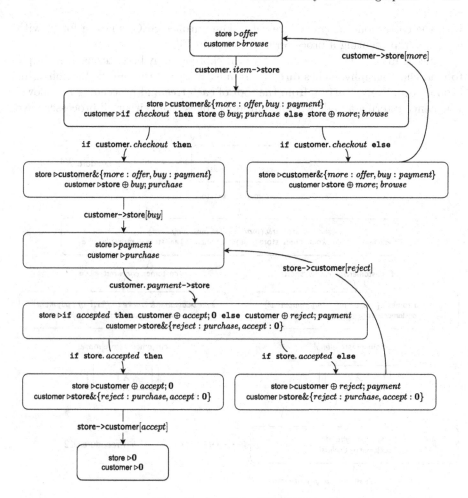

Fig. 1. The SEG of the network from Example 2.

Choreography Construction. The main idea for generating a choreography from a SEG is that edges correspond to choreography actions, so the choreography essentially describes all paths in the SEG. The choreographic way of representing loops is by means of procedures, so each loop in the SEG should become a procedure definition. To achieve this, we first *unroll* the graph by splitting every *loop node* – the nodes that close a loop[2] – into two: a *exit node*, which is the target of all edges previously pointing to the loop node, and a *entry node*, which is the source of all edges previously pointing from the loop node. Entry nodes are given distinct procedure names, and exit nodes are associated

---

[2] Formally, every node with at least two incoming edges – plus the starting node, if it has any incoming edges.

with the corresponding procedure calls. The unrolled SEG is now a forest with each tree representing a procedure, as shown in Fig. 2.

Since transition labels are similar to the choreography body terms, it is simple to read choreography bodies directly from each tree of the unrolled graph. This is done recursively, starting from the root of each tree and proceeding as follows: when encountering a node with no outgoing edges, then either all processes have

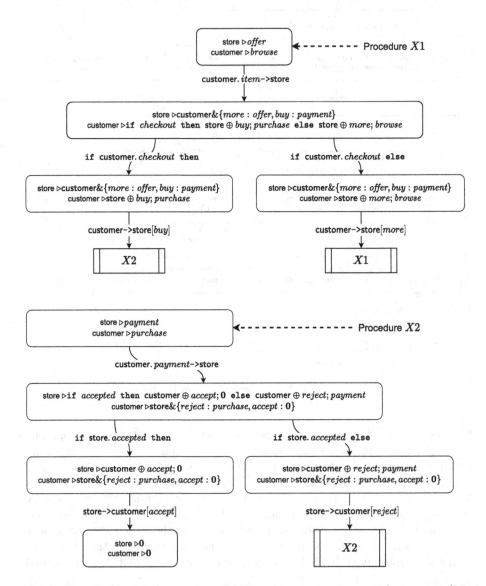

Fig. 2. The unrolling of the graph of Fig. 1 resulting in two trees, each corresponding to a procedure in the SEG to be extracted. For readability, the exit node corresponding to the invocation of $X2$ is depicted twice.

terminated, in which case we return **0**, or the node is an exit node, in which case we return the corresponding procedure invocation. If there is one outgoing edge, that edge represents an interaction, so we return the choreography body that starts with the transition label for that edge and continues as the result of the recursive invocation on the edge's target. If there are two outgoing edges, then we return a conditional choreography body whose two continuations are the results of the recursive calls targets of the two edges, as dictated by those edges' labels.

Example 4. By reading the trees in Fig. 2 in the manner described, we obtain the choreography given earlier in Example 3, where procedures *Buy* and *Pay* are now called $X1$ and $X2$, respectively.

3   Networks and Choreographies with Process Spawning

In this section, we extend the theories of networks and choreographies with support for spawning new processes at runtime.

We start by adding three primitives to the language of behaviours, following ideas from [4].

1. *Spawning of processes.* The language of behaviours is extended with the construct spawn q with B_q continue B, which adds a new process to the network with a new, unique name. The new process gets main behaviour B_q, and inherits its parent's set of procedures, while the parent continues executing B. This term also binds q (a process variable) in B.

2. *Advertising processes.* Since names of newly spawned processes are only known to their parents, we need terms for communicating process names. Process p can "introduce" q and r to each other (send each of them the other's name) by executing term q <-> r; B, while q and r execute the dual actions p?t; B_q and p?t; B_r. Here t is again a variable, which is bound in the continuations B_q and B_r.

3. *Parameterised procedures.* To be able to use processes spawned at runtime in procedures, their syntax is changed so that they can take process names as parameters.

We do not distinguish process names from process variables syntactically, as this simplifies the semantics. We assume as usual that all binders in the same term bind distinct variables, and work up to α-renaming. However, we allow a variable to occur both free and bound in the same term – this is essential for our algorithm.

As previously, the semantics includes a state function σ, mapping each process to a value (its memory state). The new ingredient is a graph of connections $\mathcal{G}$ between processes, connecting pairs of process that are allowed to communicate. The choice of the initial graph allows for modelling different network topologies. We use the notation p $\leftrightarrow$ q $\in \mathcal{G}$ to denote that p and q are connected in $\mathcal{G}$, and

$\mathcal{G} \cup \{p \leftrightarrow q\}$ to denote the graph obtained from $\mathcal{G}$ by adding an edge between p and q.

Figure 3 includes some representative rules of this extended semantics.[3]

$$\frac{p \leftrightarrow q \in \mathcal{G} \quad e \downarrow_p^\sigma v}{p \triangleright q!e; B_1 \mid q \triangleright p?; B_2, \sigma, \mathcal{G} \xrightarrow{p.v \to q} p \triangleright B_1 \mid q \triangleright B_2, \sigma[q \mapsto v], \mathcal{G}} \; \text{N|COM}$$

$$\frac{p \leftrightarrow q \in \mathcal{G} \quad p \leftrightarrow r \in \mathcal{G}}{p \triangleright q \Leftrightarrow r; B_p \mid q \triangleright p?r; B_q \mid r \triangleright p?q; B_r, \sigma, \mathcal{G}} \; \text{N|INTRO}$$
$$\xrightarrow{p.q \Leftrightarrow r}$$
$$p \triangleright B_p \mid q \triangleright B_q \mid r \triangleright B_r, \sigma, \mathcal{G} \cup \{q \leftrightarrow r\}$$

$$\frac{}{p \triangleright \textbf{spawn } q \textbf{ with } B_q \textbf{ continue } B, \sigma, \mathcal{G}} \; \text{N|SPAWN}$$
$$\xrightarrow{p \text{ spawns } q}$$
$$p \triangleright B \mid q \triangleright B_q, \sigma, \mathcal{G} \cup \{p \leftrightarrow q\}$$

Fig. 3. New semantics of networks, selected rules.

Rule N|COM describes a communication. Process p wants to send the result of evaluating e to process q, and q is expecting to receive from p. These processes can communicate, and the result v of evaluating e at p is sent and stored in q (premise $e \downarrow_p^\sigma v$). The difference from the previous semantics is the presence of the additional premise $p \leftrightarrow q \in \mathcal{G}$, which checks that these two processes are allowed to communicate.

Rule N|INTRO is similar, but process names are communicated instead, and the communication graph is updated. For simplicity, instead of explicitly substituting variables for process names, we assume that the behaviours of q and r have previous been α-renamed appropriately (this kind of simplifications based on α-renaming are standard in process calculi [18]).

Rule N|SPAWN creates a new process q into the network with a unique name, and adds an edge between it and its parent to the network. Note that q is distinct from other process names in the network.

Choreographies get two corresponding actions: p **spawns** q; C and p.q <> r; C. Procedures also become parameterized. At the choreography level we do not require process variables except in procedure definitions (which are replaced by process names when called); we assume that all names of spawned processes are unique (again treating **spawn** actions as binders and α-renaming in procedure bodies when needed at invocation time).

The corresponding rules for the semantics are given in Fig. 4.

Example 5. We illustrate a network with process spawning by writing Example 1 in our language. The client sends a request to an entry-point, which then

---
[3] For the complete semantics, see the technical report [9].

$$\frac{p \leftrightarrow q \in \mathcal{G} \quad e \downarrow_p^\sigma v}{p.e \rightarrow q; C, \sigma, \mathcal{G} \xrightarrow{p.v \rightarrow q} C, \sigma[q \mapsto v], \mathcal{G}} \text{ C|COM}$$

$$\frac{p \leftrightarrow q \in \mathcal{G} \quad p \leftrightarrow r \in \mathcal{G}}{p.q \leftrightarrow r; C, \sigma, \mathcal{G} \xrightarrow{p.q \leftrightarrow r} C, \sigma, \mathcal{G} \cup \{q \leftrightarrow r\}} \text{ C|INTRO}$$

$$\frac{}{p \text{ spawns } q; C, \sigma, \mathcal{G} \xrightarrow{p \text{ spawns } q} C, \sigma, \mathcal{G} \cup \{p \leftrightarrow q\}} \text{ C|SPAWN}$$

Fig. 4. New semantics of choreographies, selected rules.

spawns an instance to handle the request, which gets introduced to the client. The instance sends the client the result, and the client either makes another request or terminates the connection. Additional requests spawn new instances, since requests may differ in kind – this is handled by the previous instance to reduce load on the entry-point.

```
client {                          | entry {
    def X(s){                     |     def X(this){
        s?w; w?; if more          |         spawn worker with
            then w⊕next; X(w)      |             this?client; client!res;
            else w⊕end; 0         |             client&{ next: X
    }                             |             (worker), end: 0 }
    main{ entry!req; X(entry) }   |         continue worker <-> client; 0
}                                 |     }
                                  |     main{ client?; X(entry) }
                                  | }
```

After the initial communication and procedure call, variable w in client needs to be renamed to worker in order for the next communication to reduce.

4 Extraction with Process Spawning

In the presence of spawning, the intuitive process of extraction described earlier no longer works: since a network can generate an unbounded number of new processes, there is no guarantee that the SEG is finite and, as a consequence, that the procedure terminates.

However, we observe that since networks are finite and can only reduce to networks built from their subterms, there is only a finite number of possible behaviours for processes that are spawned at runtime. Therefore we can keep SEGs finite if we allow renaming processes when connecting nodes. This intuition is key to our development.

Example 6. Consider the network from Example 5 and its SEG, shown in Fig. 5. The dotted part shows the network that would be generated by symbolic execution as described earlier. By allowing renaming of processes, we can close a loop by applying the mapping {client ↦ client, entry/worker0 ↦ entry}. The parameters w and worker are both variables mapping to entry/worker0, and since entry has terminated, the remapping makes the dotted node equivalent to the second node of the SEG, as shown by the loop. For simplicity we only show the process variables that are changed by the mapping, i.e., we omit client ↦ client.

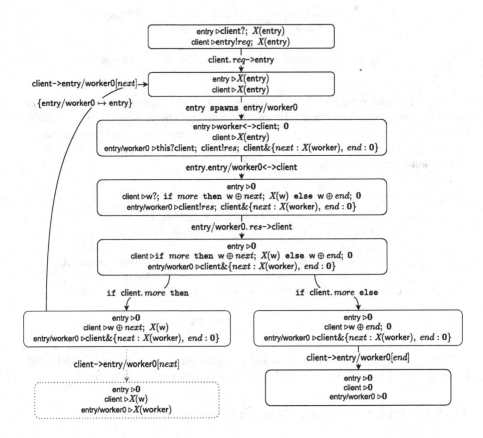

Fig. 5. The SEG of the network in Example 5.

4.1   Generating SEGs

Formally, we define an abstract semantics for networks that makes two changes with respect to the concrete semantics given above. First, we remove all information about states σ (and as a consequence about the actual values being communicated), as in [2]. Secondly, we now treat *all* process names as variables, and replace the communication graph $\mathcal{G}$ by a partial function γ mapping pairs of a process name and a process variable to process names: intuitively, $\gamma(\mathsf{p}, \mathsf{q})$

returns the name of the actual process that p locally identifies as q. If $\gamma(p,q)$ is undefined, then p does not know who to communicate with. We assume that initially $\gamma(p,p) = p$ for all p, and that, for all p and q, either $\gamma(p,q) = q$ (meaning that p knows q's name and is allowed to communicate with it) or $\gamma(p,q)$ is undefined (meaning that p is not connected to q and cannot communicate with it) – this allows us to model different initial network topologies. Figure 6 shows the abstract versions of the rules previously shown.

$$\frac{r \downarrow_p^\gamma q \quad s \downarrow_q^\gamma p}{p \triangleright r!e; B_1 \mid q \triangleright s?; B_2, \gamma \xrightarrow{p.e \to q} p \triangleright B_1 \mid q \triangleright B_2, \gamma} \ \text{N}|\text{Com}$$

$$\frac{s \downarrow_p^\gamma q \quad t \downarrow_p^\gamma r \quad u \downarrow_q^\gamma p \quad v \downarrow_r^\gamma p}{p \triangleright s <> t; B_p \mid q \triangleright u?w; B_q \mid r \triangleright v?x; B_r, \gamma} \ \text{N}|\text{Intro}$$
$$\xrightarrow{p.q <> r}$$
$$p \triangleright B_p \mid q \triangleright B_q \mid r \triangleright B_r, \gamma[\langle q,w\rangle \mapsto r][\langle r,x\rangle \mapsto u]$$

$$\frac{}{p \triangleright \textbf{spawn } q \textbf{ with } B_q \textbf{ continue } B, \gamma} \ \text{N}|\text{Spawn}$$
$$\xrightarrow{p \text{ spawns } q}$$
$$p \triangleright B \mid r \triangleright B_q, \gamma[\langle p,q\rangle \mapsto r][\langle r,p\rangle \mapsto p]$$

Fig. 6. Abstract semantics of networks, selected rules

Example 7. It is easy to check that the SEG shown in Fig. 5 follows the rules in Fig. 6. Initially, the variable mapping is the identity, and this remains unchanged after the first communication.

γ	entry	client	worker	w
entry	entry	client	—	—
client	entry	client	—	—

When entry spawns the new process entry/worker0, this name is associated to entry's local variable worker according to rule N|SPAWN. So the variable mapping is now given by the following table.

γ	entry	client	worker	w
entry	entry	client	entry/worker0	—
client	entry	client	—	—
entry/worker0	entry	—	—	—

Next, entry introduces entry/worker0 and client to each other; client uses the local name w for the new process. According to rule N|INTRO, the variable mapping is now the following.

γ	entry	client	worker	w
entry	entry	client	entry/worker0	—
client	entry	client	—	entry/worker0
entry/worker0	entry	client	—	—

To determine whether we can close a loop in the SEG, we need the following definitions.

Definition 1. *Two networks N and N' are equivalent if there exists a total bijective mapping M from processes in N to processes in N', such that, for all processes* p:

- *if* p *has main behaviour B, then $M(\mathsf{p})$ has main behaviour $M(B)$ (where M is extended homeomorphically to behaviours);*
- *if* p *has not terminated and $X(\tilde{\mathsf{q}}) = B$ is a procedure definition in* p, *then $X = M_{\mathsf{q}}(B)$ is a procedure definition in $M(\mathsf{p})$, where M_{q} maps every process in $\tilde{\mathsf{q}}$ to itself and every other process* r *to $M(\mathsf{r})$.*

To close a loop in the SEG, we also need to look at the variable mappings γ.

Definition 2. *Two nodes N, γ and N', γ' in a SEG are behaviourally equivalent if:*

- *There exists a series of reductions $\tilde{\lambda}$ in the SEG such that $N, \gamma \xrightarrow{\tilde{\lambda}}^{*} N', \gamma'$;*
- *There exists a mapping function M that proves N and N' are equivalent.*
- *If $M(\mathsf{p}) = \mathsf{q}$, $\gamma(\mathsf{p}, \mathsf{a}) = \mathsf{b}$, $\gamma'(\mathsf{q}, \mathsf{a}) = \mathsf{c}$, and there is a reduction accessible from N, γ that evaluates $\gamma^{*}(\mathsf{p}, \mathsf{a})$ for some intermediary γ^{*}, then $M(\mathsf{b}) = \mathsf{c}$.*

The last point of the definition only applies to variables actually evaluated in reductions of N. This makes extraction more efficient (as more nodes are equivalent): a variable might have been used for a previous step in the evolution up to N, σ, but if it remains unused thereafter it does not affect the behaviour anymore, and can be ignored.

Lemma 1. *Let N, γ and N', γ' be behaviourally equivalent nodes in a SEG for a given network. The graph obtained by redirecting all edges coming into N', γ' to N, γ and removing the nodes that are no longer accessible from the root is also a SEG for the original network.*

Our implementation simply looks for a suitable N, γ when N', γ' is generated, and records the mapping M in the edge leading to N, γ.

Termination. As we mentioned at the start of this section, our algorithm can only generate a finite number of behaviours for each process involved in the network. This is enough to guarantee termination, following the arguments in [2], unless the number of processes in the network is allowed to grow unboundedly.

This situation can occur if processes are spawned in a loop, faster than they terminate, making the number of processes increase for every iteration. Such networks embody a resource leak, and they cannot be extracted by our theory. To ensure termination, our algorithm must be able to detect resource leaks, which is an undecidable problem. We deal with it as follows: when a new candidate node is generated, we check whether there is a *surjective* mapping with the properties described above such that there are at least two process values mapped to the same process name. If this happens, the algorithm returns failure. The interested reader can find some examples of networks with resource leaks in the technical report [9].

4.2 Generating the Choreography

Building a choreography from a SEG is similar to the original case. The main change deals with procedure calls: we use the variable mappings in edges that close loops to determine their parameters and arguments.

When unrolling the SEG, each node corresponding to a procedure definition gets a list of parameters corresponding to the process names[4] that appear in the co-domain of any variable mapping in an edge leading to that node. Each procedure call is then appended to the reverse images of these processes by the mapping in the edge leading to it. Note that the edges do not contain process names that are mapped to themselves; as such, processes that are the same in all maps will not appear as arguments to the extracted procedure. A consequence of this is that some procedures may get an empty set of arguments.

After this transformation the choreography can again be extracted by recursively traversing the resulting forest.

We formulate the correctness of our extraction procedure in terms of strong bisimilarity [19].

Theorem 1. *If C is a choreography extracted from a network N, then $C \sim N$.*

Example 8. We return to the network in Example 5, whose SEG was shown in Fig. 5. The only loop node has two incoming edges, one with empty (identity) mapping and another with {entry/worker0 $\mapsto$ entry}. Therefore this node is extracted to a procedure $X1$ with one process variable entry. The original call simply instantiates this parameter as itself, while the recursive call replaces it with entry/worker0.

The choreography extracted from this SEG is thus the following.

```
def X1(entry) {
    entry spawns entry/worker0;  entry.entry/worker0 <-> client;
```

---

[4] Assuming some predefined ordering of process names.

```
    entry/worker0.res -> client;
    if client.more
        then client -> entry/worker0[next]; X1(entry/worker0)
        else client -> entry/worker0[end]; 0
}
main { client.req -> entry; X1(entry) }
```

4.3   Implementation and Limitations

The extension of the original extraction algorithm to networks with process spawning has been implemented in Java. It can successfully extract the networks in the examples given here, as well as a number of randomly generated tests following the ideas from [3]. Due to space constraints, we do not report on the details of our testing strategy, which is an extension of the strategy presented in detail in [3], extended in the natural way to include networks with process spawning and introduction.

Since our language only allows for tail recursion, divide-and-conquer algorithms such as mergesort are currently still not extractable, and our next plan is to extend the algorithm to deal with general recursion. This is not a straightforward extension, as our way of constructing the SEG has no way of getting past a potentially infinite recursive subterm to its continuation.[5]

Another example of an unextractable network, which does not use general recusion, is the following.

```
s {
    def X(p,t){
        if cont then spawn q with X(t,q) continue q?; p!m; 0 else p!m; 0
    }
    main{ X(p,s) }
} |
p{s?; stop}
```

Although the spawned processes behave as their parent, the entire network never repeats itself, and extraction fails: extracting a choreography would require closing a loop where some processes did not reduce. This is essentially the same limitation already discussed in [3], and cannot be avoided: given that the problem of determining whether a network can be represented by a choreography is in general undecidable [2], soundness of our algorithm implies that such networks will always exist.

5   Conclusion

We showed how the state-of-the-art algorithm for choreography extraction [2,3] could be extended to accommodate for networks with process spawning. This

---

[5] This was also the reason for only including tail recursion in the original work [2].

adaptation requires allowing processes names to change dynamically, so that the total number of networks that needs to be consider remains finite. The resulting theory captures examples including loops where processes that are spawned at runtime take over for other processes that terminate in the meantime. This extension also required adding parameterised procedures to the network and choreography language, and including a form of resource leak detection to ensure termination.

A working implementation of choreography extraction with process spawning is available at [10].

References

1. Carbone, M., Montesi, F., Schürmann, C.: Choreographies, logically. Distrib. Comput. **31**(1), 51–67 (2017). https://doi.org/10.1007/s00446-017-0295-1
2. Cruz-Filipe, L., Larsen, K.S., Montesi, F.: The paths to choreography extraction. In: Esparza, J., Murawski, A.S. (eds.) FoSSaCS 2017. LNCS, vol. 10203, pp. 424–440. Springer, Heidelberg (2017). https://doi.org/10.1007/978-3-662-54458-7_25
3. Cruz-Filipe, L., Larsen, K.S., Montesi, F., Safina, L.: Implementing choreography extraction. CoRR abs/2205.02636 (2022). https://arxiv.org/abs/2205.02636. Submitted for publication
4. Cruz-Filipe, L., Montesi, F.: Procedural choreographic programming. In: Bouajjani, A., Silva, A. (eds.) FORTE 2017. LNCS, vol. 10321, pp. 92–107. Springer, Cham (2017). https://doi.org/10.1007/978-3-319-60225-7_7
5. Cruz-Filipe, L., Montesi, F.: A core model for choreographic programming. Theor. Comput. Sci. **802**, 38–66 (2020). https://doi.org/10.1016/j.tcs.2019.07.005
6. Honda, K., Yoshida, N., Carbone, M.: Multiparty asynchronous session types. J. ACM **63**(1), 9 (2016). https://doi.org/10.1145/2827695
7. International Telecommunication Union: Recommendation Z.120: Message sequence chart (1996)
8. Kjær, B.A.: Implementing choreography extraction in Java. Bachelor thesis, University of Southern Denmark (2020)
9. Kjær, B.A., Cruz-Filipe, L., Montesi, F.: From infinity to choreographies: extraction for unbounded systems. CoRR abs/2207.08884 (2022). https://arxiv.org/abs/2207.08884. Technical report
10. Kjær, B.A.: Choreographic extractor (2022). https://doi.org/10.5281/zenodo.6554763
11. Lange, J., Tuosto, E.: Synthesising choreographies from local session types. In: Koutny, M., Ulidowski, I. (eds.) CONCUR 2012. LNCS, vol. 7454, pp. 225–239. Springer, Heidelberg (2012). https://doi.org/10.1007/978-3-642-32940-1_17
12. Lange, J., Tuosto, E., Yoshida, N.: From communicating machines to graphical choreographies. In: Rajamani, S.K., Walker, D. (eds.) Proceedings of the 42nd Annual ACM SIGPLAN-SIGACT Symposium on Principles of Programming Languages, POPL 2015, Mumbai, 15–17 January 2015, pp. 221–232. ACM (2015). https://doi.org/10.1145/2676726.2676964
13. Montesi, F.: Choreographic programming. Ph.D. Thesis, IT University of Copenhagen (2013). https://www.fabriziomontesi.com/files/choreographic-programming.pdf
14. Montesi, F.: Introduction to Choreographies. Cambridge University Press (2022). Accepted for publication

15. Object Management Group: Business process model and notation (2011). http://www.omg.org/spec/BPMN/2.0/
16. Object Management Group: Unified modelling language, version 2.5.1 (2017)
17. Safina, L.: Formal methods and patterns for microservices. Ph.D. thesis, University of Southen Denmark (2019)
18. Sangiorgi, D.: πI: a symmetric calculus based on internal mobility. In: Mosses, P.D., Nielsen, M., Schwartzbach, M.I. (eds.) CAAP 1995. LNCS, vol. 915, pp. 172–186. Springer, Heidelberg (1995). https://doi.org/10.1007/3-540-59293-8_194
19. Sangiorgi, D.: Introduction to Bisimulation and Coinduction. Cambridge University Press (2011). https://doi.org/10.1017/CBO9780511777110

Logic Programming

Typed SLD-Resolution: Dynamic Typing for Logic Programming

João Barbosa(✉)[ID], Mário Florido[ID], and Vítor Santos Costa[ID]

LIACC, INESC, Dep. de Ciência de Computadores Faculdade de Ciências,
Universidade do Porto, rua do Campo Alegre s/n 4169-007, Porto, Portugal
{joao.barbosa,amflorido,vscosta}@fc.up.pt

Abstract. The semantic foundations for logic programming are usually separated into two different approaches. The operational semantics, which uses SLD-resolution, the proof method that computes answers in logic programming, and the declarative semantics, which sees logic programs as formulas and its semantics as models. Here, we define a new operational semantics called TSLD-resolution, which stands for Typed SLD-resolution, where we include a value "wrong", that corresponds to the detection of a type error at run-time. For this we define a new typed unification algorithm. Finally we prove the correctness of TSLD-resolution with respect to a typed declarative semantics.

Keywords: Logic programming · Operational semantics · Types

1 Introduction

Types play an important role in the verification and debugging of programming languages, and have been the subject of significant research in the logic programming community [2,3,9,12,14,15,18,20,23,25,26,28,29]. Most research has been driven by the desire to perform compile-time checking. One important line of this work views types as approximation of the program semantics [7,9,14,28,29]. A different approach relies on asking the user to provide the type information, thus filtering the set of admissible programs [2,18,23,26]. In practice, static type-checking is not widely used in actual Prolog systems, but Prolog systems do rely on dynamic typing to ensure that system built-in parameters are called with acceptable arguments, such as *is/2*. In fact, the Prolog ISO standard defines a set of predefined types and typing violations [10].

Motivated by these observations, we propose a step forward in the dynamic type checking of logic programs: to extend unification with a type checking mechanism. Type checking will thus become a core part of the resolution engine. This extension enables the detection of several bugs in Prolog programs which are rather difficult to capture in the standard untyped language, such as the unintended switch of arguments in a predicate call. This approach can also be used to help in the tracing of bugs in the traditional Prolog *Four-Port Model* debugging

A. Villanueva (Ed.): LOPSTR 2022, LNCS 13474, pp. 123–141, 2022.
https://doi.org/10.1007/978-3-031-16767-6_7

approach. In classical programming languages, type-checking essentially captures the use of functions on arguments of a type different from the expected. The parallel in logic programming is to capture type errors in queries applied to arguments of a different type. This is the essence of our new operational mechanism, here called *Typed SLD (TSLD)*. Following Milner's argument on wrong programs [22], type errors will be denoted by an extra value, *wrong*; unification may succeed, fail, or be *wrong*. As discussed in prior work, a three-valued semantics provides a natural framework for describing the new unification [2]. We name the new evaluation mechanism, that extends unification with type checking thus performing dynamic typing, *Typed SLD (TSLD)*. Let us now present a simple example of the use of TSLD-resolution:

Example 1. Consider the following program consisting of the three facts:

```
p(0).
p(1).
p(a).
```

Let □ stand for success, *false* for failure and *wrong* for a run-time error. Assuming that constants 1 and *a* have different types (in this case, *int* and *atom*, respectively), the TSLD-tree for the query $p(1)$ is:

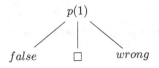

Fig. 1. TSLD-tree

In the following we prove that TSLD-resolution is correct with respect to a new typed declarative semantics for logic programming based on the existence of several different semantic domains, for the interpretation of terms, instead of the usual Herbrand universe domain. The use of different domains for the semantics of logic programming is not new [18], but before it was used in a prescriptive typing approach where types were mandatory for every syntactic objects: functors, variables, and predicates. Here we assume that only constants and function symbols have predefined types. Type correctness in the form of a reformulation of subject-reduction for SLD-resolution was defined in [11] for a typed version of logic programs where also every syntactic objects must be typed statically. To semantically deal with dynamic typing here we define a new version of SLD (Typed SLD) and prove its soundness with respect to a new declarative semantics. In another previous work [26] dynamic type checking of Prolog predicates was done in two different scenarios: on calls from untyped to typed code using program transformation, and on calls to untyped code from typed code to check whether the untyped code satisfies previously made type annotations. In this previous work type annotations for predicates were necessary in both scenarios and the semantic soundness of these run-time checks was not studied. Here we do a semantic study of dynamic typing and use it to show that a new operational mechanism detecting run-time errors is sound. For this we use predefined types only for constants and function symbols.

The paper is organised as follows. Section 2 reviews some preliminary background concepts with the necessary definitions and results on the theory of types and logic programming, and sets the grounds for subsequent developments. In Sect. 3 we present the important new notion of *typed unification*, present the use of different *types* for constant symbols, and show that typed unification extends standard first order unification in the sense that when it succeeds the result is the same. Section 4 presents *TSLD-resolution*. We define the notion of *TSLD-derivation step* and *TSLD-tree*, showing how run-time type errors are detected during program evaluation. We also distinguish the notion of a type error in the program from the notion of a type error in the query with respect to a program. In Sect. 5, we define a new declarative semantics for logic programming based on our previous work [2] using a three-valued logic which uses the value *wrong* to denote run-time type errors, define ill-typed programs and queries, and show that TSLD-resolution is sound with respect to this declarative semantics. Finally, in Sect. 6, we conclude and point out some research directions for future work. A version of this paper with the full proofs can be found in [4].

2 Preliminary Concepts

In this section we will present concepts that are relevant both to the definitions of the operational and declarative semantics for logic programming. These concepts include the three-valued logic that will be used throughout the paper, defined initially in [17], and the definition of our syntax for types, terms, and programs.

2.1 Three-Valued Logic

The three-valued logic used in this paper is the Weak Kleene logic [17], later interpreted by [6] and [5]. As in our previous work [2] the third value is called *wrong* and represents a (dynamic) type error. In this logic, the value *wrong* propagates through every connective, which is a behaviour we want the type error value to have. In Table 1, we describe the connectives in the logic.

Table 1. Connectives of the three-valued logic - conjunction and disjunction

∧	true	false	wrong
true	true	false	wrong
false	false	false	wrong
wrong	wrong	wrong	wrong

∨	true	false	wrong
true	true	true	wrong
false	true	false	wrong
wrong	wrong	wrong	wrong

The negation of logic values is defined as: $\neg true = false$, $\neg false = true$ and $\neg wrong = wrong$. And implication is defined as: $p \to q \equiv (\neg p) \vee q$.

Note that whenever the value *wrong* occurs in any connective in the logic, the result of applying that connective is *wrong*.

2.2 Types

In this paper we fix the set of base types *int, float, atom* and *string*, an enumerable set of compound types $f(\sigma_1, \cdots, \sigma_n)$, where f is a function symbol and σ_i are types, and an enumerable set of functional types of the form $\sigma_1 \times \cdots \times \sigma_n \to \sigma$, where σ_i and σ are types.

We use this specific choice of base types because they correspond to types already present, to some extent, in Prolog. Some built-in predicates already expect integers, floating point numbers, or atoms.

2.3 Terms

The alphabet of logic programming is composed of symbols from disjoint classes. For our language of terms we have an infinite set of variables **Var**, an infinite set of function symbols **Fun**, parenthesis and the comma [1].

Terms are defined as follows:

- a variable is a term,
- if f is an n-ary function symbol and $t_1, \ldots, t_n$ are terms, then $f(t_1, \ldots, t_n)$ is a term,
- if f is a function symbol of arity zero, then f is a term and it is called a constant.

A ground term is a term with no variables. In the rest of the paper we assume that ground terms are assumed to be typed, meaning that each constant has associated to it a base type and for any ground compound term $f(t_1, \cdots t_n)$, the function symbol f (of arity $n \geq 1$) has associated to it a functional type of the form $\sigma_1 \times \cdots \times \sigma_n \to f(\sigma_1, \cdots, \sigma_n)$. Note that variables are not statically typed, but, as we will see in the forthcoming sections, type checking of the use of variables will be made dynamically through TSLD-resolution.

2.4 Programs and Queries

We now extend our language of terms to a language of programs by adding an infinite set of predicate symbols **Pred** and the reverse implication $\leftarrow$.

The definition of atoms, queries, clauses and programs is the usual one [1]:

- an atom is either a predicate symbol p with arity n, applied to terms $t_1, \ldots, t_n$, which we write as $p(t_1, \ldots, t_n)$. We will represent atoms by H, A, B;
- a query is a finite sequence of atoms, which we will represent by $Q, \bar{A}, \bar{B}$;
- a clause is of the form $H \leftarrow \bar{B}$, where H is an atom of the form $p(t_1, \ldots, t_n)$ and $\bar{B}$ is a query;
- a program is a finite set of clauses, which we will represent by P.

The interpretation of queries and clauses is quantified. Every variable that occurs in a query is assumed to be existentially quantified and every variable that occurs in a clause is universally quantified [1].

3   Typed Unification

Solving equality constraints using a unification algorithm [21,24] is the main computational mechanism in logic programming. Logic programming usually uses an untyped term language and assumes a semantic universe composed of all semantic values: the Herbrand universe [1,16].

However, in our work, we assume that the semantic values are split among several disjoint semantic domains and thus equality only makes sense inside each domain. Moreover each type will be mapped to a non-empty semantic domain. To reflect this, unification may now return three different outputs. Besides being successful or failing, unification can now return the *wrong* value. This is the logical value of nonsense and reflects the fact that we are trying to perform unification between terms with different types corresponding to a type error during program evaluation.

A substitution is a mapping from variables to terms, which assigns to each variable X in its domain a term t. We will represent bindings by $X \mapsto t$, substitutions by symbols such as $\theta, \eta, \delta \ldots$, and applying a substitution θ to a term t will be represented by $\theta(t)$. We say $\theta(t)$ is an instance of t.

Substitution composition is represented by $\circ$, i.e., the composition of the substitutions θ and η is denoted $\theta \circ \eta$ and applying $(\theta \circ \eta)(t)$ corresponds to $\theta(\eta(t))$. We can also calculate substitution composition, i.e., $\delta = \theta \circ \eta$ as defined below [1].

Definition 1 (Substitution Composition). *Suppose θ and η are substitutions, such that $\theta = [X_1 \mapsto t_1, \ldots, X_n \mapsto t_n]$ and $\eta = [Y_1 \mapsto t_1', \ldots, Y_m \mapsto t_m']$. Then, composition $\eta \circ \theta$ is calculated by following these steps:*

- *remove from the sequence $X_1 \mapsto \eta(t_1), \ldots, X_n \mapsto \eta(t_n), Y_1 \mapsto t_1', \ldots, Y_m \mapsto t_m'$ the bindings $X_i \mapsto \eta(t_i)$ such that $X_i = \eta(t_i)$ and the elements $Y_i \mapsto t_i'$ for which $\exists X_j . Y_i = X_j$*
- *form a substitution from the resulting sequence.*

A substitution θ is called a unifier of two terms t_1 and t_2 iff $\theta(t_1) = \theta(t_2)$. If such a substitution exists, we say that the two terms are unifiable. In particular, a unifier θ is called a most general unifier (mgu) of two terms t_1 and t_2 if for every other unifier η of t_1 and t_2, $\eta = \delta \circ \theta$, for some substitution δ.

First order unification [24] assumes an untyped universe, so unification between any two terms always makes sense. Therefore, it either returns a mgu between the terms, if it exists, or halts with failure.

We argue that typed unification only makes sense between terms of the same type. Here we will extend a previous unification algorithm [21] to define a *typed unification algorithm*, where failure will be separated into *false*, where two terms are not unifiable but may have the same type, and *wrong*, where the terms cannot have the same type.

Definition 2 (Typed Unification Algorithm). *Let t_1 and t_2 be two terms, and F be a flag that starts true. We create the starting set of equations as*

$S = \{t_1 = t_2\}$, and we will rewrite the pair (S, F) by applying the following rules until it is no longer possible to apply any of them, or until the algorithm halts with wrong. If no rules are applicable, then we output false if the flag is false, or output the solved set S, which can be seen as a substitution.

1. $(\{f(t_1, \ldots, t_n) = f(s_1, \ldots, s_n)\} \cup Rest, F) \rightarrow (\{t_1 = s_1, \ldots, t_n = s_n\} \cup Rest, F)$
2. $(\{f(t_1, \ldots, t_n) = g(s_1, \ldots, s_m)\} \cup Rest, F) \rightarrow wrong$, if $f \neq g$ or $n \neq m$
3. $(\{c = c\} \cup Rest, F) \rightarrow (Rest, F)$
4. $(\{c = d\} \cup Rest, F) \rightarrow (Rest, false)$, if $c \neq d$, and c and d have the same type
5. $(\{c = d\} \cup Rest, F) \rightarrow wrong$, if $c \neq d$, and c and d have different types
6. $(\{c = f(t_1, \ldots, t_n)\} \cup Rest, F) \rightarrow wrong$
7. $(\{f(t_1, \ldots, t_n) = c\} \cup Rest, F) \rightarrow wrong$
8. $(\{X = X\} \cup Rest, F) \rightarrow (Rest, F)$
9. $(\{t = X\} \cup Rest, F) \rightarrow (\{X = t\} \cup Rest, F)$, where t is not a variable and X is a variable
10. $(\{X = t\} \cup Rest, F) \rightarrow (\{X = t\} \cup [X \mapsto t](Rest), F)$, where X does not occur in t and X occurs in $Rest$
11. $(\{X = t\} \cup Rest, F) \rightarrow (Rest, false)$, where X occurs in t and $X \neq t$

Let us illustrate with an example.

Example 2. Let t_1 be $g(X, a, f(1))$ and t_2 be $g(b, Y, f(2))$. We generate the pair $(\{g(X, a, f(1)) = g(b, Y, f(2))\}, true)$, and proceed to apply the rewriting rules.
$(\{g(X, a, f(1)) = g(b, Y, f(2))\}, true) \rightarrow_1$
$(\{X = b, a = Y, f(1) = f(2)\}, true) \rightarrow_{10}$
$(\{X = b, Y = a, f(1) = f(2)\}, true) \rightarrow_1$
$(\{X = b, Y = a, 1 = 2\}, true) \rightarrow_5$
$(\{X = b, Y = a\}, false) \rightarrow false.$

The successful cases of this algorithm are the same as for first order unification [21]. We will prove this result in the following theorem.

Theorem 1 (Conservative with respect to term unification). *Let t_1 and t_2 be two terms. If we apply the Martelli-Montanari algorithm (MM algorithm) to t_1 and t_2 and it returns a set of solved equalities S, then the typed unification algorithm applied to the same two terms is also successful and returns the same set of equalities.*

The following theorem proves typed unification detects run-time type errors.

Theorem 2 (Ill-typed unification). *If the output of the typed unification algorithm is wrong, then there is no substitution θ such that $\theta(t_1)$ and $\theta(t_2)$ have the same type.*

Example 3. Let $t_1 = f(1, g(h(X, 2)), Y)$ and $t_2 = f(Z, g(h(W, a)), 1)$. The typed unification algorithm outputs *wrong*. We can see in Table 2 that there is no substitution θ such that $\theta(t_1) = \theta(t_2)$, nor any substitution θ such that $\theta(t_1)$ has the same type as $\theta(t_2)$, since the highlighted terms cannot have the same type for any substitution.

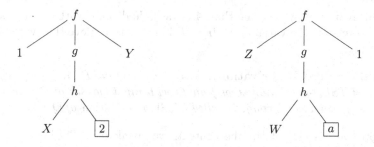

Fig. 2. Tree representation terms t_1 and t_2

4   Operational Semantics

The operational semantics of logic programming describes how answers are computed. Here we define Typed SDL-resolution (TSLD) which returns the third value *wrong* whenever it finds a type error. We start by defining a TSLD-derivation step, which is a variation on the basic mechanism for computing answers to queries in the untyped semantics for logic programming, the SLD-derivation step. The major difference is the use of the typed unification algorithm. Then we create TSLD-derivations by iteratively applying these singular steps. After this, we introduce the concept of TSLD-trees and use it to represent the search space for answers in logic programming. Finally, we interpret the contents of the TSLD-tree.

4.1   TSLD-Derivation

To compute in logic programming, we need a program P and a query Q. We can interpret P as being a set of statements, or rules, and Q as being a question that will be answered by finding an instance $\theta(Q)$ such that $\theta(Q)$ follows from P. The essence of computation in logic programming is then to find such θ [1].

   In our setting the basic step for computation is the TSLD-derivation step. It corresponds to having a non-empty query Q and selecting from Q an atom A. If A unifies with H, where $H \leftarrow \bar{B}$ is an input clause, we replace A in Q by $\bar{B}$ and apply an mgu of A and H to the query.

Definition 3 (TSLD-derivation step). *Consider a non-empty query $Q = \bar{A}_1, A, \bar{A}_2$ and a clause c of the form $H \leftarrow \bar{B}$. Suppose that A unifies (using typed unification) with H and let θ be a mgu of A and H. A is called the* selected *atom of Q. Then we write*

$$\bar{A}_1, A, \bar{A}_2 \underset{c}{\Longrightarrow} \theta(\bar{A}_1, \bar{B}, \bar{A}_2)$$

and call it a TSLD-derivation step. $H \leftarrow \bar{B}$ is called its input clause. *If typed unification between the selected atom A and the input clause c outputs wrong (or false) we write the TSLD-derivation step as $Q \Longrightarrow wrong$ (or $Q \Longrightarrow false, \bar{A}_1, \bar{A}_2$).*

In this definition we assume that A is variable disjoint with H. It is always possible to rename the variables in $H \leftarrow \bar{B}$ in order to achieve this, without loss of generality.

Definition 4 (TSLD-derivation). *Given a program P and a query Q a sequence of TSLD-derivation steps from Q with input clauses of P reaching the empty query, false, or wrong, is called a TSLD-derivation of Q in P.*

If the program is clear from the context, we speak of a TSLD-derivation of the query Q and if the input clauses are irrelevant we drop the reference to them. Informally, a TSLD-derivation corresponds to iterating the process of the TSLD-derivation step. We say that a TSLD-derivation is *successful* if we reach the empty query, further denoted by $\Box$. The composition of the mgus $\theta_1, \ldots, \theta_n$ used in each TSLD-derivation step is the *computed answer substitution* of the query. A TSLD-derivation that reaches *false* is called a *failed derivation* and a TSLD-derivation that reaches *wrong* is called an *erroneous derivation*.

In a TSLD-derivation, at each TSLD-derivation step we have several choices. We choose an atom from the query, a clause from the program, and a mgu. It is proven in [1] that the choice of mgu does not affect the success or failure of an SLD-derivation, as long as the resulting mgu is idempotent. Since for TSLD-derivations the successes are the same as the ones in a corresponding SLD-derivation, then the result still holds for TSLD.

The *selection rule*, i.e., how we choose the selected atom in the considered query, does not influence the success of a TSLD-derivation either [1], however if you stopped as soon as unification returns false, it could prevent us from detecting a type error, in a later atom. Let us show this in the following example.

Example 4. Consider the logic program P consisting of only one fact, $p(X, X)$, and the selection rule that chooses the leftmost atom at each step. p Then, if we stopped when reaching *false*, the query $Q = p(1, 2), p(1, a)$ would have the TSLD-derivation $Q \implies false$, since typed unification between $p(X, X)$ and $p(1, 2)$ outputs *false*. However, the query $Q\prime = p(1, a), p(1, 2)$ has the TSLD-derivation $Q \implies wrong$, since typed unification between $p(X, X)$ and $p(1, a)$ outputs *wrong*.

In fact, as the comma stands for conjunction, and since $wrong \wedge false = false \wedge wrong = wrong$, we have to continue even if typed unification outputs *false* in a step, and check if we ever reach the value *wrong*. In general, for any selection rule S we can construct a query Q such that it is necessary to continue when typed unification outputs *false* for some atom in Q. Therefore, when we reach the value *false* in a TSLD-derivation step, we continue applying steps until either we obtain a value *wrong* from typed unification or we have no more atoms to select. In this last case, we can safely say that we reached *false*. This guarantees independence of the selection rule. For the following example we use the selection rule that always chooses the leftmost atom in a query, which is the selection rule of Prolog.

Example 5. p Let us continue Example 4. The TSLD-derivation for Q is $Q \implies false, p(1, a) \implies wrong$. Let $Q'' = p(1, 2), p(1, 1)$. Then the TSLD-derivation is $Q'' \implies false, p(1, 1) \implies false$.

Note that when we get to $false$ for a typed unification in a TSLD-derivation, we can only output $false$ or $wrong$, so either way it is not a successful derivation.

The selected clause from the program is another choice point we have at each TSLD-derivation step. We will discuss the impact of this choice in the next section.

4.2   TSLD-Tree

When we want to find a successful TSLD-derivation for a query, we need to consider the entire search space, which consists of all possible derivations, choosing all possible clauses for a selected atom. We are considering a fixed selection rule here, so the only thing that changes between derivations is the selected clause. We say that a clause $H \leftarrow \bar{B}$ is *applicable* to an atom A if H and A have the same predicate symbol with the same arity.

Definition 5 (TSLD-tree). *Given a program P and a query Q, a TSLD-tree for $P \cup \{Q\}$ is a tree where branches are TSLD-derivations of $P \cup \{Q\}$ and every node Q has a child for each clause from P applicable to the selected atom of Q.*

Prolog uses the leftmost selection rule, where one always selects the leftmost atom in the query, and since the selection rule does not change the success of a TSLD-derivation we will use this selection rule in the rest of the paper.

Definition 6 (TSLD-tree classification).

- *If a TSLD-tree contains the empty query, we call it* successful.
- *If a TSLD-tree is finite and all its branches are erroneous TSLD-derivations, we call it* finitely erroneous.
- *If a TSLD-tree is finite and it is not successful nor finitely erroneous, we say it is* finitely failed.

Example 6. Let program P be:

```
p(1).
p(2).
q(1).
q(a).
r(X) :- p(X),q(X).
```

and let query Q be $r(1)$. The TSLD-tree for Q and P is the following successful TSLD-tree:

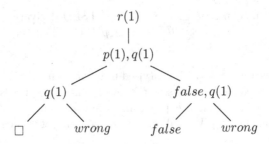

We will present two auxiliary definitions which are needed to clearly define the notion of a type error in a program.

Definition 7 (Generic Query). *Let Q be a query and P a program. We say that Q is a* generic query *of P iff Q is composed of an atom of the form $p(X_1, \ldots, X_n)$ for some predicate symbol p that occurs in the head of at least one clause in P, where $X_1, \ldots, X_n$ are variables that occur only once in the query.*

Example 7. Let P be the program defined as follows:

```
p(X,X).
q(X) :- p(1,a).
```

Then, given the generic query $Q_2 = q(X_1)$, we have the following TSLD-derivation: $q(X_1) \implies p(1,a) \implies wrong$.

Definition 8 (Blamed Clause). *Given a program P and a query Q, a clause c is a* blamed clause *of the TSLD-tree for $P \cup \{Q\}$ if all derivations where c is a input clause are erroneous.*

The blamed clause is a clause in the program which causes a type error. A similar notion was first defined for functional programming languages with the blame calculus [27].

Example 8. Let P be the following program, with clauses c_1, c_2, and c_3, respectively:

```
p(1).
q(a).
q(X) :- p(a).
```

Then for the query $p(2), q(b)$, we have the following TSLD-tree:

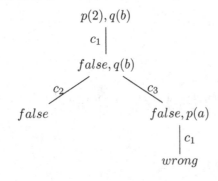

In this case, c_3 is a blamed clause, since every derivation that uses it eventually reaches *wrong*. Note that c_1 is not a blamed clause, because the leftmost branch of the TSLD-tree uses c_1 but is *false*.

Definition 9 (Blamed Set). *Suppose we have a program P. We call the blamed set of P the set of blamed clauses of each generic query of P.*

Definition 10 (Type Error in the Program). *Suppose we have a program P. We say that P has a type error if at least one clause c in the blamed set of P is a blamed clause in every TSLD-tree where it occurs for $P \cup \{Q\}$, where Q is a generic query. We call c an erroneous clause of P.*

Note that if a program does not have a type error, then there is no *blamed clause* in the blamed set of P that always leads to erroneous derivations.

Example 9. Assume the same program from Example 8. Let $Q_1 = p(X1)$ and $Q_2 = q(X1)$ be generic queries of P. The TSLD-trees for $P \cup \{Q_1\}$ and $P \cup \{Q_2\}$ are:

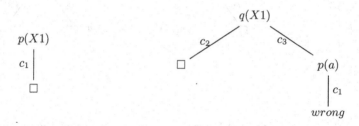

As we can see, the blamed set of P is $\{c_1, c_3\}$, and c_3 is an *erroneous clause* of P. Note that c_1 is not an erroneous clause of P since in the leftmost TSLD-tree, it is used but not a blamed clause.

Intuitively, having a type error in the program means that somewhere in the program we will perform typed unification between two terms that do not have the same type.

Consider a generic query $Q = p(X_1, \ldots, X_n)$. For some derivation, after one step, we will have $\theta(\bar{B})$, where $H \leftarrow \bar{B}$ is a clause in P and θ is a unifier of $p(X_1, \ldots, X_n)$ and H. Since θ, or any other idempotent MGU of $p(X_1, \ldots, X_n)$ and H, is a renaming of $\{X_1 \mapsto t_1, \ldots, X_n \mapsto t_n\}$, where $H = p(t_1, \ldots, t_n)$, and since the variables $X_1, \ldots, X_n$ do not occur in $\bar{B}$ because the clause is variable disjoint from the query by definition, then $\theta(\bar{B}) = \bar{B}$.

After selecting the *erroneous clause* c, every TSLD-derivation is such that $Q_0 \implies \cdots \implies Q_n \implies$ *wrong*. Thus, at step Q_n, the selected atom comes from the program and every mgu applied up to this point is from substitutions arising from the program itself and not the query. Therefore, the type error was in the program.

Definition 11 (Type Error in the Query). *Let P be a program and Q be a query. If there is no type error in P and the TSLD-tree is finitely erroneous, then we say that there is a* type error in the query Q *with respect to P.*

If there is no type error in the program P but the TSLD-tree is finitely erroneous, then that error must have occurred in a unification between terms from the query and the program. We then say that the type error is in the query.

Example 10. Now suppose we have the following program:

```
p(1).
q(a).
q(X) :- p(X).
```

Let us name the clauses c_1, c_2, and c_3, respectively. The following trees are the TSLD-tree for generic queries, and the TSLD-tree for the query $Q = q(1.1)$.

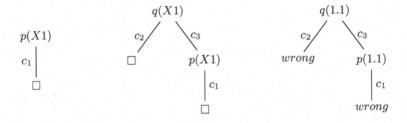

From the two leftmost TSLD-trees, we can conclude that the program has no *erroneous clause*, which means that there is no type error in the program. The rightmost tree is finitely erroneous, therefore there is a type error in query Q.

5   Declarative Semantics

The declarative semantics of logic programming is, in opposition to the operational one, a definition of what the programs compute. The fact that logic programming can be interpreted this way supports the fact that logic programming is declarative [1]. In this section, we will introduce the concept of interpretations, which takes us from the syntactic programs we saw and used so far into the semantic universe, giving them meaning. With this interpretation we will redefine a declarative semantics for logic programming first defined in [2] and prove a connection between both the operational and the declarative semantics.

5.1   Domains

Let U be a non-empty set of semantic values, which we will call the universe. We assume that the universe is divided into domains such that each ground type is mapped to a non-empty domain. Thus, U is divided into domains as follows: $U = Int + Float + Atom + String + A_1 + \cdots + A_n + F + Bool + W$, where Int is the domain of integer numbers, $Float$ is the domain of floating point numbers, $Atom$ is the domain of non-numeric constants, $String$ is the domain of strings, A_i are domains for trees, where each domain has trees whose root is the same functor symbol and its n-children belong to n domains and F is the domain of functions. Moreover, we define $Bool$ as the domain containing $true$ and $false$, and W as the domain with the single value $wrong$, corresponding to a run-time error. We will call Int, $Float$, $Atom$, and $String$ the base domains, and $A_1, \ldots, A_n$ the tree domains. In particular, we can see that constants are separated into several predefined base domains, one for each base type, while complex terms, i.e. trees, are separated into domains depending on the principal function symbol (root) and the n-tuple inside the parenthesis (n-children).

5.2   Interpretations

Every constant of type T is associated with a semantic value in one of the base domains, Int, $Float$, $Atom$, or $String$, corresponding to T. Every function symbol f of arity n in our language is associated with a mapping f_U from any n-tuple of base or tree domains $\delta_1 \times \cdots \times \delta_n$ to the domain $F(\delta_1, \ldots, \delta_n)$, which is the domain of trees whose root is f and the n-children are in the domains δ_i.

To define the semantic value for terms, we will first have to define states. States, Σ, are mappings from variables into values of the universe. We also define a function $domain$ that when applied to a semantic value returns the domain it belongs to. The semantic value of a term is defined as follows:

$$\llbracket X \rrbracket_\Sigma = \Sigma(X)$$
$$\llbracket c \rrbracket_\Sigma = c_U$$
$$\llbracket f(t_1, \ldots, t_n) \rrbracket_\Sigma = f_U(\llbracket t_1 \rrbracket_\Sigma, \ldots, \llbracket t_n \rrbracket_\Sigma)$$

An *interpretation* I associates every predicate symbol p with a function $I(p)$ in F, such that the output of the function $I(p)$ is the domain $Bool$ and the input is a union of tuples of domains. For each tuple that is in its domain, the function $I(p)$ either returns $true$ or $false$. We will use $\llbracket \rrbracket_{I,\Sigma}$ to denote the semantics of an *expression E*, which can be an atom, a query, or a clause, in an interpretation I, and define it as follows:

$$
\begin{aligned}
\llbracket p(t_1, \ldots, t_n) \rrbracket_{I,\Sigma} &= \textbf{if}(domain(\llbracket t_1 \rrbracket_\Sigma), \ldots, domain(\llbracket t_n \rrbracket_\Sigma)) \subseteq domain(I(p)) \\
&\quad \textbf{then } I(p)(\llbracket t_1 \rrbracket_\Sigma, \ldots, \llbracket t_n \rrbracket_\Sigma) \\
&\quad \textbf{else } wrong \\
\llbracket A_1, \ldots, A_n \rrbracket_{I,\Sigma} &= \llbracket A_1 \rrbracket_{I,\Sigma} \wedge \cdots \wedge \llbracket A_n \rrbracket_{I,\Sigma} \\
\llbracket q(t_1, \ldots, t_n) : -\bar{B} \rrbracket_{I,\Sigma} &= (\llbracket \bar{B} \rrbracket_{I,\Sigma} \rightarrow (\llbracket q(t_1, \ldots, t_n) \rrbracket_{I,\Sigma}))
\end{aligned}
$$

Note that if the clause is of the form $H \leftarrow$, then its semantics is equivalent to that of H.

5.3 Models

The term language and their semantic values are fixed, thus each interpretation I is determined by the interpretation of the predicate symbols. Interpretations differ from each other only in the functions $I(p)$ they associate to each predicate p defined in P. We now define a *context* as a set Δ of pairs of the form $X : D$, where X is a variable that occurs only once in the set, and D is a domain. We say that Σ complies with Δ if every binding $X : v$ in Σ is such that $(X : D) \in \Delta$ and $v \in D$.

An interpretation I is a *model* of E in the context Δ iff for every state Σ that complies with Δ, $[\![E]\!]_{I,\Sigma} = true$. We will denote this as $\Delta \models [\![E]\!]_I$. Given a program P, we say that an interpretation I is a model of P in context Δ if I is a model of every clause in P in context Δ. Here we assume, without loss of generality, that all clauses are variable disjoint with each other. If two expressions E_1 and E_2 are such that every model of E_1 in a context Δ is also a model of E_2 in the context Δ, then we say that E_2 is a semantic consequence of E_1 and represent this by $E_1 \models E_2$.

Suppose two interpretations I_1 and I_2 are models of program P in some context Δ. Suppose, in particular, that for some predicate p of P the associated function is $I_1(p)$ for I_1 and $I_2(p)$ for I_2. Let us call T_i the set of tuples of terms for which $I_i(p)$ outputs *true*, and F_i to the set of tuples of terms for which $I_i(p)$ outputs *false*. We say that I_1 is smaller than I_2 if $T_1 \subseteq T_2$ and, if $T_1 = T_2$, then $F_1 \subseteq F_2$.

We say that a model I of P in context Δ is *minimal* if for every other model I' of P in context Δ, I is smaller than I'.

Example 11. Consider the program P defined below:

```
father(john,mary).
father(phil,john).
grandfather(X,Y) :- father(X,Z), father(Z,Y).
```

Suppose that interpretation I_1 is such that $I_1(p)$ is associated with *grandfather* and $I_1(p) :: Atom \times Atom \rightarrow Bool$. Also, suppose that $I_2(p)$ is associated to *grandfather* in I_2, with the same domain. Suppose that $I_3(p)$, associated in I_3 with *grandfather*, is such that $I_3(p) :: Atom \times Atom \cup Int \times Int \rightarrow Bool$. Let the sets $T_1 = \{(phil, mary)\}$, $T_2 = \{(phil, mary), (john, caroline)\}$, and $T_3 = \{(phil, mary)\}$ be the sets of accepted tuples for $I_1(p)$, $I_2(p)$, and $I_3(p)$, respectively.

Thus, if these interpretations associate the same function $I(q) :: Atom \times Atom \rightarrow Bool$ to *father*, and $T = \{(john, mary), (phil, john)\}$ the set of accepted tuples for $I(q)$, then all I_i are models of P in context $\Delta = \{X : Atom, Y : Atom, Z : Atom\}$. In fact, all states Σ that comply with Δ are such that $[\![grandfather(X,Y) : -father(X,Z), father(Z,Y)]\!]_{I_i,\Sigma}$ is true, for all $i = 1, 2, 3$.

But note that $T_1 \subseteq T_2$, and $T_1 = T_3$, but $F_1 \subseteq F_3$. In fact, any smaller domain or set T_k would not model P. Therefore I_1 is the minimal model of P.

5.4   Type Errors

To calculate the set of accepted tuples for a given interpretation we will use the immediate consequence operator T_P. The T_P operator is traditionally used in the logic programming literature to iteratively calculate the minimal model of a logic program as presented in [1,13,19]. The application $T_P \uparrow \omega(\emptyset)$ calculates the least fixed point of this operator, which corresponds to the minimal model of program P in the untyped semantics of logic programming.

Since for us interpretations for predicates are typed, $T_P \uparrow \omega(\emptyset)$ does not generate an interpretation by itself. Instead it generates a set of atoms S. Then we say that any interpretation I derived from S is such that for all predicates p occurring in S, $I(p) :: (D_{(1,1)} \times \cdots \times D_{(1,n)}) \cup \cdots \cup (D_{(k,1)}, \ldots, D_{(k,n)}) \rightarrow Bool$, where for all i there is at least one atom $p(v_1, \ldots, v_n) \in S$ such that $v_1 \in D_{(i,1)}, \ldots, v_n \in D_{(i,n)}$. Note that these interpretations may not be models of P using our new definition of a model. We are now able to define the notion of *ill-typed program*.

Definition 12 (Ill-typed Program). *Let P be a program. If no interpretation derived from $T_P \uparrow \omega(\emptyset)$ is a model of P, we say that P is an ill-typed program.*

Example 12. Let P be the program defined as:

```
p(1).
p(a).
q(X) :- p(1.1).
```

Then $S = T_P \uparrow \omega(\emptyset) = \{p(1), p(a)\}$. So any interpretation I derived from S is such that $I(p) :: Int \cup Atom \rightarrow Bool$. Therefore for any context Δ, for every Σ that complies with Δ, $[\![q(X) : -p(1.1)]\!]_{I,\Sigma} = wrong$. Therefore no such I is a model of P.

The reason why $T_P \uparrow \omega(\emptyset)$ is always a minimal model of P in the untyped semantics, comes from the fact that whenever a body of a clause is *false* for all states, then the clause is trivially *true* for all states. However in our semantics, since we are separating these cases into *false* and *wrong*, the *wrong* ones do not trivially make the formula *true*, making it *wrong* instead. These are the ill-typed cases.

Lemma 1 (Erroneous Clause Type Error). *Suppose there is a type error in the program with erroneous clause $H \leftarrow A_1, \ldots, A_m$. Then, $\exists A_i = p(t_1, \ldots, t_n)$ such that $\forall p(s_1, \ldots, s_n) \in T_P \uparrow \omega(\emptyset).\forall \Sigma.\exists j. domain([\![t_j]\!]_\Sigma) \neq domain([\![s_j]\!]_\Sigma)$.*

Effectively what this means is that if there is a type error in the program, then the erroneous clause is such that it will not be used to calculate the $T_P \uparrow \omega(\emptyset)$, since at least one of the atoms in its body will never be able to be used in an application of T_P. We can also have a ill-typed query, and we define it as follows.

Definition 13 (Ill-typed Query). *Let P be a program. If any interpretation I derived from $T_P \uparrow \omega(\emptyset)$, such that I models P in some context Δ, is such that I is not a model of Q in the context Δ, then we say that Q is an ill-typed query with respect to P.*

5.5 Soundness of TSLD-resolution

In this section we will prove that TSLD-resolution is sound, i.e. if there is a successful derivation of a query Q in program P with a correct answer substitution θ, then every model of P is also a model of $\theta(Q)$; if there is a type error in the program, then the program is ill-typed; and if there is a type error in the query, the query is ill-typed with respect to the program. To prove this we will introduce the following auxiliary concept.

Definition 14 (Resultant). *Suppose we have a TSLD-derivation step $Q_1 \implies \theta(Q_2)$. Then we define the resultant associated to this step as $\theta(Q_1) \leftarrow Q_2$.*

Lemma 2 (Soundness of resultants). *Let $Q_1 \implies \theta(Q_2)$ be a TSLD-derivation step using input clause c and r be the resultant associated with it. Then:*

1. *$c \models r$;*
2. *for any TSLD-derivation of $P \cup \{Q\}$ with resultants $r_1, \ldots, r_n$, $P \models r_i$ (for all $i \geq 0$).*

Proof of this lemma for the SLD-resolution is in [1]. Since for unifiable terms the typed unification algorithm behaves like first-order unification, the proof still holds.

Theorem 3 (Soundness of TSLD-resolution). *Let P be a program and Q a query. Then:*

1. *Suppose that there exists a successful derivation of $P \cup \{Q\}$, with the correct answer substitution θ. Then $P \models \theta(Q)$.*
2. *Suppose there is a type error in the program. Then P is ill-typed.*
3. *Suppose there is a type error in the query. Then Q is an ill-typed query with respect to P.*

A short note about completeness. As for untyped SLD-resolution, completeness is related to the search for answers in a TSLD-tree. If we use Prolog sequential, top-down, depth-first search with backtracking, then it may result in incompleteness for same cases where the TSLD-tree is infinite, because the exploration of an infinite computation may defer indefinitely the exploration of some alternative computation capable of yielding a correct answer.

6   Conclusions and Future Work

We presented an operational semantics for logic programming, here called TSLD-resolution, which is sensitive to run-time type errors. In this setting type errors are represented by a new value, here called *wrong*, which is added to the usual *fail* and *success* results of evaluation of a query for a given logic program. We have then adapted a previously defined declarative semantics for typed logic programs using a three-valued logic and proved that TSLD-resolution is sound with respect to this semantics. All these new concepts, TSLD, typed unification and the new declarative semantics, revisit and partially extend well-known concepts form the theory of logic programming.

Specially Interpreted Functors: in this paper functors are uninterpreted, such as in Prolog, in the sense that they are just symbols used to build new trees. An obvious extension of this work is to extend the system to dynamically detect type errors relating to the semantic interpretation of some specific functors, for instance the list constructor. For this, we would have for the list constructor not the Herbrand-based interpretation $[\,|\,] :: \forall A, B.A \times B \rightarrow [A|B]$, but the following interpretation $[\,|\,] :: \forall A.A \times list(A) \rightarrow list(A)$. Moreover, we would have the empty list $[\,]$ with type $\forall D.list(D)$. This would necessarily change the typed unification algorithm by introducing a new kind of constraints. As an example, consider the unification $[1|2] = [1|2]$, where the second argument in both terms is not a list: considering a specially interpreted list constructor the result should be *wrong*, although the traditional untyped result is *true*. The same issues appear for arithmetic expressions. Arithmetic interpretations of $+, -, \times$, and $/$ can be introduced in the typed unification algorithm, so that in this context, unifications such as $a + b = a + b$ would now return *wrong* instead of *true*. These extensions are left for future work.

Using TSLD in Practice: we plan to integrate TSLD into the YAP Prolog System [8]. This will enable further applications of the method to large scale Prolog programs. One important point of this integration it to add explicit type declarations to all the implicitly typed Prolog built-in predicates. Finally, one could also wonder how to apply TSLD to the dynamic typing of constraint logic programming modules, adding new types mapped to constraint domains.

References

1. Apt, K.R.: From Logic Programming to Prolog. Prentice-Hall Inc., Upper Saddle River (1996)
2. Barbosa, J., Florido, M., Costa, V.S.: A three-valued semantics for typed logic programming. In: Proceedings 35th International Conference on Logic Programming (Technical Communications), ICLP 2019 Technical Communications, Las Cruces, NM, USA, 20–25 September 2019. EPTCS, vol. 306, pp. 36–51 (2019)
3. Barbosa, J., Florido, M., Costa, V.S.: Data type inference for logic programming. In: De Angelis, E., Vanhoof, W. (eds.) LOPSTR 2021. LNCS, pp. 16–37. Springer, Cham (2022). https://doi.org/10.1007/978-3-030-98869-2_2
4. Barbosa, J., Florido, M., Santos Costa, V.: Typed SLD-resolution: dynamic typing for logic programming. arXiv (2022)
5. Beall, J.: Off-topic: a new interpretation of weak-kleene logic. Australas. J. Logic **13**(6) (2016)
6. Bochvar, D., Bergmann, M.: On a three-valued logical calculus and its application to the analysis of the paradoxes of the classical extended functional calculus. Hist. Philos. Logic **2**(1–2), 87–112 (1981)
7. Bruynooghe, M., Janssens, G.: An instance of abstract interpretation integrating type and mode inferencing. In: Fifth International Conference and Symposium, Washington, 1988, pp. 669–683 (1988)

8. Costa, V.S., Rocha, R., Damas, L.: The YAP prolog system. Theor. Pract. Log. Program. **12**(1–2), 5–34 (2012)
9. Dart, P.W., Zobel, J.: A regular type language for logic programs. In: Pfenning, F. (ed.) Types in Logic Programming, pp. 157–187. The MIT Press, Cambridge (1992)
10. Deransart, P., Ed-Dbali, A., Cervoni, L.: Prolog - the Standard: Reference Manual. Springer, Heidelberg (1996). https://doi.org/10.1007/978-3-642-61411-8
11. Deransart, P., Smaus, J.-G.: Well-typed logic programs are not wrong. In: Kuchen, H., Ueda, K. (eds.) FLOPS 2001. LNCS, vol. 2024, pp. 280–295. Springer, Heidelberg (2001). https://doi.org/10.1007/3-540-44716-4_18
12. Drabent, W., Małuszyński, J., Pietrzak, P.: Using parametric set constraints for locating errors in CLP programs. Theor. Pract. Logic Program. **2**(4–5), 549–610 (2002). https://doi.org/10.1017/S1471068402001473
13. van Emden, M.H., Kowalski, R.A.: The semantics of predicate logic as a programming language. J. ACM **23**(4), 733–742 (1976)
14. Frühwirth, T.W., Shapiro, E.Y., Vardi, M.Y., Yardeni, E.: Logic programs as types for logic programs. In: Proceedings of the Sixth Annual Symposium on Logic in Computer Science (LICS '91), Netherlands, 1991, pp. 300–309 (1991)
15. Hanus, M.: Multiparadigm languages. In: Computing Handbook, Third Edition: Computer Science and Software Engineering, vol. 66, pp. 1–17. Springer, Cham (2014)
16. Herbrand, J.: Recherches sur la théorie de la démonstration. Numdam (1930). http://eudml.org/doc/192791
17. Kleene, S.C.: On notation for ordinal numbers. J. Symbolic Logic **3**(4), 150–155 (1938)
18. Lakshman, T.L., Reddy, U.S.: Typed Prolog: a semantic reconstruction of the Mycroft-O'Keefe type system. In: Logic Programming, Proceedings of the 1991 International Symposium, San Diego, California, USA (1991)
19. Lloyd, J.W.: Foundations of Logic Programming. Springer-Verlag, Berlin (1984). https://doi.org/10.1007/978-3-642-96826-6
20. Lu, L.: On Dart-Zobel algorithm for testing regular type inclusion. Sigplan Not. **36**(9), 81–85 (2001)
21. Martelli, A., Montanari, U.: An efficient unification algorithm. ACM Trans. Program. Lang. Syst. **4**(2), 258–282 (1982). https://doi.org/10.1145/357162.357169
22. Milner, R.: A theory of type polymorphism in programming. J. Comput. Syst. Sci. **17**(3), 348–375 (1978)
23. Mycroft, A., O'Keefe, R.A.: A polymorphic type system for Prolog. Artif. Intell. **23**(3), 295–307 (1984)
24. Robinson, J.A.: A Machine-Oriented Logic Based on the Resolution Principle. J. ACM **12**(1), 23–41 (1965)
25. Schrijvers, T., Bruynooghe, M., Gallagher, J.P.: From monomorphic to polymorphic well-typings and beyond. In: Hanus, M. (ed.) LOPSTR 2008. LNCS, vol. 5438, pp. 152–167. Springer, Heidelberg (2009). https://doi.org/10.1007/978-3-642-00515-2_11
26. Schrijvers, T., Santos Costa, V., Wielemaker, J., Demoen, B.: Towards typed prolog. In: Garcia de la Banda, M., Pontelli, E. (eds.) ICLP 2008. LNCS, vol. 5366, pp. 693–697. Springer, Heidelberg (2008). https://doi.org/10.1007/978-3-540-89982-2_59

27. Wadler, P., Findler, R.B.: Well-typed programs can't be blamed. In: Castagna, G. (ed.) ESOP 2009. LNCS, vol. 5502, pp. 1–16. Springer, Heidelberg (2009). https://doi.org/10.1007/978-3-642-00590-9_1

28. Yardeni, E., Frühwirth, T.W., Shapiro, E.: Polymorphically typed logic programs. In: Pfenning, F. (ed.) Types in Logic Programming, pp. 63–90. The MIT Press (1992)

29. Zobel, J.: Derivation of polymorphic types for Prolog programs. In: Logic Programming, Proceedings of the Fourth International Conference, Melbourne (1987)

On Correctness of Normal Logic Programs

Włodzimierz Drabent[1,2][✉] [iD]

[1] Institute of Computer Science, Polish Academy of Sciences, Ul. Jana Kazimierza 5,
PL – 01-248 Warszawa, Poland
[2] Department of Computer and Information Science, Linköping University,
SE – 581 83 Linköping, Sweden
drabent@ipipan.waw.pl

Abstract. We present sufficient conditions for correctness of logic programs with negation (normal programs). We focus on the Kunen semantics, this declarative semantics is a closest one to what is implemented in Prolog (negation by finite failure) when floundering is avoided. We also recall an existing result for the well-founded semantics.

Keywords: Logic programming · Negation · Program correctness · Kunen semantics

1 Introduction

We consider logic programs with negation (called also general, or normal logic programs). There are three main semantics for such programs: the Kunen semantics (logical consequences of program completion in 3-valued logic), the well-founded semantics, and stable model semantics. Here we consider the former two; the contribution of this report concerns the Kunen semantics. It is the semantics most closely related to what happens in Prolog when unsound usage of negation (implemented by \+) is avoided, for instance by taking care that only ground negative literals are selected.

We consider specifications similar to those of [11] but restricted to Herbrand interpretations only. By program correctness we mean, informally speaking, that whenever Q (an instance of an initial query) is obtained as an answer of the program, then Q is compatible with the specification. Also, if failure of a query Q is obtained then $\neg Q$ is compatible with the specification. As the operational semantics one may consider SLDNF-resolution, or any other mechanism sound w.r.t. the Kunen semantics (like any generalization of SLDNF-resolution to constructive negation).

For the Kunen semantics we present two ways of proving program correctness. The first is similar to that of previous work. As its predecessor, it is only applicable when the least fixed point of the 3-valued immediate consequence operator is, informally speaking, a subset of the specification. This weakness is overcome

A. Villanueva (Ed.): LOPSTR 2022, LNCS 13474, pp. 142–154, 2022.
https://doi.org/10.1007/978-3-031-16767-6_8

in the second sufficient condition for correctness, which is the main contribution of this paper. For comparison we recall the (possibly not widely known) sufficient condition of [12] for correctness w.r.t. the well-founded semantics.

2 Preliminaries

Basic Notions. We use the standard definitions and notation of logic programming [1,2]. A maybe nonstandard notion is (computed or correct) answer; by this we mean a query to which a (computed or correct) answer substitution has been applied. We assume a fixed set of function symbols (including constants) and predicate symbols. $\mathcal{HU}$ stands for the Herbrand universe, and $\mathcal{HB}$ for the Herbrand base; $ground(P)$ is the set of ground instances of the clauses of a program P. $\mathbb{N}$ is the set of natural numbers. We deal with normal [16] programs (called also "general" [1]), and we usually call them just "programs".

4-valued Logic. We will refer to Belnap's 4-valued logic. The truth values are the subsets of the set of two standard truth values $\mathbf{t}$ and $\mathbf{f}$. The subsets $(\emptyset, \{\mathbf{t}\}, \{\mathbf{f}\}, \{\mathbf{t}, \mathbf{f}\})$ will be denoted by $\mathbf{u}, \mathbf{t}, \mathbf{f}, \mathbf{tf}$, respectively. The rationale for the four values is that a query, apart from succeeding ($\mathbf{t}$) and failing ($\mathbf{f}$), may diverge ($\mathbf{u}$); additionally a specification may permit it both to succeed and to fail ($\mathbf{tf}$). Given a set of ground atoms $S \in \mathcal{HB}$, let $\neg S$ stand for $\{\neg A \mid A \in S\}$. A 4-valued Herbrand interpretation is a subset of $\mathcal{HB} \cup \neg\mathcal{HB}$. (We will often skip the word "Herbrand".) If such interpretation does not contain both A and $\neg A$ (for any $A \in \mathcal{HB}$) then it is said to be 3-valued. Consider an interpretation $I \subseteq \mathcal{HB} \cup \neg\mathcal{HB}$, and a ground atom $A \in \mathcal{HB}$. The truth value $v \subseteq \{\mathbf{t}, \mathbf{f}\}$ of A in I is determined as follows: $\mathbf{t} \in v$ iff $A \in I$, and $\mathbf{f} \in v$ iff $\neg A \in I$. We may briefly say that A is v in I, e.g. p is $\mathbf{tf}$ and q is $\mathbf{u}$ in $\{p, \neg p\}$.

Further introduction to the 4-valued logic may possibly be skipped at the first reading, as most of technical details in the paper will be expressed in the standard two-valued first order logic. The truth values of possibly nonground atoms in an interpretation and a variable valuation are defined in a usual way. The negation of $\mathbf{t}$ is $\mathbf{f}$ (and vice-versa), and each of $\mathbf{u}, \mathbf{tf}$ is the negation of itself. To define $\wedge$ and $\vee$ let us employ the truth-ordering $\leq_t$ on $\{\mathbf{u}, \mathbf{t}, \mathbf{f}, \mathbf{tf}\}$; under $\leq_t$ the set is a complete lattice. In this ordering $v_1 \leq_t v_2$ when 1. if $\mathbf{f} \in v_2$ then $\mathbf{f} \in v_1$ and 2. if $\mathbf{t} \in v_1$ then $\mathbf{t} \in v_2$. So $\mathbf{f} \leq_t \emptyset \leq_t \mathbf{t}$, $\mathbf{f} \leq_t \mathbf{tf} \leq_t \mathbf{t}$ and $\emptyset, \mathbf{tf}$ are incomparable. An informal explanation of $v_1 \leq_t v_2$ is that v_1 is "less true or more false" than v_2 [14]. Now $v_1 \wedge v_2$ and $v_1 \vee v_2$ are, respectively, the greatest lower bound and the least upper bound of $\{v_1, v_2\}$ (w.r.t. $\leq_t$). See [19] or [14] for further explanations. For dealing with program completion, connectives $\leftarrow$ and $\leftrightarrow$ are defined in a nonstandard way, we skip the details. We write $I, \vartheta \models_4 F$ (respectively $I \models_4 F$) to state that the truth value of a formula F in an interpretation I and a variable valuation ϑ (resp. all variable valuations) contains $\mathbf{t}$.

Using Standard Logic. In this work we prefer to avoid dealing with technical details of 4-valued logic. Instead we would employ an encoding in the standard 2-valued logic. Such approach is maybe less elegant, but it seems convenient to work within a well-known familiar logic. We extend the underlying alphabet by adding new predicate symbols, a distinct new symbol p' for each predicate symbol p. We introduce the following notation [7,10]:

Let $\mathcal{F}$ be a query, the negation of a query, a clause, or a program. Then $\mathcal{F}'$ is $\mathcal{F}$ with p replaced by p' in every negative literal of $\mathcal{F}$ (for any predicate symbol p, except for =). Similarly, $\mathcal{F}''$ is $\mathcal{F}$ with p replaced by p' in every positive literal. If $I \in \mathcal{HB}$ is a (2-valued) Herbrand interpretation then I' is the interpretation obtained from I by replacing each predicate symbol p by p'. Let Q be a query and $\mathcal{Q}$ be Q or $\neg Q$; consider a 4-valued interpretation $I = X \cup \neg(\mathcal{HB} \setminus Y)$ (where $X, Y \in \mathcal{HB}$). We have $I \models_4 \mathcal{Q}$ iff $X \cup Y' \models \mathcal{Q}'$ iff $X' \cup Y \models \mathcal{Q}''$.

Immediate Consequence Operator. For a sequence $\vec{L}$ of literals, we will often write $L \in \vec{L}$ to state that L is a literal from $\vec{L}$. Given a normal program P, the (4-valued) immediate consequence operator $T4_P$ [19] can be defined as follows. For an $I \subseteq \mathcal{HB} \cup \neg\mathcal{HB}$, $T4_P(I)$ contains an atom A iff $ground(P)$ contains a clause $A \leftarrow \vec{L}$ so that each $L \in \vec{L}$ is in I; $T4_P(I)$ contains a negative literal $\neg A$ iff for each clause $A \leftarrow \vec{L} \in ground(P)$ the negation of some literal $L \in \vec{L}$ is in I. Note that when applied to 3-valued interpretations, the operator becomes the standard 3-valued immediate consequence operator [13]. In a usual way we define $T4_P \uparrow \alpha$ (for an ordinal α): $T4_P \uparrow 0 = \emptyset$, $T4_P \uparrow (\alpha + 1) = T4_P(T4_P \uparrow \alpha)$ for successor ordinals, and $T4_P \uparrow \alpha = \bigcup_{\beta < \alpha} T4_P \uparrow \beta$ for any limit ordinal. Each $T4_P \uparrow \alpha$ is 3-valued. As $T4_P$ is monotone (w.r.t. $\subseteq$), it has its $\subseteq$-least fixed point, which is $T4_P \uparrow \alpha$ for some α. The least fixed point is the central notion of so called Fitting semantics [13] (which is usually expressed by means of a 3-valued operator).

Semantics of Negation in Prolog. Here we present a brief discussion, for missing details see e.g. [1,5]

A natural way of adding negation to Prolog was negation as failure (more precisely, negation as finite failure, NAFF). This means deriving $\neg Q$ if a query Q finitely fails, i.e. has a finite SLD-tree without answers. (In Prolog, \+Q fails if Q succeeds, and succeeds when Q terminates without any answer.) NAFF makes it possible to deal with normal programs and queries. In an appropriate generalization of SLD-resolution, if a negative literal $\neg A$ is selected in a query Q_i then Q_i has a descendant when A finitely fails (and the descendant is Q_i with $\neg A$ removed). For Q_i to be a leaf of a failed tree it is necessary that truth of A can be derived. This means A is ground and succeeds (or more generally, A succeeds with a most general answer). Otherwise (A does not finitely fail, and is not found to be true) Q_i is a floundered node; such node cannot be a leaf of a failed tree. These ideas are formalized as SLDNF-resolution and its variants (cf. e.g. [1,16,17]). Usually one simply requires that any selected $\neg A$ is ground. It is responsibility of the programmer to assure that floundering is avoided (this is not checked by the built-in \+).

Apparently NAFF was introduced as an operational device without any logical semantics. A main attempt to provide such semantics was the program completion [3]. SLDNF-resolution is sound w.r.t. the completion. However the completion of a program may "imply too much". A program completion may be inconsistent (e.g. $comp(\{p \leftarrow \neg p\})$ is $p \leftrightarrow \neg p$). It may imply conclusions that are far from any desired semantics of programs. For instance, consider a program $P = \{p \leftarrow \neg p, \neg q. \; q \leftarrow q\}$. Its completion has q as a logical consequence, but it does not seem reasonable to derive q from the program.

The solution was given by Kunen [15], by considering logical consequences of the completion in a 3-valued logic of Kleene. (The logic may be seen as Belnap's logic without the truth value **tf**.) Given a program P, soundness (of some operational semantics) w.r.t. the Kunen semantics means that if a query Q fails then $comp(P) \models_3 \neg Q$, and if Q is a computed answer then $comp(P) \models_3 Q$.

The Kunen semantics can be considered to be the right declarative semantics of NAFF and SLDNF-resolution. First, SLDNF-resolution is sound w.r.t. the Kunen semantics, and is complete for wide classes of programs and queries. Moreover, natural ways of augmenting SLDNF-resolution by constructive negation [6,20] are sound and complete w.r.t. this semantics. Also, it can be shown that floundering is the only reason for incompleteness of SLDNF-resolution w.r.t. the Kunen semantics [7].

This is an important property of the Kunen semantics.

Theorem 1 ([15, see also 1]). *Assume that in the underlying language the set of function symbols (including constants) is infinite. For any normal program P and a first order formula F not containing $\leftarrow$ and $\leftrightarrow$,*

$$comp(P) \models_3 F \quad \textit{iff} \quad T4_P \uparrow n \models_4 F \quad \textit{for some finite } n.$$

The theorem also holds for a finite set of function symbols, provided that a weak domain closure axiom is added to the equality theory (which is a part of $comp(P)$).

Example 2. Here we show that a single Herbrand interpretation $T4_P \uparrow \omega$ does not characterize the Kunen semantics (when nonground queries/answers are considered). Let $P = \{p(X) \leftarrow q(X). \; p(X) \leftarrow \neg q(X). \; q(0). \; q(s(X)) \leftarrow q(X). \}$. We have that $T4_P \uparrow \omega \models p(X)$, as $T4_P \uparrow n = \{q(s^i(0)), \neg q(s^i(t)), p(s^j(0)), p(s^j(t)) \mid i < n, j < n{-}1, t \in \mathcal{HU}$, and the main symbol if t is neither 0, nor $s \}$ (thus each atom $p(u) \in \mathcal{HB}$ is in $T4_P \uparrow \omega$). However, $comp(P) \not\models_3 p(X)$.

Note that, under SLDNF-resolution, each atom $A \in T4_P \uparrow \omega$ is a computed answer (for A as a query), and for each negative literal $\neg A \in T4_P \uparrow \omega$, query A finitely fails (unless floundering occurs).

3   Program Correctness

We begin with discussing specifications. Then we present two sufficient conditions for correctness of normal programs. The first one is based on [11], the second one is more precise and is a contribution of this work.

3.1   Specifications

Definition 3. *A* **specification** *is a pair* (St, Snf) *where* $St, Snf \in \mathcal{HB}$.

The (4-valued) interpretation corresponding to specification (St, Snf) *is*
$I^4(St, Snf) = St \cup \neg(\mathcal{HB} \setminus Snf)$.

The letters nf, t stand for "not false", and "true". The intuition about a specification as above is that $A \in St$ means that A can be (an instance of) an answer of the program; and $A \notin Snf$ means that the query A can fail (and that $\neg A$ can be an instance of an answer). Hence any atom $A \in St \setminus Snf$ is allowed both to succeed and fail; from a 4-valued point of view such atom is **tf** in $I^4(St, Snf)$. Similarly, any $A \in Snf \setminus St$ is neither allowed to succeed, nor to fail; its truth value in $I^4(St, Snf)$ is **u**. (Also, the atoms from $St \cap Snf$ are **t**, and those from $(\mathcal{HB} \setminus Snf) \setminus St$ are **f** in $I^4(St, Snf)$.) The idea of a specification as pair of interpretations comes from [11].

Example 4. A possible specification of a program defining the list membership predicate m is (St_m, Snf_m), where

$$Snf_m = \{\, m(e_i, [e_1, \ldots, e_n]) \in \mathcal{HB} \mid 1 \le i \le n \,\},$$
$$St_m = Snf_m \cup \{\, m(e, t) \in \mathcal{HB} \mid t \text{ is not a list} \,\}.$$

So we require that for a ground $m(e, t)$ to be true, e must be an element of a list t, if t is a list. Any ground atom not of the form $m(e_i, [e_1, \ldots, e_n])$ (where $1 \le i \le n$) is allowed to be false. If t is not a list then any $m(e, t) \in \mathcal{HB}$ is allowed to be true or false.

From the 4-valued point of view, atoms $m(e, t) \in \mathcal{HB}$, where t is not a list, are **tf** in $I^4(St_m, Snf_m)$. Atoms $m(e_i, [e_1, \ldots, e_n]) \in \mathcal{HB}$ (where $1 \le i \le n$) are **t**, and atoms $m(e, [e_1, \ldots, e_n]) \in \mathcal{HB}$ where $e \notin \{e_1, \ldots, e_n\}$ are **f** in $I^4(St_m, Snf_m)$.

Definition 5. *A program P is* **correct** *w.r.t. a specification* $spec = (St, Snf)$ *if for any query Q*

(i) if $comp(P) \models_3 Q$ then $Snf' \cup St \models Q'$
(ii) if $comp(P) \models_3 \neg Q$ then $Snf' \cup St \models \neg Q''$

Remember that $I \models Q$ (for a 2-valued Herbrand interpretation $I \in \mathcal{HB}$) means that, for any ground instance $L_1, \ldots, L_n$ of Q, if L_i is a positive literal then $L \in I$, and if $L_i = \neg A$ is a negative literal then $A \notin I$ (for $i = 1, \ldots, n$).

For an atomic query $Q = A$, the conditions of Definition 5 reduce to

$$\begin{aligned} &\text{if } comp(P) \models_3 A \text{ then } St \models A, \\ &\text{if } comp(P) \models_3 \neg A \text{ then } Snf \models \neg A. \end{aligned} \tag{1}$$

In this paper we prefer to employ the standard 2-valued logic, as it is more familiar. When we express the definition in the 4-valued logic, the conditions become:

$$\begin{aligned} &\text{if } comp(P) \models_3 Q \text{ then } I^4(St, Snf) \models_4 Q, \\ &\text{if } comp(P) \models_3 \neg Q \text{ then } I^4(St, Snf) \models_4 \neg Q. \end{aligned} \tag{2}$$

Note that our notion of correctness is relevant for actual computations (abstracted by SLDNF-resolution). This is because SLDNF-resolution is sound w.r.t. the Kunen semantics: $comp(P) \models_3 Q$ whenever Q is an SLDNF-computed answer of P, and $comp(P) \models_3 \neg Q$ whenever Q fails. From a point of view of Prolog programming, program correctness means the following. Let us consider atomic queries, and assume that a program P is correct w.r.t. (St, Snf). If A is an atomic answer of P, and floundering has not occurred during the computation, then $St \models A$. If an atomic query A fails (without floundering), then $Snf \models \neg A$.

It immediately follows from (2) by Theorem 1 that:

Lemma 6. *A program P is correct w.r.t. a specification spec iff $T4_P \uparrow \omega \subseteq I^4(St, Snf)$.*

The lemma shows a certain limitation of the kind of specifications used here. As in Example 2, for a program P and, say, an atomic query A, it is possible that for each ground instance $A\theta$ we have $comp(P) \models_3 A\theta$, but $comp(P) \not\models_3 A$. A detail of this kind cannot be expressed by a specification: in such case, $St \models A$ for each specification $spec = (St, Snf)$ w.r.t. which P is correct.

3.2 Sufficient Condition for Correctness 1

Here we present a sufficient condition which basically is a simplification of that of [11]. Simplifying is possible due to a restriction to Herbrand interpretations.

We first introduce a notion of a weakly covered atom. The notion of a covered atom is used in incompleteness diagnosis and in reasoning about program completeness [8, 18]. Roughly – a covered atom is made true by a clause of a program, assuming that the body atoms are valuated according to the specification. A weakly covered atom, informally speaking, cannot be made false.

Definition 7. *An atom $A \in \mathcal{HB}$ is **weakly covered** by a clause C w.r.t. a specification $spec = (St, Snf)$ if there exists a ground instance $A \leftarrow L_1, \ldots, L_n$ $(n \geq 0)$ of C such that for each $i \in \{1, \ldots, n\}$, if L_i is a positive literal then $L_i \in Snf$, and if L_i is a negative literal then the atom $\neg L_i \notin St$.*

Theorem 8 (Correctness 1). *A program P is correct w.r.t. a specification $spec = (St, Snf)$ if*

1. *$St \cup Snf' \models P'$, and*
2. *each atom $A \in Snf$ is weakly covered by P w.r.t. spec.*

We present three proofs of the theorem, as they are concise, and two of them relate Theorem 8 to other results.

Proof 1. The theorem follows from Theorem 11 below.

Proof 2. Conditions 1,2 imply that $I^4(spec)$ is a pre-fixed point of $T4_P$, hence a superset of the least fixed point, hence a superset of any $T4_P \uparrow n$. Now the correctness follows by Theorem 1.

Proof 3. The theorem follows from [11, Theorem 4.6] (as condition 2 implies that $St \cup Snf' \cup \{=(t,t) \mid t \in \mathcal{HU}\} \models \text{ONLY-IF}(P'')$). $\qquad\square$

148   W. Drabent

Note: From Proof 2 if follows that Theorem 8 provides a sufficient condition for correctness w.r.t. the Fitting semantics (which is given by the least fixed point of $T3_P$). The theorem differs from that of [11] in its condition 2. The previous version requires that each formula from a certain set of formula is true in an interpretation; the set $(\text{ONLY-IF}(P''))$ is related to the completion of P. This makes it possible to deal with specifications which are non-Herbrand interpretations.

Example 9 (based on [11]). Consider the program SS [19]:

$$ss(L,M) \leftarrow \neg nss(L,M)$$
$$nss(L,M) \leftarrow m(X,L), \neg m(X,M)$$
$$m(X,[X|L]) \leftarrow$$
$$m(X,[Y|L]) \leftarrow m(X,L)$$

(ss stands for subset, nss for not subset, m for member). Let us take (St, Snf) as a specification, where

$$St = St_{ss} \cup St_{nss} \cup St_m, \qquad Snf = Snf_{ss} \cup Snf_{nss} \cup Snf_m,$$
$$St_{ss} = \{\, ss(l,m) \in \mathcal{HB} \mid l \text{ and } m \text{ are lists} \rightarrow l \subseteq m \,\},$$
$$Snf_{ss} = \{\, ss(l,m) \in \mathcal{HB} \mid l \text{ and } m \text{ are lists} \wedge l \subseteq m \,\},$$
$$St_{nss} = \{\, nss(l,m) \in \mathcal{HB} \mid l \text{ and } m \text{ are lists} \rightarrow l \not\subseteq m \,\},$$
$$Snf_{nss} = \{\, nss(l,m) \in \mathcal{HB} \mid l \text{ and } m \text{ are lists} \wedge l \not\subseteq m \,\},$$

and St_m, Snf_m are as in Example 4. Here by $l \subseteq m$ we mean that all elements of list l are elements of list m; we will say briefly that l is a subset of m.

The specification (St, Snf) states (among others) that – for any program P correct w.r.t (St, Snf), and any lists l, m – if $comp(P) \models_3 ss(l,m)$ then l is a subset of m, and if $comp(P) \models_3 \neg ss(l,m)$ then l is not a subset of m. (The specification says nothing about an $ss(l,m)$ where l or m is not a list.)

We apply Theorem 8 to prove correctness of SS w.r.t. (St, Snf). Let us look at the details related to the second clause and to literals $nss(l,m)$. For condition 1, consider a ground instance $C = nss(l,m) \leftarrow m(x,l), \neg m(x,m)$ of the clause. Assume that the body of C' is true in $St \cup Snf'$, i.e. $m(x,l) \in St$ and $Snf' \models \neg m'(x,m)$, so $m(x,m) \notin Snf$. Hence if l is a list then x is its member. Also, $m(x,m)$ is not of the form $m(e_i,[e_1,\ldots,e_n])$ (for some $1 \le i \le n$); thus if m is a list then x is not its member. Thus if both l,m are lists then x is a member of l but not of m, hence $nss(l,m) \in St_{nss}$. We showed that $St \cup Snf' \models C'$ for any ground instance C of the second clause of SS.

Consider now an atom $nss(l,m) \in Snf_{nss}$. Both l and m are lists such that $l \not\subseteq m$. Hence some $x \in \mathcal{HU}$ is a member of l but not of m. Thus $m(x,l) \in Snf_m \subseteq Snf$, and $m(x,l) \notin St_m$ (and thus $m(x,l) \notin St$). So $nss(l,m)$ is weakly covered by clause instance C as above (for the given l,m,x).

We skip the rest of the proof, dealing with condition 1 for the remaining clauses of SS, and condition 2 for the atoms from $Snf_{ss} \cup Snf_m$.

For programs without negation, a specification is a single Herbrand interpretation (cf. e.g. [8]). For such programs, condition 1 of Theorem 8 becomes the sufficient condition for correctness w.r.t. specification St of [4] ($St \models P_+$ implies $St \models Q$ for any answer Q of a definite clause program P_+). Condition 2 becomes a part of a sufficient condition for completeness of a definite clause program w.r.t. specification Snf [8]. This is because for such programs the notions "weakly covered w.r.t. (St, Snf)" and "covered w.r.t. Snf" coincide.

Note the following informal explanation of the theorem. Any ground atomic answer A of P should be in St. Such answer is the head of a clause $A \leftarrow \vec{L} \in ground(P)$ with the body literals also obtained from P. For each such clause we make an inductive assumption that the literals are permitted by specification (St, Snf) (i.e. that $St \cup Snf' \models \vec{L}'$), and require that A is in St. This is condition 1 of Theorem 8. Briefly, it says that only correct atoms can be produced out of correct literals. Also, any atom $A \in Snf$ should not fail, so there must be a clause in P able to produce A out of literals that should not fail. This is condition 2.

The author argued for an opinion that condition 1 is a formalization of a natural way of a programmer's reasoning about the declarative semantics of logic programs (cf. e.g. [8,9]). The opinion was expressed for definite clause programs, but applies also to normal programs. So the condition can be used (possibly at informal level) in everyday programming for reasoning about program correctness. We may expect the same about condition 2. The former version of the theorem [11] seems less suitable for practical informal applications.

3.3 Sufficient Condition for Correctness 2

Now we are going to strengthen the proof method, in order to capture the difference between $T4_P \uparrow \omega$ and the least fixed point of $T4_P$. We need a generalization of the notion of level mapping, often used in reasoning about program termination. By a level mapping we will mean a function $| \ |: \mathcal{HB} \rightarrow \mathbb{N} \cup \{\omega\}$. It what follows we assume that $1 + \omega = \omega$. To extend a level mapping for literals let $|\neg A| = |A|$.

The intention of the following definition is to describe a restriction on the level of a true (respectively non-false) atom $A \in \mathcal{HB}$ and the levels of atoms on which the truth (non-falsity) of A depends. Informally speaking, the truth of an atom follows from a ground clause with body $\vec{L}$ so that $St \cup Snf' \models \vec{L}'$. (The latter means that each literal of $\vec{L}$ is in $I^4(St, Snf)$.) Conversely, to find out falsity of an atom A, we have to consider all the clauses with head A.

Definition 10. *A level mapping* $| \ |: \mathcal{HB} \rightarrow \mathbb{N} \cup \{\omega\}$ *is* **adjusted** *to a program P and a specification $spec = (St, Snf)$ if*

1. *for each $A \in St$,*

$$|A| \leq 1 + \min \left\{ \max\{|L| : L \in \vec{L}\} \ \middle| \ \begin{array}{l} A \leftarrow \vec{L} \in ground(P), \\ St \cup Snf' \models \vec{L}' \end{array} \right\},$$

2. *for each $A \in \mathcal{HB} \setminus Snf$,*

$$|A| \leq 1 + \max \left\{ \min\{|L| \ \middle| \ \begin{array}{l} L \in \vec{L}, \\ St \cup Snf' \models (\neg L)' \end{array}\} \ \middle| \ A \leftarrow \vec{L} \in ground(P) \right\},$$

3. *for each $A \in Snf \setminus St$, $|A| = \omega$*

(where $\max \emptyset = 0$, $\min \emptyset = \omega$).

So if $A \in \mathcal{HB}$ is not an instance of any clause head in P then $|A|$ is arbitrary when $A \in St$ and $|A| \leq 1$ when $A \in \mathcal{HB} \setminus Snf$.

Note that a simpler version of the definition is obtained by dropping (one or both) conditions of the form $St \cup Snf' \models \dots$. A level mapping satisfying the simpler definition satisfies the original one (as without these conditions the minimum taken in 1 or in 2 is not greater than that in the original definition).

Theorem 11 (Correctness 2). *A program P is correct w.r.t. a specification* $spec = (St, Snf)$ *if there exists a level mapping $|\ |$ adjusted to P and spec, such that*

1. *for each $A \leftarrow \vec{L} \in ground(P)$, if $St \cup Snf' \models \vec{L'}$ then $A \in St$ or $|A| = \omega$;*
2. *for each $m \in \mathbb{N}$ and each $A \in Snf$ there exists $A \leftarrow \vec{L} \in ground(P)$ such that for each $L \in \vec{L}$, $|L| > m$ or $St' \cup Snf \models L'$.*

Note that condition $St' \cup Snf \models L'$ can be equivalently represented as $L \in Snf$ if L is a positive literal, and $A \notin St$ if $L = \neg A$ is negative; in both cases $\neg L \notin I^4(spec)$. So $St' \cup Snf \models L'$ iff $\neg L \notin I^4(spec)$.

PROOF: We show that $T4_P \uparrow n \subseteq I^4(spec)$ and that $L \in T4_P \uparrow n$ implies $|L| \leq n$, by induction on n. The base case of $n = 0$ is obvious. Assume the property holds for the numbers less than n.

Assume $A \in T4_P \uparrow n \cap \mathcal{HB}$. So there exists $A \leftarrow \vec{L} \in ground(P)$, such that each literal L of $\vec{L}$ is in $T4_P \uparrow (n-1)$. By the inductive assumption, $L \in I^4(spec)$ and $|L| \leq n - 1$. So if L is positive then $L \in St$, and if L is negative then $\neg L \notin Snf$; also $\max\{|L| : L \in \vec{L}\} \leq n - 1$, hence $|A| \leq 1 + (n - 1) < \omega$. Thus by condition 1 of the theorem, $A \in St \subseteq I^4(spec)$.

Assume $A \in Snf$. By condition 2 (for $m = n - 1$), there exists $A \leftarrow \vec{L} \in ground(P)$, such that for each $L \in \vec{L}$, one of the two cases holds:

1. $|L| > n - 1$. So $\neg L \notin T4_P \uparrow (n-1)$, by the inductive assumption.
2. $St' \cup Snf \models L'$, hence $\neg L \notin I^4(spec)$; by the inductive assumption, $\neg L \notin T4_P \uparrow (n-1)$.

Thus by the definition of $T4_P$ we obtain that $A \in Snf$ implies $\neg A \notin T4_P \uparrow n$. Conversely, if $\neg A \in T4_P \uparrow n \cap \neg \mathcal{HB}$ then $A \notin Snf$, i.e. $\neg A \in I^4(spec)$.

Take now a $\neg A \in T4_P \uparrow n \cap \neg \mathcal{HB}$. So for each clause $A \leftarrow \vec{L} \in ground(P)$ the negation of some L from $\vec{L}$ is in $T4_P \uparrow (n-1)$. By the inductive assumption, $|L| \leq n - 1$ and $\neg L \in I^4(spec)$ (i.e. $St \cup Snf' \models (\neg L)'$). Hence

$$\min\{|L| : L \in \vec{L}, \ St \cup Snf' \models (\neg L)'\} \leq n - 1.$$

Thus $|A| \leq n$.   □

Example 12. Let P be $\{\, p \leftarrow q(X).\ q(s(X)) \leftarrow q(X).\,\}$. Let $St = \emptyset$, $Snf = \{p\}$. Specification $spec = (St, Snf)$ states that no atom may succeed, and each atom but p may fail. Note that $T4_P \uparrow \omega$ is not a fixed point of $T4_P$; the least fixed point is $T4_P \uparrow \omega + 1 = \neg \mathcal{HB}$. Hence Theorem 8 is inapplicable here. Let us construct a level mapping and a correctness proof using Theorem 11.

Condition 1 of Theorem 11 obviously holds (as the (positive) body of each clause is false in St). For condition 2, we need to consider ground instances of the first clause, they are of the form $p \leftarrow q(t)$, with arbitrary $t \in \mathcal{HU}$. Note that $q(t) \notin Snf$. Hence to show condition 2, we need that for each $m \in \mathbb{N}$ there exists an atom $q(t)$ which $|q(t)| > m$. Let us find an appropriate level mapping.

Let $\mathcal{HU}_{\neg s}$ be the set of all terms with the main function symbol distinct from s. Assume $u \in \mathcal{HU}_{\neg s}$. Then $|q(u)| \leq 1$ (by Definition 10, as no clause in $ground(P)$ has the head $p(u)$). For $q(s^i(u))$ (where $i > 0$) we have $|q(s^i(u))| \leq 1 + |q(s^{i-1}(u))|$ (by Definition 10, as there is a single clause in $comp(P)$ with the head $q(s^i(u))$, and it has a single body atom). Thus a suitable level mapping is e.g. $|q(s^i(u))| = i$, for any $u \in \mathcal{HU}_{\neg s}$ and $i \geq 0$. Now condition 11 of the Theorem holds. Thus P is correct w.r.t. $spec$. Note that this cannot be shown by applying Theorem 8.

Comment. In this section, a decision was made that $|A| = |\neg A|$. As a result, atoms from $St \setminus Snf$ have to satisfy both conditions 1, 2 of Definition 10. This may be inconvenient in some cases. A possible improvement is to allow $|A| \neq |\neg A|$, and use condition 2 of Definition 10 (with $|A|$ replaced by $|\neg A|$) to constrain $|\neg A|$. (For $A \in Snf \setminus St$ it remains that $|\neg A| = |A| = \omega$).

4   Correctness for the Well-Founded Semantics

A sufficient conditions for correctness under the well-founded semantics (WFS) was presented by Ferrand and Deransart [12]. Here we translate that result into our terminology. Note that what is usually understood as correctness, they split into two notions. Roughly, by correctness they mean that succeeding ground atoms are in the specification. By weak completeness they mean (something equivalent in our setting to) each failing ground atom being in $\mathcal{HB} \setminus Snf$.

The well-founded model of a program P, represented as a subset of $\mathcal{HB} \cup \neg \mathcal{HB}$, will be denoted by $WF(P)$. A definition of correctness under the well-founded semantics can be obtained from that for the Kunen semantics (Definition 5) by replacing $comp(P) \models_3$ by $WF(P) \models_3$. Here is an equivalent and simpler formulation.

Definition 13. A program P is **correct** under the well-founded semantics w.r.t. a specification $spec = (St, Snf)$ when $WF(P) \subseteq I^4(spec)$.

Their correctness criterion employs a more general notion of level mapping – its values may be taken from an arbitrary well-ordered set $(W, \prec)$.

Theorem 14 ([12]).   A program P is correct w.r.t. a specification $spec =$ (St, Snf) under the well-founded semantics provided that

1. $St \cup Snf' \models P'$, and
2. there exists a level mapping $|\ |: Snf \rightarrow W$ as above such that $\forall A \in Snf$ $\exists A \leftarrow \vec{L} \in ground(P)$ such that
   (a) $St' \cup Snf \models \vec{L}'$, and
   (b) for each positive literal L from $\vec{L}$, $|L| \prec |A|$.

Note the similarity between the sufficient conditions under the Kunen semantics (Theorems 8, 11) and the well-founded semantics (Theorem 14). Condition 1 is the same in Theorem 8 and Theorem 14. It differs from that of Theorem 11 only by special treatment of clause heads with an infinite level (in Theorem 11). Condition 2a of Theorem 14 is equivalent to condition 2 of Theorem 8. This condition is required in Theorem 11 to hold only for body literals with sufficiently small $|\ |$. In Theorems 8, 14 a single clause is considered for each atom from Snf; while in Theorem 11 it may be an infinite set of clauses. The level mappings in Theorem 14 are more general than those that we apply. Moreover, what matters in Theorem 11 is $|A|$ for $A \in St \cup (\mathcal{HB} \setminus Snf)$, while here it is $|A|$ for $A \in Snf$.

Example 15. Consider the program $P = \{p \leftarrow q(X).\ q(s(X)) \leftarrow q(X).\}$ from Example 12, and $spec = (\emptyset, \emptyset)$. Note that $WF(P) = \neg \mathcal{HB}$. The specification states that each atom fails. Both conditions of Theorem 14 trivially hold, thus P is correct w.r.t. $spec$ under WFS.

Example 16. Consider a program P:
$$p(a) \leftarrow \neg p(x)$$
$$p(x) \leftarrow p(x)$$
$$p(b) \leftarrow \neg p(b)$$
(and assume that a and b are not the only function symbols of the underlying language). Consider a specification $spec = (St, Snf) = (\{p(a)\}, \{p(a), p(b)\})$. It states that $p(a)$ should be true, $p(b)$ neither true nor false, and all the remaining atoms should be false. We apply Theorem 14. Condition 1 is obvious, for the first clause due to $St \models p(a)$, and for the third one due to $Snf' \not\models \neg p'(b)$. Let c a term distinct from a and b. For condition 2a note that $p(a)$ is the head of a clause with the body $\neg p(c)$, and $St' \models \neg p'(c)$, and that $p(b)$ is the head of a clause with the body $\neg p(b)$ and $St' \models \neg p'(b)$; for these two clauses condition 2b holds vacuously. Note that $WF(P) = \{p(a), \neg p(t) \mid t \in \mathcal{HU},\ t \neq a,\ t \neq b\}$.

5   Conclusions

This paper discusses reasoning about correctness of normal (or general) logic programs. They are a reasonable abstraction of Prolog programs with negation. Reasoning about completeness is a subject of future work.

As the underlying declarative semantics, the Kunen semantics is chosen. This semantics is arguably the closest one to SLD-resolution combined with negation as finite failure; we discuss this issue in Sect. 2. In such context, a need for a 4-valued logic arises. The Kunen semantics is 3-valued, and additionally a specification may allow an atom both to be false and to be true; thus it is natural to employ the 4-valued logic of Belnap. In particular, it may be convenient to consider specifications which are 4-valued Herbrand interpretations. However, to simplify the approach by employing a familiar logic, we deal with technical details within the standard 2-valued first order logic. So, for instance, we view a specification as a pair of 2-valued Herbrand interpretations (i.e. a pair of sets of ground atoms).

We simplified a sufficient condition for program correctness from [11], by restricting it to Herbrand interpretations. We showed that it seems suitable for (informal) reasoning about program correctness in actual programming. This condition however implies correctness w.r.t. the Fitting semantics, given by the least fixed point of the 3-valued (or 4-valued) immediate consequence operator. So it cannot be used to show that certain answers are actually not implied by the Kunen semantics, and not produced by SLDNF-resolution (when floundering does not occur). The main contribution of this paper is a more precise sufficient condition for correctness of normal programs w.r.t. the Kunen semantics. We also compare our sufficient conditions with that of [12] for the well-founded semantics.

References

1. Apt, K., Bol, R.: Logic programming and negation: a survey. J. Logic Program. **19/20**, 9–71 (1994)
2. Apt, K.R.: From Logic Programming to Prolog. International Series in Computer Science, Prentice-Hall, Hoboken (1997)
3. Clark, K.: Negation as failure. In: Gallaire, H., Minker, J. (eds.) Logic and Databases. Springer, Boston (1978). https://doi.org/10.1007/978-1-4684-3384-5_11
4. Clark, K.L.: Predicate logic as computational formalism. Technical report 79/59. Imperial College, London (1979)
5. Doets, K.: From Logic to Logic Programming. The MIT Press, Cambridge, MA (1994)
6. Drabent, W.: What is failure? An approach to constructive negation. Acta Informatica **32**(1), 27–59 (1995). https://doi.org/10.1007/BF01185404
7. Drabent, W.: Completeness of SLDNF-resolution for non-floundering queries. J. Logic Program. **27**(2), 89–106 (1996)
8. Drabent, W.: Correctness and completeness of logic programs. ACM Trans. Comput. Log. **17**(3), 18:1-18:32 (2016). https://doi.org/10.1145/2898434
9. Drabent, W.: Logic + control: on program construction and verification. Theor. Pract. Logic Program. **18**(1), 1–29 (2018). https://doi.org/10.1017/S1471068417000047
10. Drabent, W., Martelli, M.: Strict completion of logic programs. N. Gener. Comput. **9**, 69–79 (1991). https://doi.org/10.1007/BF03037151
11. Drabent, W., Miłkowska, M.: Proving correctness and completeness of normal programs – a declarative approach. Theor. Pract. Logic Program **5**(6), 669–711 (2005). https://doi.org/10.1017/S147106840500253X

12. Ferrand, G., Deransart, P.: Proof method of partial correctness and weak completeness for normal logic programs. J. Logic Program. **17**, 265–278 (1993)
13. Fitting, M.: A Kripke-Kleene semantics for logic programs. J. Logic Program. **2**(4), 295–312 (1985)
14. Fitting, M.: Bilattices and the semantics of logic programming. J. Log. Program. **11**(1&2), 91–116 (1991). https://doi.org/10.1016/0743-1066(91)90014-G
15. Kunen, K.: Negation in logic programming. J. Log. Program. **4**(4), 289–308 (1987)
16. Lloyd, J.W.: Foundations of Logic Programming. Springer, Heidelberg (1987). Second, extended edition, https://doi.org/10.1007/978-3-642-83189-8
17. Nilsson, U., Małuszyński, J.: Logic, Programming and Prolog 2nd edn. John Wiley & Sons Ltd. (1995). http://www.ida.liu.se/~ulfni/lpp/
18. Shapiro, E.: Algorithmic Program Debugging. The MIT Press, Cambridge (1983)
19. Stärk, R.F.: From logic programs to inductive definitions. In: Hodges, W., Hyland, M., Steinhorn, C., Truss, J. (eds.) Logic: From Foundations to Applications. European Logic Colloquium '93, pp. 453–481. Clarendon Press, Oxford (1996). ISBN 978-0-19-853862-2
20. Stuckey, P.: Constructive negation for constraint logic programming. In: 6th Annual IEEE Symposium on Logic in Computer Science (LICS'91), pp. 328–339 (1991). https://doi.org/10.1109/LICS.1991.151657

Author Index

Printed in the United States
by Baker & Taylor Publisher Services

Printed in the United States
by Baker & Taylor Publisher Services